A READER'S GUIDE TO Geoffrey Chaucer

A READER'S GUIDE TO
Geoffrey Chaucer

BY MURIEL BOWDEN

OCTAGON BOOKS

A DIVISION OF HIPPOCRENE BOOKS, INC.

New York 1987

Reprinted 1971

Second Octagon printing 1977
Third Octagon printing 1980
Fourth Octagon printing 1983
Fifth Octagon printing 1987

OCTAGON BOOKS
A DIVISION OF HIPPOCRENE BOOKS, INC.

LIBRARY OF CONGRESS CATALOG CARD NUMBER: 75-111635
ISBN 0-88254-860-3

TO ALL WHO SHARE MY INTEREST IN
GEOFFREY CHAUCER
AND TO BARNARD COLLEGE
AS A TRIBUTE ON THE OCCASION OF ITS
SEVENTY-FIFTH ANNIVERSARY

PREFACE

THIS BOOK has grown from two sources: first from my interest in the questions which students have asked me over the years concerning Chaucer as a man, rather than as a poet; and second, from my profound belief in the truism that no great artist is dependent upon his genius alone—he must take matter and color also from his physical and cultural surroundings, both of which are obviously modified by the artist's position in time. Hence, the book primarily concerns the part environment played in Geoffrey Chaucer's poetry.

The book is planned in the main for those who are new readers of Chaucer and whose knowledge of the life and thought of the fourteenth century has perforce been somewhat limited; it should be read in conjunction with—or closely following— the study of an up-to-date, fully annotated text of the poet's works, as, for example, F. N. Robinson's *Works of Geoffrey Chaucer* (2nd edition, Boston, 1957). The line references I give follow the conventions of the Robinson edition, including the parenthetical Skeat references, and all my quotations from

Chaucer are taken from Professor Robinson's rendering of the texts. (In the *Legend of Good Women* I have considered only the *F Prologue*.) I have also followed the Robinson order in placing my treatment of the *Canterbury Tales* before my treatment of other works, but Parts II, III and IV are sufficiently independent for the student to read them in any order.

Following Part IV, a selected glossary is to be found in which two kinds of words appear: those which are now obsolete, as, for example, *swynken;* and, second, those which exist as words in Modern English, but which have changed in meaning, either partially or wholly, since Chaucer's day, as, for example, *defenden* and *knave*. The words selected have had to be limited in number, of course; I have selected only those which my students have found difficult to interpret properly.

The bibliography following the glossary is, like the latter, limited in scope, for I am obliged to omit the mention of many books, and I have mentioned no articles. However, nearly all the books in my brief list themselves contain bibliographies, so that a new reader will be enabled to pursue in detail any matters which particularly interest him, and the more experienced reader will be enabled to re-examine whatever he wishes.

My great debt in preparing the book is to all the many Chaucer scholars, both past and present. Such debt must be at least acknowledged here, although it can be neither adequately measured nor adequately repaid.

MURIEL BOWDEN

New York, 1964

CONTENTS

PART I

General Observations on the Milieu of Geoffrey Chaucer— His Time and His Place

TO UNDERSTAND the particular influence which fourteenth-century English life had upon Chaucer, we should at first glance briefly at the temper of the late Middle Ages in a more general sense. What sort of world was this, peopled by what sort of men and women? Today man understands his physical surroundings more fully than did his medieval ancestor; hence modern man is able—or at least feels that he is able—to take precautions against many of the dangers which beset him. Medieval man, in striking contrast, lived in the unending fear of "battle, murder, and sudden death," of monstrous devils lying in wait for him around every corner, of a material and terrible hell, of the storms and convulsions of nature, of the rigors of every winter, and of the horrors of pestilence and famine.

Fears of that sort, exceedingly violent in themselves, bred a species of violence in the medieval mind, so that the average man of intelligence saw nearly everything in the light of exaggerated contrast: human beings were deemed to be either extremely good or extremely bad, they were either Fortune's favorites, or Fortune's victims, they were either brilliantly happy or bowed down in black despair; statements had to be wholly true or wholly false, decisions had to be based on the most literal and stern interpretation of justice or on completely unthinking "mercy." Furthermore, those intense and uncompromising attitudes were complicated by the fact that in the Middle Ages what one believed in and acted upon on Monday was not at all necessarily the same as what one believed in and acted upon on Tuesday.

Besides accepting as wholly natural what we today regard as startling contrasts, medieval man—especially anyone in the "educated" classes—relied on formulae. Everyone who could read (or who could listen to another's reading) was able to find a book telling him how to behave in his particular estate; ethic and etiquette were one, and politeness, which had at first sprung from religion, now became a complicated and self-justifying set of formalities. Hence the setting up of the ideal pattern (a pattern, which if we are to believe the evidence of narratives and sermons, was rarely followed in actual life) became a virtue in itself, for it brought preservation to the ideal and assurance—even a sort of insurance—to mankind.

The fears, the extremes, the rituals thus all played a general part in forming the mind of any man living in the late Middle Ages. But what about Geoffrey Chaucer, who is both "any man" and a great genius, living in his particular circumstances?

All modern editions of Chaucer's works give us the facts of his life in detail, but in this book we shall be concerned only with those facts which influenced Chaucer to write as he did when he did. His genius was innate, of course, and independent of time and place: the mature Chaucer writes of the universal, of the unchanging—of men and women and their inner reactions to human situations, of man's eternal hope and eternal despair, of man's anger, lust, and love. But every writer needs concrete form and substance in which to dress the abstractions of his universality, and he is thus forced to introduce "a local habitation and a name." From what ambiance, then, did Chaucer, the man, take his special shapes and his embellishments?

To answer that question, we shall begin by considering three divisions of the poet's life in which marked external influences were at work to shape his style and content: first, we have Chaucer's boyhood; second, we have Chaucer's service with Prince Lionel; and third, we have Chaucer's journey (or, possibly, journeys) to Italy, ushering in his life in London and elsewhere as a mature artist and man of affairs.

We do not know exactly when, or exactly where, Chaucer was born, but we do know that his birth took place some time between 1340 and 1344, and that much (if not all) of his early boyhood must have been spent in London where John Chaucer, the poet's father, resided and conducted his business. Both those known facts are important to our purpose, for fourteenth-century London at mid-century was enjoying a few rare years of optimism.

England may be said to have come of age as a unified nation by the year 1350. The great victory over the French at Crécy in 1346, followed by a series of other military successes, encouraged Englishmen for at least a decade to think of themselves as a closely knit, invincible force, and—truly medieval —they were as extravagant in their feeling that all was materially well as they were soon to feel that all was materially ill. Edward III, in chivalric majesty, was now sitting securely on his throne in Westminster, adjacent to London, attended by his hero son, the Black Prince. Pride and prosperity walked hand in hand. The time, brief though it was, was one of mental expansion, of believing that all good things could be achieved; savor for life was abroad in the land, and London was the heart and mind of that land: what London stood for was also what England stood for. Further, the great wholesale merchants of London (the vintners, the fishmongers, the grocers, the mercers, the goldsmiths) although constituting a relatively small proportion of the population, had now reached a tacitly accepted, powerful eminence, for these men had become the bankers of the nation and the dictatorial rulers of politics. They were shrewdly intelligent in getting what they wanted, they were possessed of considerable formal education (many of them had studied law as preparation for both business and politics), they were frequent recipients of royal gifts and subsidies, and they often had an interest in the arts and an appreciation of courtly amenities. We can be sure that John Chaucer, although not one of the wealthiest or the most prominent of the merchants, shared the characteristics of his class. He had enjoyed some royal favor, having held the not unimportant post of Deputy to the King's Butler* at Southampton; he had also served as Collector of Customs at various ports from time to time. Naturally he would have been ambitious for a son who gave promise (small Geoffrey must always have been a "likely lad"!) and might therefore rise —such was the temper of the times—to very great heights indeed. And the first step for John Chaucer to take towards a realization of his ambition for his son was to provide the child with as superior an education as could be obtained.

Fourteenth-century London had three elementary schools of good "academic" standing which were attended by the sons of the well-to-do, and we know that Geoffrey Chaucer attended one of those schools (we do not know which) before continuing his education in a much higher sphere. The three schools

---

* The post of "King's Butler" was that of a court official who supervised the management of the royal wine cellars. Hence, such an official had some power over the wine trade of the country.

must have offered the same curriculum more or less: reading, religion, Latin, French and arithmetic—and perhaps even some "natural science." Chaucer gives evidence in all his mature work of being extraordinarily well read and of having many wide and deep intellectual interests. Were not the foundations for those interests firmly laid in the London school?

Another influence at work in Chaucer's early boyhood—an influence more subtle than schooling, perhaps, but equally as strong—surely was the city itself. The child, imbued with imaginative power, must have walked each day through the excitements of London's narrow, crooked streets (only Cheapside was broad and straight): streets lined with open-fronted shops displaying their tempting wares, the shops interrupted here and there by one of London's many churches, or by the stately façade of a merchant's house, or by an imposing hall of one of the Gilds. On an ordinary day there were always clamorous, seething crowds, for the walled city of London in Chaucer's time had the large population of 40,000 pent up in the relatively small area of approximately one and one-half square miles. (Medieval London occupied the space called the "City" today—the smallest of the twenty-nine divisions of modern London.) How vivid must have been the impressions of London on Geoffrey's mind! Hurrying merchants and aldermen (splashes of bright reds and greens and blues and yellows—never a pastel, for even in medieval color there had to be violent contrast), obsequiously followed by no less gaily attired gentlemen-apprentices; bawling, jostling tradesmen advertising their goods, the touts for the cook-shops loudly promising capons and geese and pasties; the thief, slipping in and out like a shadow, in search of a loosely hanging, ill-guarded purse; perhaps an occasional noble, riding arrogantly through the press on his splendidly caparisoned horse with scant regard for pedestrians. There could scarcely have been a noisier city in the whole medieval world, and we may confidently add that at the middle of the fourteenth century no other city in England could surpass London in sights and sounds provocative to the imagination of a poet.

Maybe now and then, too, the child who was Geoffrey Chaucer played truant and, instead of finding his way to school, allowed himself to be drawn by the magic of one of his father's lately arrived ships, moored below Thames Street, ships which bore rich wine from the sunny vineyards of the faraway south, and which were manned by exotic, alien sailors, maybe bearded like the Shipman of whom the poet was later to write, who would be eager to regale a wondering, round-eyed child with "perilous tales" of remote lands and seas. Man has always found pleasure in accounts, both historical and fictional, of shoes and ships and sealing wax; surely we may imagine that the boy Geoffrey's fondness for a story must have been nurtured by the sailors' yarns he probably heard as a London child.

The second division in Chaucer's life to influence his writing, his service with Prince Lionel, was brought about certainly by John Chaucer's continuing ambitions for Geoffrey. Obviously we cannot tell when the idea of securing a place for the boy as page (later to advance to "squire") in a Royal Household first entered the elder Chaucer's mind, or what steps he took to realize such a lofty aim (not many noblemen could aspire to it), but some time in the 1350's found Geoffrey Chaucer in totally different surroundings from those of his London boyhood. Prince Lionel, Earl of Ulster, the third son of Edward III, had married the Countess Elizabeth of Ulster; to their circle were attracted not only the dignitaries of Church and State—many of whom were patrons of arts and letters—but artists, including writers, as well. The setting was richly ornate, in which tangible beauties were illuminated by the light of discriminating minds. In such an august and overwhelming environment there was undoubtedly a very great deal for the child of the London vintner to learn even while most of the London memories retreated temporarily before the intricate rules and ceremonies and the suavity and glitter of courtly behavior. But here again the boy was father to the poet and man of sensitive insight and intelligence. Geoffrey Chaucer did not fail—we have the evidence of his work—to "read, mark, learn, and inwardly digest" whatever took place in his golden surroundings as page and squire.

In his portrait of a fictional squire in the *Canterbury Tales,* Chaucer mentions a number of accomplishments of that delightful and life-like character, but what must have been the most rewarding and absorbing accomplishment for Chaucer himself in his own courtly education is not on the list of acquisitions of his Squire. Chaucer says in such connection only that his Squire knows how to "wel endite," [I (A) 95] that is, how to compose very well the lyrics for songs. Fourteenth-century squires were expected to perfect themselves as far as possible in the art of writing verse, a fact which is well attested by the contemporary literature—nearly every knight seems to have written a poem in honor of his lady, as does the Man in Black (presumably none other than John of Gaunt, brother to Prince Lionel) in Chaucer's own *Book of the Duchess,* as he "best koude" [BD, 1156 ff.] To become fully proficient in literary attainments, squires—at least, those who were talented—made a thorough study of the French rhetoricians, of Latin authors, especially Ovid and Virgil, and of the great French authors (for example, Guillaume de Lorris of *Le Roman de la Rose,* Deschamps, Froissart, and Machaut). Thus was the foundation laid for Chaucer's first poems, a foundation never to be abandoned entirely, even in later poems where the modern reader might think of Chaucer as breaking completely with French tradition.

That Chaucer wrote much verse in his early, experimental

period is evidenced by his friend and contemporary, John Gower. Gower speaks of Chaucer as being the disciple and poet of Venus, a poet who in "the floures of his youthe" had filled the land with ditties and "songes glade." [Gower, *Confessio Amantis*, VIII, ll. 2942*-2945*.] However, those glad songs are lost to us today; we can only imagine how closely they must have reflected the teaching the poet received in Prince Lionel's service. The first poem which we can actually examine for reflection of courtly French influence is the *Book of the Duchess* [See below, Part III], not written until 1369. All Chaucer's work, however, gives evidence in varying degree of a compelling memory of his life as a page and squire, more definite usually, and hence less difficult to detect, than a memory of his life as a child in London, strong though that memory had to be.

It is not known when Chaucer left Prince Lionel's service: he may have done so after the Countess' death in 1363, or he may have remained for a longer time with Prince Lionel who died in 1368. If the association did continue, Chaucer could have visited Italy in the Prince's company before his "first" known journey (of 1373), the journey which is usually spoken of as the beginning of the poet's Italian Period. Or if he left the Prince's household earlier in the decade, Chaucer in all likelihood attended one of London's two law schools, probably the so-called Inner Temple. No records of the law schools prior to 1500 survive, but Speght, a late-sixteenth-century editor of Chaucer's works, speaks of a Master Buckley, the keeper of the records of the Inner Temple, having seen a record in his "house" of a fine imposed on Geoffrey Chaucer for "beatinge a Franciscane Fryer."

Chaucer at some time must have been contemplating a career in the civil service, for which some legal training was a necessary qualification. A military life does not appear to

* Line numerals asterisked refer to the first version.

have been Chaucer's métier; squires usually became knights as the final step in their training, and Chaucer never attained knighthood. (A medieval squire may be roughly compared to a twentieth-century second lieutenant, and a knight to an officer of higher rank.) He did see fighting in France, once during the winter of 1359-60, at which time he was taken prisoner and later ransomed, and again in 1369; but the ten-year gap between those two engagements is further indication that Chaucer had either no aptitude or no inclination for a soldier's career. He seems to have been much more useful to the Crown as an informal ambassador, for after 1360 he served a number of different times in that capacity. Moreover, warfare plays no real part in Chaucer's works, provided we except his admiration, many times expressed, for knightly prowess.

Nor does Chaucer's marriage to Philippa Roet, probably taking place in the 1360's, appear to have directly affected his writing, although indirectly it may have done so by bringing the poet greater financial security and hence greater freedom of mind. Philippa Roet, whose sister was Katherine Swynford, the mistress and later the third wife of the Duke of Lancaster, received a "pension" and numerous gifts from the Duke, and it is to be supposed that Chaucer shared in those favors.

The third and last division of Chaucer's life with which we shall be concerned begins in 1373. It was then that Chaucer was sent to Italy "on the King's business," and during his stay in that country he fell deeply in love with Italian literature, a literature in which actuality was usually treated extremely imaginatively, as it is, for example, in the works of Boccaccio. Further, Italy could boast of a towering genius, the unique Dante, then only fifty years dead, who wrote his poetry as an imitation of life in the classical sense, and who produced a technical "realism" through brilliant selection of detail. Because of his admiration for and study of the great

Italian, Chaucer became much indebted to him, for although Chaucer never wrote in Dante's grand style, many of the English poet's lines, specifically indicated in the notes to Chaucer, texts are based on passages drawn from Dante's works. One cannot say, of course, that Chaucer learned from "the wise poete of Florence" [III (D) 1125] his portrait painter's skill in stressing only those details which will make the subject come alive—in contradistinction to the camera's "passport snap" in which all details are equally stressed and which, we say, "looks nothing like the subject"; but surely that skill of Chaucer's was strengthened, and perhaps enriched, by his reading of the Italian poet. Chaucer derived a great deal also from Boccaccio; we shall probably never really know why Chaucer did not name that author whom he apparently so much admired.

Italy, then, began a new era in writing for Geoffrey Chaucer. Although he did not wholly forget the French models of his earlier days, Chaucer now charmed his audience by an increasingly naturalistic, ironic, and philosophical flavor in his poetry, a flavor which reaches across the centuries to us today: we meet the inimitable eagle of the *House of Fame*, the delightfully matter-of-fact birds of the *Parliament of Fowls*, the haunting, psychological actualities of *Troilus and Criseyde*, and the three-dimensional men and women of the *Canterbury Tales*, and all are real to us. As Dryden said: "Chaucer followed nature everywhere, but was never so bold as to go beyond her."

Another environmental influence on Chaucer during the third division of his life is again London, but not the optimistic city of Chaucer's boyhood. The London of Chaucer's maturity was deeply pessimistic for the most part, for the times saw the deteriorating close of Edward III's reign and all the disasters, both at home and abroad, while Richard II occupied the throne. Edward III, during the last years of his life, was in failing health—the strong king had become weak, dominated by two unscrupulous and over-ambitious sons; national confidence reached a very low ebb at the time of Edward's death, and Richard, the young grandson, with no natural taste for kingship, did little—or perhaps was without the power—to stop the decline. London, beset by many kinds of grave calamities, was far from happy during the last quarter of the fourteenth century. Londoners in this period were seriously worried by the lack of any decisive English victories in the war with France and by the fear of a possible French invasion on a large scale. They were apprehensive about the instability of the English Crown, as Richard was intermittently threatened by Gloucester and Bolingbroke for some time before the deposition in 1399, and about the ruthless decrees of the Merciless Parliament bringing death or exile to many. They were discomposed by the great bloodshed following the admission of the peasant mob to the city in 1381, and by the frequent armed conflicts among the London citizens themselves—conflicts resulting either from the political rivalries of the Gilds, or from protests over unpopular civil or ecclesiastical measures.

But no matter what its temper, the city was still tne city: crowded, tumultuous, colorful, always provocative to the imagination and always loved by her citizens, no matter how much discouraged, or how angry, or how fearful they might be. Chaucer, a thoroughly sophisticated and urban individual of his time, dwelling in relative comfort over the Aldgate entrance to London during the first part of this quarter century, could and did observe life both within and without his city, noisy London from one window, and the long road leading to Mile End and East Anglia from an opposite window. To some modern readers of Chaucer it may at first seem strange that Chaucer would say almost nothing explicit about current misfortunes and upheavals, if he were really so much a part of the London scene. There is no oddness in Chaucer's omitting such references, however; the poet was now fully mature, and the polished work upon which he was then engaged had no fitting place in it for London disasters. But in a different sense, London was undoubtedly an environmental influence upon the poet. As a busy civil servant, Chaucer had to be daily in touch with men of affairs, constantly aware of all walks of fast-paced life; further, as is pointed out above, London was the intellectual center of England, and Chaucer's native many-sided interests—in human nature and in the ways men act, in philosophy, in religion, in science—widened and deepened inevitably because of his residence there.

Thus Geoffrey Chaucer wrote as he did not only because of his unique and luminous power, but also because of his situation in time and place in the long, so-far-unbroken line of human existence. The genius is timeless; the man, of necessity, is local. We shall examine—or re-examine—in the following pages Chaucer's poetic works with those facts in mind.

PART II
The Canterbury Tales

ONE ❖ The Influence of Chaucer's Chivalric World

SOMETIMES THE MODERN READER has a conception of medieval chivalry derived solely from romantic stories of plumed knights and fair ladies: the knights, surrounded by elaborate pageantry, engage with success in daring feats of an impossibly exaggerated character, spurred on by the noblest sentiments of love. Although pageantry did play a great part in actual fourteenth-century chivalry, as did also prowess in battle and—to a lesser extent—love for a lady, those matters represent only half the true meaning of chivalry in Chaucer's day. To acquire a better understanding, one must first examine the origin of the term "chivalry," or "knighthood."

Medieval man rightly claimed that the underlying idea of chivalry went back to Graeco-Roman antiquity, and that Christians had espoused it through the very nature of their faith; chivalry, in theory, was a moral code based on decent behavior. In practice, however, there was little adherence to such a code before the end of the eleventh century:

"knights" were merely mounted soldiers, and their lack of moral standards was frequently notorious. But in the year 1095, Pope Urban II, preaching in Rome to the knights of the First Crusade on their way to the Holy Land, spoke of those knights as having hitherto been mercenary plunderers. Because of the sacred nature of their current expedition, where the Cross had joined with the Sword, the Pope besought the crusaders to make complete change in their way of life. "Become wise, provident, temperate, learned, peacemaking, truth-seeking, pious, just and pure," he exhorted them, urging that they desert their cruelty and rapacity, thus becoming genuine soldiers of Christ, willing to wage war only on the infidel. We know from our history, of course, that Pope Urban's words had little effect on the behavior of the knights he addressed; nevertheless, the sermon wrought a kind of miracle, for it brought about an immediate revitalization of an ideal which Christendom had long allowed to fall into desuetude. Fidelity to both God and His Church and to one's temporal lord, a love for one's Christian neighbor —and hence pity for the afflicted and the weak—and a willingness to sacrifice the self in righteous cause, were all ethics which at once gained a new strength in men's minds and formed the initial medieval concept of ideal "knighthood," or "chivalry." To be worthwhile, an ideal must, of course, be beyond man's grasp, but it must also be within his comprehension as a good towards which he should strive. Part of the miracle created by Pope Urban was that his world truly desired to immediately set up a standard based on his precepts. "Orders of Chivalry" were quickly formed by groups of knights, and the centuries to follow in the Middle Ages saw many manuals which laid down regulations for such chivalric organizations. Most of the manuals are complex in their prescriptive detail, but there is little qualitative variation among them. Unless he had his title bestowed upon him in the "field," a practical short cut, or if he were a civilian who had performed some special service (such as the impulsive knighting by Richard II of Walworth, Brembre and Philipot during the Peasants' Revolt), a knight was expected to go through the relatively long period of training as page and squire in the household of a nobleman or of a knight of standing. That training included all the polite and formalized accomplishments of Chaucer's Squire, besides the particular concentration given to the young man's preparation for a military life.

Thus the good knight in literature will surely possess all the moral attributes of the ideal, as well as all the skills called for in the elaborate Rules, and, as a result, will usually seem totally "unreal" to a modern reader who misses the symbolical implications. Chaucer's courtly contemporaries, on the other hand, could have had no difficulty in separating the literal from the figurative, for they were accustomed to meeting both in one setting. Knightly life was basically aristocratic and ornately ritualistic, but it also embraced a hard core of factual acceptance.

That knighthood was so largely made up of set forms leads us to the introduction of the fair lady, although by an indirect path. As long as the knight was steadily occupied with warfare, there was room for little else in his life. But as the twelfth century advanced, warfare decreased in frequency, and leisure time correspondingly increased. To avoid too many hours of idleness there were war games: jousting, and a series of jousts, called a tournament; and, as always, when young men and young women are together in affluent idleness, there was the pleasure of dalliance. Gradually, the two amusements merged: the young man, when he fought, did so in honor of his lady, he was her faithful servant in all that he did. Love affairs grew to be as important as the fighting for Church and State. So-called "courtly love," in all its elaborate ramifications, became an accepted mode of behavior which fascinated both laymen and clerics who dwelt in this strangely interwoven world of solid facts, frivolous entertainments and deep concern for ethical and religious problems.

The fourteenth century, the hard-minded and pragmatic grandchild of the twelfth, stressed the facts in its modus vivendi, although it was still keenly aware of the ethical problems; the devotion to the fair lady, on the other hand, had disappeared from actuality to some extent, although not from the literature of the period. Consequently, when Chaucer writes of his Knight as a "real" person on a pilgrimage, love affairs are omitted as inappropriate as they would be in actuality, and the Knight appears to us as a flesh-and-blood figure for all his chivalric "perfections." In some of the Tales, however, where the knight is intended to represent the fictional, there is a decorous blend of ethics and love affair.

Many of Chaucer's friends were chivalric figures of historical import, and we do not need to turn to fiction to be aware of their actions. Throughout the ages there have always been men of great courage and rectitude who have lived as nearly as they could according to their religious and ethical beliefs, and who have been admired and loved by those with whom they have come in contact. Chaucer gives us the picture of exactly that sort of man [I (A) 42-78], placing him first in the list of pilgrims, not so much, we feel, because of the Knight's superior social position, as because of the beauty of the Knight's virtues. Here is indeed someone who is actually and metaphorically a *chevalier sans peur et sans reproche*. Chaucer tells us that his Knight has always "loved chivalrie": he has also, as a part of chivalry, loved "trouthe," or the keeping of his word; "honour"; "freedom," or material generosity; and "curteisie," or love for his neighbor as himself. Further, the Knight is "worthy . . . [but] wys" (that is, brave, but prudent); in his personal deportment, he is "as meeke as is a mayde," and he has "nevere yet no vileynye ne sayde/In al his lyf unto no maner wight."

The account of the Knight's activities and the description of his appearance support the statements about his character. The military campaigns and engagements which Chaucer mentions specifically as experienced by the Knight are all actual crusades, thereby attesting the Knight's adherence to Pope Urban's command that the good knight should take arms only against the infidel. Chaucer's Knight has been at the siege of Algezir in southern Spain, and has fought in Belmarye and Tramyssene in north Africa, all crusading campaigns of the 1340's against the Moors. In the 1360's the Knight has been present at the celebrated taking of Alexandria from the Saracens, as well as at the taking of the rich cities of Lyeys and Satalye in Asia Minor. The latter three cities were won by a force under the renowned and chivalric Peter of Cyprus, a king to whom Chaucer pays tribute in the *Monk's Tale,* and who is described by Guillaume de Machaut as *"li bons roys et tres vaillant homme."* Finally, probably in the 1380's, Chaucer's Knight has seen honorable action "in Pruce / In Lettow . . . and in Ruce," now termed Prussia, Lithuania, and Russia, all crusading expeditions initiated by the Teutonic Knights against the heathen, barbaric tribes.

In connection with the campaigns of the 1380's, Chaucer adduces a powerful piece of evidence regarding the Knight's great prowess. The Knight has "ful ofte tyme . . . the bord bigonne / Aboven alle nacions in Pruce," meaning probably that he has been singled out by the Teutonic Knights to head their famous "table of honor," a much coveted and unusual distinction accorded an especially valorous soldier. Even if "ful ofte tyme" is the poet's hyperbole, we may accept it paradoxically as very real and literal praise of the Knight's prowess. In like fashion, when Chaucer tells us that the

Knight has fought in "lystes thries, and ay slayn his foo" we may again have some poetical exaggeration, but again pointing up the true valor of the Knight. Chaucer is here referring to the medieval chivalric custom, highly familiar to both him and his audience, in which one or more champions were chosen to contend against the same number from the enemy's force, the winners or winner to decide the victory for the entire army. Obviously the choice for such combat could fall only upon the most celebrated among the knights.

That Chaucer's Knight is properly modest in bearing is implied by the soberness of his costume, although his horses —his own mount, his son's and the Yeoman's—are valuable, and by his wearing a gipon of "fustian," a coarse material designed to stand up under hard service. His dress also gives further small evidence of his piety, that is, of his eagerness to make his pilgrimage to Canterbury, probably to give thanks to St. Thomas for some successful undertaking. Chaucer states that the Knight's tunic is "al bismotered" (soiled) from his coat of mail; so intent is the Knight "to doon his pilgrymage" that he has not even taken the time to remove his battle dress completely before he arrives at the Tabard Inn in Southwark.

Although he is personally "meek," the Knight is aware that he should uphold the dignity of knighthood. Rules of the chivalric Orders state that a knight must always possess "good" horses, as does Chaucer's Knight, and that his office demands that he be accompanied on every journey by at least one squire and an attendant of lesser rank, and Chaucer's Knight is so escorted. Furthermore, when the cut falls to him to tell the first Tale (probably through design, for the entire company of pilgrims would give him the place of honor), the Knight graciously and readily accepts the assignment as a dignity belonging to his position in life. And we should here contrast the Knight's noble awareness of what

is fitting with January's attitude in the *Merchant's Tale.*
January is termed a "knight" by the pompous and not very
discerning Merchant, but Chaucer would expect his audience
to look beneath the surface and recognize January as being
the antithesis of the ideal. January, that lascivious old man,
lives luxuriously, because he believes that that way of living
"longeth to a knyght"; his "housynge" and his "array" are
fashioned as richly as a king's [IV (E) 2024-2027].—How
different from our pilgrim Knight!

There can be nothing idle or accidental in Chaucer's delineation of his Knight: that truly "parfit" and "gentil" man represents what anyone in the fourteenth century would recognize
as a "good servant of the Lord," always to be met somewhere
in the real world, one of the humble in heart but mighty
in virtue, not frequently met, alas, but unmistakable when
encountered. Chaucer is here writing straight from his environment.

In searching for a basic narrative to use for the *Knight's
Tale,* Chaucer found a happy choice in Boccaccio's *Il Teseida.*
True, an affair of the heart is very much present in the plot,
and at first glance that does not seem altogether appropriate
to Chaucer's Knight, but through his genius, Chaucer transforms Boccaccio's classical epic and love story into a chivalric picture of medieval life. Chaucer's representation is "real"
in the sense that it mirrors selected portions of an ordered,
aristocratic world, the reality strengthened—paradoxically,
if one wishes so to think—by the very fact that that world
often exists only as an ideal. In the Middle Ages the dream
is frequently the bulwark to the business, and the business to
the dream; there is no clear demarcation between them. Some
twentieth-century critics have claimed that the *Knight's Tale*
does not "fit" the teller because of its stately style and philosophical overtones. The Knight, those critics say, is a simple
soldier, not a man of letters, and hence, from the point of view

of verisimilitude, he could not have told his Tale in such a polished literary form, nor would he have been "interested" in so doing. But how "simple" is the chivalric knight of the fourteenth century? Chivalry, in all its enormously complex—and "polished"—implications, is surely inseparable from the mind of every good knight of the Middle Ages. And certainly even the most literal-minded of us today must acknowledge that both professional soldiers and sailors of our own times have been able to write books which have literary value.

Chaucer uses the character of Theseus as the unifying chivalric force in the *Knight's Tale*. The poet is not at all concerned with representing Theseus as a hero of ancient Athens; instead, Theseus emerges as a medieval knight, as much of Chaucer's own times as Chaucer himself. Of course, Theseus is quite different from the Knight of the pilgrimage, although, as a chivalric figure, he must be depicted as sharing a number of that worthy's moral attributes. Theseus is much more flamboyant and more authoritative than Chaucer's Knight; after all, the narrative demands that he be a royal personage, whereas the Knight is but a "commoner." When Theseus rides forth he is rightly "gay" in all his clothing and in his accoutrements; he must glitter and dazzle, bearing his golden pennon; all must be in keeping with his exalted position in life. Indeed, as "lord and gouvernour" of Athens his spectacular splendor is as true to the actual chivalric picture as is the retiring modesty of the pilgrim Knight. And of course royal chivalric figures were as much a part of Chaucer's environment as the good knights he knew of less lofty origins.

Theseus' prowess in battle is less specifically stressed—perhaps more taken for granted—than is the Knight's, but it is given a prominent place at the beginning of the *Knight's Tale*. Theseus has been in his time "swich a conqueror" that there is none greater "under the sonne." He has won very many rich countries through "his wysdom and his chivalrie";

he has killed the monstrous Minotaur, a tremendous feat, and when he proceeds against Thebes, he slays King Creon himself, in "pleyn bataille" or, as we would say, in fair fight. Theseus' compassion is introduced to us almost as soon as his prowess. He interrupts his triumphal return from conquest in Scythia to listen courteously to the wailing, black-clad ladies, and swears with "herte pitous" that as "trewe knyght" he will immediately avenge their wrongs. And later in the Tale [I (A) 1761] Chaucer again emphasizes the virtue of compassion by reminding his audience that "pitee renneth soone in gentil herte," a sentiment familiar to the fourteenth century and one of which the poet is fond, for he repeats it in the *Man of Law's Tale* [II (B) 660], in the *Merchant's Tale* [IV (E) 1986], and in the *Squire's Tale* [V (F) 479], and— outside the *Canterbury Tales*—in the *Legend of Good Women* [F 503]. For Theseus, in his nobility of character, takes pity on the suppliant Hippolyte and her ladies (and thus on Palamon and Arcite, who have *not* behaved in knightly fashion); his anger vanishes, and the two young men are generously forgiven [I (A) 1748-1844].

Theseus is also imbued with consideration for the happiness of others. After Arcite's fatal accident following the tournament with Palamon, Theseus—although he is himself grief-stricken—publicly makes light of the disaster for a time, in order that the three days of feasting, gayety and lavish presentation of gifts may be cloudlessly enjoyed by all the visitors.

Theseus, like the Knight, possesses material generosity, or "fredom." After the fall of Thebes, Theseus gives permission to his men to share in the spoils of war; Perotheus, obtaining Arcite's release from prison, is not required by Theseus to pay ransom; later, because he is appreciative of the excellent service given by the disguised Arcite as squire, Theseus supplies the young man with gold "to mayntene his degree." And certainly, when Theseus has the lists erected for the tournament, he spares no expense. All the skilled geometricians and arithmeticians, all the celebrated painters and sculptors are summoned and given "mete and wages" to produce a veritably royal structure. Which leads us inevitably to Chaucer's own interest and undoubted knowledge of the many tournaments staged in London during his lifetime—a facet of chivalry which evidently caught his imagination with all its pomp and circumstance.

For in spite of the Church's opposition to the spending of money on the vanities of the world, Londoners always loved a show, the more elaborate and sumptuous the better. A celebration of any kind, even an airing of a grievance, was an excuse for a procession, and except for a coronation a royal tournament was the best excuse of all. The child Geoffrey, in his early London days, must have been ecstatically aware of all the excitements of such occasions. The streets would be decorated with bright banners; if the occasion were especially important, the banners would not be of serge, but of purple silk and cloth-of-gold, the streets would be strewn with flowers when the season permitted, and fountains—constructed for the event—might be playing. Everywhere there would be music and laughter and joyous cries, troubles forgotten until the morrow; everywhere there would be deep velvets and shining silks in gem-like colors. The streets of London must have presented an extraordinary, harmonious dissonance, weaving together voluptuous and intoxicating sound and sights. The replicas of the Surcoat and of the Funeral Achievements of the Black Prince, now hanging above the Prince's tomb in Canterbury Cathedral, can give us an idea of the brilliance of the colors and of the beauty of design of chivalric dress.

As a young man, Chaucer must have taken part himself in festival occasions, maybe riding as a squire in Prince Lionel's retinue in a ceremonial procession, a procession which might easily include the gorgeously appareled ladies of the court on their palfreys, all on the way to attend one of the series of royal jousts to be staged at Smithfield, that great open space lying outside the city to the northwest.

Chaucer, the poet, shows without question that a love of spectacle lay at the roots of his being, and that in true medieval fashion, for men of the Middle Ages were indeed consistently inconsistent, he willingly accepted some of the vanities of fourteenth-century chivalry, even as he extolled the austerities of an earlier code. In his pleasure in magnificent display, Chaucer apparently ignored the fact that the Church condemned tournaments, an attitude based not only on the fact that they encouraged gross expenditure of money which should have gone towards almsgiving and other good deeds, but also on the score that tournaments frequently resulted in the deaths of the participants, either by accident or by malice aforethought.

In the *Knight's Tale*, Chaucer gives positive evidence of his own interest in and approval of royal tournaments by giving us what might be termed an exciting "eyewitness" description of the preparations for the contest and of the contest itself. In the morning, at dawn, on the day of the great tournament between Palamon and Arcite, Chaucer says*:

> Of hors and harneys noyse and claterynge
> Ther was in hostelryes al aboute;
> And to the paleys rood ther many a route
> Of lordes upon steedes and palfreys.
> Ther maystow seen devisynge of harneys
> So unkouth and so riche, and wroght so weel
> Of goldsmythrye, of browdynge, and of steel;
> The sheeldes brighte, testeres, and trappures,
> Gold-hewen helmes, hauberkes, cote-armures;

* For definitions of difficult words, see Selected Glossary, pp. 196-206.

Lordes in parementz on hir courseres.
Knyghtes of retenue, and eek squieres
Nailynge the speres, and helmes bokelynge:
Giggynge of sheeldes, with layneres lacynge
(There as nede is they weren no thyng ydel);
The fomy steedes on the golden brydel
Gnawynge, and faste the armurers also
With fyle and hamer prikynge to and fro;
Yemen on foote, and communes many oon
With shortes staves, thikke as they may goon;
Pypes, trompes, nakers, clariounes,
That in the bataille blowen blody sounes:
The paleys ful of peple up and doun,
Heere thre, ther ten, holdynge hir questioun. . . .

[*I (A) 2492-2514*]

The description of the tournament itself is no less vivid. Theseus is first pictured seated at a window of his palace, in full view of the vast crowds, "arrayed right as he were a god in trone," awaiting the arrival of the young Theban knights. A herald trumpets for silence, and Theseus proclaims his "myghty dukes wille": the tournament is not to be held under the guise of a battle to the death, for there is to be no deliberate slaying (a not uncommon command in actuality— perhaps as some recognition of the ecclesiastical position regarding tournaments); only long swords and maces are to be used; a stake is to be set up on each side to which the wounded of the opposing side are to be brought, by force if necessary, and the tournament is ended when either Arcite or Palamon is so captured. Following his proclamation, Theseus, flanked by the young Thebans, heads the stately procession to the lists; he is followed by the queen and Emily and a great company of knights and ladies, through streets which have been hung with cloth of gold—no inexpensive serge banners for this momentous occasion!

After the procession reaches the lists, Theseus mounts to his high seat, and all the honored guests take their places. Then

> . . . westward, thurgh the gates under Marte,
> Arcite, and eek the hondred of his parte,
> With baner reed is entred right anon;
> And in that selve moment Palamon
> Is under Venus, estward in the place.
> With baner whyt, and hardy chiere and face.
>
> [*I (A) 2581-2586*]

The two young Thebans are perfectly matched in bravery, estate and age; as the chivalric code demands, neither has the advantage.

> And in two renges faire they hem dresse.
> Whan that hir names rad were everichon,
> That in hir nombre gyle were ther noon,
> Tho were the gates shet, and cried was loude:
> 'Do now youre devoir, yonge knyghtes proude!'
> The heraudes lefte hir prikyng up and doun;
> Now ryngen trompes loude and clarioun.
> There is namoore to seyn, but west and est
> In goon the speres ful sadly in arrest;
> In gooth the sharpe spore into the syde.
> Ther seen men who kan juste and who kan ryde;
> Ther shyveren shaftes upon sheeldes thikke;
> He feeleth thurgh the herte-spoon the prikke.
> Up spryngen speres twenty foot on highte;
> Out goon the swerdes as the silver brighte;
> The helmes they tohewen and toshrede;
> Out brest the blood with stierne stremes rede;
> With myghty maces the bones they tobreste.
> He thurgh the thikkeste of the throng gan threste;
> Ther stomblen steedes stronge, and doun gooth al;
> He rolleth under foot as dooth a bal;
> He foyneth on his feet with his tronchoun,

And he hym hurtleth with his hors adoun;
He thurgh the body is hurt and sithen take,
Maugree his heed, and broghte unto the stake:
As forward was, right there he most abyde.
[*I (A) 2594-2619*]

And so the fighting continues throughout the day, with brief
interludes called by Theseus for rest and refreshment. The
plot demands, of course, that Arcite, fighting under Mars,
"the stierne god armypotente," win the contest, although both
knights are considered to be equally valiant.

The general "equality" of Palamon and Arcite must be
apparent throughout the *Knight's Tale,* since the two young
men are to be shown in chivalric rivalry: no knight should
contend with another of less strength than himself. At the beginning of the Tale, Palamon and Arcite are depicted as

Two yonge knyghtes liggynge by and by,
Bothe in oon armes, wroght ful richely, . . .
[For they] weren of the blood roial
Of Thebes, and of sustren two yborn.
[*I (A) 1011-1012, 1018-1019*]

Both are imprisoned "in angwissh and in wo," for "ther may
no gold hem quite"; both fall in love at first sight with Emily,
who is fairer than the lily. Although many critics have
stressed "differences" in Palamon and Arcite, saying, for example, that the former is the more contemplative man, and
that the latter is more the man of action, it seems to the
present writer that Chaucer has placed his own emphasis on
similarities rather than on any dissimilarities. It is true, of
course, that Chaucer is too much the portrayer of the actual
to depict two cousins as being completely identical, but it is
none the less true that in the *Knight's Tale* Chaucer intended
the chivalric equation to be paramount.

Palamon and Arcite are sworn brothers, that is, each has

pledged to support the other in any situation which may arise
—indeed each has pledged to give up his very life for the
other should it prove necessary. Whether or not Chaucer intended his audience to interpret the breaking of that pledge,
upon their both falling in love with the same girl, as a seriously reprehensible act, is unknown. But the keeping of one's
word was an extremely important part of the chivalric code,
and it seems unlikely that Chaucer and his contemporaries—
no matter how they might act themselves in "real" life—
would accept as ethical the fictional Arcite's argument addressed to the outraged Palamon:

'. . . who shal yeve a lovere any lawe?
Love is a gretter lawe, by my pan,
Than may be yeve to any erthely man;
And therfore positif lawe and swich decree
Is broken al day for love in ech degree.
A man moot nedes love, maugree his heed.
He may nat fleen it, thogh he sholde be deed. . . .'
            [*I (A) 1164-1170*]

Further, surely by the time he was writing the *Canterbury
Tales*, Chaucer distinguished one kind of love from another;
he had talked gravely of the woes emanating from the physical
love between man and woman, the loves that are "thise
wrecched worldes appetites" [*Troilus and Criseyde*, V, 1851];
if, then, the poet is showing in the *Knight's Tale* any actual disapproval of the breaking of the vow between Palamon and Arcite, there is a possible added reason, small though it may be, for
deploring the act: the cause gives little excuse for the result. We
must remember again that the fourteenth century saw nothing
strange in a sharp cleavage between the theory of the code and
the practice of what took place in daily living, and although
Chaucer observed life-as-it-is with great fidelity—indeed, the
nature of his genius was such that he was impelled to portray

men and women exactly as they are—he still admired, and had to be aware of the emphases on, conventional chivalric beliefs and ideals. We may smile today over the artificially excessive promises in sworn brotherhood and the "natural" breakdown of such promises if two young "brothers" turn out to be rivals in love; we may smile even when Palamon (the "gentil" Palamon!) links Arcite to himself as guilty in their duty to Theseus. "Do not give either of us mercy," begs Palamon, "but slay us both," because, as he continues—

'. . . though thow knowest it lite,
This is thy mortal foo, this is Arcite,
That fro thy lond is banysshed on his heed,
For which he hath deserved to be deed.
For this is he that cam unto thy gate
And seyde that he highte Philostrate.
Thus hath he japed thee ful many a yer,
And thou hast maked hym thy chief squier; . . .
I make pleynly my confessioun
That I am thilke woful Palamoun
That hath thy prisoun broken wikkedly. . . .
Wherfore I axe deeth and my juwise;
But sle my felawe in the same wise,
For both han we deserved to be slayn.'
    [*I (A) 1723-1730, 1733-1735, 1739-1741*]

Palamon's downright implication of Arcite is obviously not chivalric in any sense, for his very human desire to put his rival out of the running has canceled all thought of the vows of sworn brotherhood. Yes, *we* may smile. But would Chaucer's audience have so done? To the present writer it seems that if there were any amusement, it would have been concealed and it would have been rueful.

There would have been no laughter on the part of Chaucer's audience, however, when Palamon and Arcite meet in the grove for the first time after Arcite's return to Athens. Here we have an encounter which, on the surface, is genuinely chival-ric. No true knight was to take advantage over another, and consequently Palamon must be supplied with clothes and food and the armor which he lacks. In knightly fashion, Arcite gives his word that he will bring Palamon, now a deadly en-emy, all that the latter needs. "And ches [choose] the beste, and leef the worste for me," Arcite adds.

The chivalric honor of Palamon and Arcite, although badly shaken by rivalry in love, is completely restored towards the close of the *Knight's Tale*. On his deathbed, Arcite advises Emily to consider Palamon, "his cosyn deere," as her suitor. Palamon, he declares, has all the knightly virtues:

> 'That is to seyen, trouthe, honour, knyghthede,
> Wysdom, humblesse, estaat, and heigh kyndrede,
> Fredom, and al that longeth to that art— . . .
> Foryet nat Palamon, the gentil man.'
> [*I (A) 2789-2791, 2797*]

Thus we are left with the conviction—even today, when "chivalry" has become less "romantic" and less often in man's mind—that here is a young knight, purged of human frailties, now showing the world that the ideal *chevalier* can be truly "actual."

Chaucer, as interested as he was in the concept of chivalry, could not have confined that interest to one Tale alone, and a number of the narratives in the *Canterbury Tales*, besides that of the Knight, indicate the poet's continuing absorption in ideas of knighthood. In such respect, the *Franklin's Tale* is second to the *Knight's Tale*. To be sure, the Franklin him-self is technically not a knight, but Chaucer shows him to be a man who venerates all the knightly virtues. "Fy on pos-sessioun," exclaims the Franklin, "but if [except] a man be vertuous withal!" [V (F) 686-687] And in the *General Prologue*, Chaucer depicts the Franklin as possessing some of

the characteristics of the Knight himself [I (A) 331-360].
The Franklin, the "St. Julien . . . in his contree," is a
"worthy" vavasour. (As far as we know, the terms *vavasour*
and *franklin* were identical in fourteenth-century England;
both terms denoted a "wealthy landowner.") The Franklin's
whole-souled hospitality corresponds to the Knight's love of
"fredom" and—again like the Knight—the Franklin is highly
successful in all his undertakings. He has presided at sessions
of the justices of the peace, and he has often been a "knyght
of the shire," or a member of Parliament; he has also been a
"shirreve," or an officer next in rank to the Lord Lieutenant of the shire, and a "contour," or special pleader in
court. The Franklin's achievements and activities, although
completely different from those of the Knight, may yet be
compared to them: each man has attained success, as has
been his duty, in that state of life unto which it has pleased God
to call him. Consequently, since the *Franklin's Tale* is decidedly chivalric in nature, we may say with conviction that
the Tale truly "fits" the teller.

The plot of the *Franklin's Tale* is drawn in large measure
from Boccaccio's *Il Filocolo*, but Chaucer's Tale as it stands
is far more serious and more subtle than the Italian source.
The lady in Boccaccio's story is worldly-wise and is shrewd
rather than virtuous; thus we have little sympathy, if any, for
her or for her husband, who seems as coldly calculating as his
wife. When the lady arrives at her would-be lover's house, she
is coy, but not reluctant, and the "secrecy [discretion]" she
has conventionally requested is nullified by the ornate retinue
escorting her. Dorigen of the *Franklin's Tale,* on the other hand,
goes in great distress to meet Aurelius, and only because Arveragus has—for the noblest motives—commanded her to keep her
promise; and she is attended only by a maid and a squire.
Here is no fanfare, but the considered resolution of a grave
dilemma. Arveragus truly believes, we are convinced, that

"trouthe is the hyest thyng that man may kepe"; he weeps as he professes his creed, and he speaks neither unadvisedly nor lightly. Indeed, Arveragus, although quite different from the Knight of the Canterbury pilgrimage, may also be described as "a verray parfit gentil knyght." Arveragus has done his noble best to serve a lady, and has so assured her of his "worthynesse" and of his "meke obeysaunce" that she has been willing to take him both for "hir housbonde" and "hir lord." Arveragus truly means what he says when he swears:

> Of his free wyl . . . as a knyght
> That nevere in al his lyf he, day ne nyght,
> Ne sholde upon hym take no maistrie
> Agayn hir wyl, ne kithe hire jalousie,
> But hire obeye, and folwe hir wyl in al,
> As any lovere to his lady shal,
> Save that the name of soveraynetee,
> That wolde he have for shame of his degree.
>
> [V (F) 745-752]

Thus, in ideal fashion, the knightly husband is both servant and lord, while his lady wife is his love as well as wife.

And theré Chaucer is writing of the "new" in his environment: the belief that physical love could—and often did—exist without sin in marriage, a belief contrary to the tenet of earlier times which held that "love" in marriage had always to be identified with lust. Chaucer, however, lived in the fourteenth century, when paradoxes and genuine contradictions troubled no one. In the *Franklin's Tale,* the poet does not hesitate to present the "old" together with the new, Aurelius embodying the former, while Dorigen and her husband embody the latter; old and new meet constantly without clash or strain and—such is the magic of Chaucer— even twentieth-century readers are hardly conscious that the poet is dealing simultaneously with two opposing schools of thought in the chivalric world. Aurelius, the squire who is "fressher" and "jolyer of array . . . than is the month of May," represents "old-fashioned," or courtly, love: the fact that the object of his utter devotion is the wife of another man does not enter his consciousness, except as it gives him "honorable" permission to offer himself as a lover. Aurelius is

> Oon of the beste farynge man on lyve:
> Yong, strong, right vertuous, and riche, and wys,
> And wel biloved, and holden in greet prys.
>
> [V (F) 932-934]

He has placed Dorigen on such a pedestal that he has not dared tell her of his love, although he has suffered for more than two years, and has celebrated his woe "in a general compleyning" by composing "layes, songes, compleintes, roundels, virelayes." (Poetic composition as a means of relieving the pangs of unrequited passion seems to be independent of historic time!) But eventually, when Arveragus is away in England, the discreet Aurelius speaks, and we are not surprised, because Dorigen is "modern," when the lady announces firmly:

> 'By thilke God that yaf me soule and lyf,
> Ne shal I nevere been untrewe wyf
> In word ne werk, as fer as I have wit;
> I wol been his to whom that I am knyt.
> Taak this for fynal answere as of me.'
>
> [V (F) 983-987]

Of course, the plot of the *Franklin's Tale* requires that Dorigen make her "unmeant" rash promise, but still—from one point of view of the Middle Ages—a promise; and the keeping of one's word, the chivalric dictum that "he that sweareth unto his neighbour and disappointeth him not, though it were to his own hindrance . . . shall never fall," is the great fusing element of the *Franklin's Tale*. In the *Friar's Tale*, the

fiend refuses to take the horses "promised" by the carter, because—the fiend explains—the carter has not "meant" the
promise; but the *Friar's Tale* is not chivalric: no knightly virtue is being extolled, and the embellishments of the folk tale
are largely in the realities of everyday living. In the *Franklin's
Tale*, however, we are for the most part in the tapestried, symbolic world, although, as has been said, that also had "reality"
for Chaucer and his contemporaries, and the poet is intent
upon telling his audience that adherence to one's word is the
most important ethic man possesses. What difference can it
make that Dorigen's "guarantee" may be absurd in the literal
sense, or that one of the actors in the narrative is somewhat
behind his own times? It is still true, Chaucer would say to
us, that "trouthe is the hyeste thyng that man may kepe,"
and he accordingly writes in high seriousness.

Dorigen, suggested possibly by the lady in Boccaccio's
narrative, is a character in her own right, although she is also
very much of an ideal figure. For his purpose in the *Franklin's Tale*, Chaucer stresses Dorigen's integrity as a loving
wife: he shows her woe and despair that she cannot escape
from her promise except through "deeth or elles dishonour,"
and that she thinks death is the better course. Arveragus, as
one would anticipate, makes the proper decision; in tears—
for this must be a hard and painful decision to prove the
point—Arveragus says to Dorigen:

'For God so wisly have mercy upon me,
I hadde wel levere ystiked for to be
For verray love which that I to yow have,
But if ye sholde youre trouthe kepe and save.'
[*V (F) 1475-1478*]

Yet Chaucer, writing in the late fourteenth century, was apparently not unmindful of an ultramodern and sophisticated
courtly audience. He has the Franklin state, presumably to

the company of pilgrims, in reference to Arveragus' command:

> Paraventure an heep of yow, ywis,
> Wol holden hym a lewed man in this
> That he wol putte his wyf in jupartie.
> Herkneth the tale er ye upon hire crie.
> She may have bettre fortune than yow seemeth;
> An whan that ye han herd the tale, demeth.
>
> [V (F) 1493-1498]

The reaction of Aurelius to Arveragus' upholding of "trouthe" is plainly chivalric. When he learns the reason for Dorigen's coming to meet him, Aurelius has great compassion in his heart, and releases the lady from her promise, giving his solemn word to her, "the trewest and the beste wyf," that he will never approach her again—as a squire, he, too, can do a knightly deed. But to satisfy the demands of chivalric action, Aurelius' sacrifice—like Arveragus'—must be a difficult one. Therefore we are told that he "curseth the tyme that evere he was born," and bewails the fact that he must pay the magician "of pured gold a thousand pound of wighte," a sum which will ruin him. In the same breath, however, Aurelius returns to exalted knightly virtue and declares, "My trouthe wol I kepe, I wol nat lye"; he will pay the magician in installments, "yeer by yeer."

The magician, a true man of his times, shows in turn, first that he understands chivalric ideals, and second, that even though he is of an inferior class, he can at least copy the behavior of a good knight. Before the situation is fully explained to him, he is amazed that Aurelius is not going to keep the "covenant"; even a candidate for knighthood is expected in theory to keep a promise. But when Aurelius gives him the details—the "gentilesse" of Arveragus, who would rather die in sorrow and distress than "that his wyf were of hir trouthe fals"; the despair of Dorigen, who has been tempted to commit suicide, but who nobly has listened to her husband's plea that she keep her "trouthe"; and Aurelius' own renunciation for the sake of the highest of motives—the magician is himself overcome by admiration, and rises to the great height of generosity in the chivalric code by excusing Aurelius from all obligation.

Chaucer's placing of the *demande d'amour* at the close of the Tale is, of course, a literary, courtly-love convention, and hence can be said to belong to his chivalric environment. The same question is posed in *Il Filocolo*, and there answered. Chaucer, apparently with intention, supplies no answer, and we wonder if the fourteenth-century audience found the same amusement we may find today in debating the matter.

The *Wife of Bath's Tale*, as Chaucer presents the plot, has been shorn largely of the chivalric features of the analogues, the widespread tales of the Loathly Lady. The *Weddynge of Sir Gawen and Dame Ragnell* and the *Marriage of Sir Gawaine* are intimately concerned with knighthood as practiced at King Arthur's court. (Gawain, nephew to Arthur, is depicted as the most chivalric of all the knights in the early legends of the Round Table, and Chaucer himself speaks in the *Squire's Tale* of "Gawayn, with his olde curteisye.") Even Gower's *Tale of Florent*, resembling the *Wife of Bath's Tale* more than the two Gawain narratives, has more of a courtly background than the Wife's story. For Gower's hero, Florent, is

A worthi knyght . . .
Nevoeu to themperour
And of his Court a Courteour: . . .
He was a man that muchel myhte,
Of armes he was desirous,
Chivalerous and amorous
And for the fame of worldes speche,
Strange aventures for to seche

He rod the Marches al aboute.

[Confessio Amantis, *Book I, ll. 1408-1417*]

In the *Wife of Bath's Tale,* it is true that the hero comes from King Arthur's court, but he is described as a "lusty bacheler" (*bacheler* here means a "young knight") of no great importance, and when we first meet him he is returning merely from a day's sport in hawking for river fowl, not from the knightly quest sought by Florent. Furthermore, to set the plot in motion, the Wife's hero commits an actual—and certainly non-chivalric—crime, for which he should lose his head, while the noble Florent has the blameless misfortune to be overcome in fair fight with enemies. However, the chivalric enters in the *Wife of Bath's Tale* when the queen and her ladies beseech the king to spare the life of the young man—we should note the parallel of the pleading ladies in the *Knight's Tale*—thus giving Arthur the chivalric opportunity to accede to their prayers and to allow the queen to set the task for the young knight of finding the answer to the question. It may also be noted that the young knight does turn homeward when the time comes, for he has given his pledge to do so; and later he recognizes that he must marry the hag, for he must keep his word. Here again is Chaucer's emphasis on "trouthe."

The two questions in the Tale are also somewhat connected with chivalry, since they are in themselves *demandes d'amour* and hence suggestive of courtly love: "What do women most desire?" and the question put by the hag to her young husband, "Will you have me ugly and old and faithful, or will you have me fair and young and possibly unfaithful?" But the answer to the first question is such an integral part of Dame Alisoun's own special philosophy (in fact, it is the reason *par excellence* why Chaucer assigns the story to her), that it tends to lose all other significance; and because the answer to the second question is not given by the hero himself, so that it becomes a mere variation of the first answer, the second also tends to slip outside any chivalric classification. Essentially, if we are to consider the *Wife of Bath's Tale* as plot alone, we must admit that the Tale is tailored by Chaucer to fit Alisoun, Wife of Bath, and consequently it has little to do with knighthood.

The sermon, which the hag unexpectedly delivers to her new husband on the wedding night, is, however, irrelevant to the plot, and has, in fact, been considered a narrative flaw by many critics. We cannot be sure why Chaucer interpolated it; the sermon certainly has no logical relation to Alisoun herself, or to the hag, or to the furtherance of the action. As the didactic and the homiletic were admired as literary ornaments, the introduction of any sermon may be simply a medieval rhetorical device, but the choice of "gentilesse" as the limiting subject seems to be because of Chaucer's own absorption in chivalric matters. The Parson, in his Tale—that long and unrelieved sermon on the Seven Deadly Sins—does include a few observations on "gentilesse," similar in idea to the observations of the hag in the *Wife of Bath's Tale* [X (I) 460-465], but of course there can be nothing literally chivalric in the "povre Persoun of a Toun." In Alisoun's tale, in the hag's discourse of over one hundred lines, there are twenty-two words connected with the concept of "gentilesse," and the whole discourse is filled with ideas which were beloved familiarities in the ethics of fourteenth-century courtly life. Chaucer, then, is here immensely influenced by the time and place in which he lived.

Other Tales show Chaucer's interest in knighthood. In the *Monk's Tale* we do not find it inappropriate that the Monk, very much a man of the world, should extol chivalric figures. Alexander the Great, that well-known hero of medieval romance, is praised by the Monk, Daun Piers, in what for that self-centered and pompous soul passes for enthusiastic terms. Alexander is "of knyghthod and of fredom flour"; there are not enough tears in the world to bewail the death of his "gentilesse" and liberality. And the Monk also pays the same kind of generalized tribute to the "chivalrie" of Peter of Cyprus and of Julius Caesar. Daun Piers, however, is far more intent on a sort of gloating pleasure over the fact that important persons have met disaster than he is on their achievements, chivalric or otherwise—after all, his own importance has been summarily set aside, by Harry Bailly, in favor of the drunken Miller after the close of the *Knight's Tale* [I (A) 3127 ff.]. But for us, there is significance in that "chivalry" does appear in the *Monk's Tale,* even though the teller, true to his nature, treats it conventionally and pallidly.

The *Man of Law's Tale,* that folk tale of the Calumniated Wife which Chaucer transforms into religious allegory (one of the few Tales not well adapted to the teller, who—if we observe him in the *General Prologue* and identify the Sergeant with the Man of Law—is undoubtedly the "war and wys" Thomas Pynchbek of actual life), has very little direct chivalric reference. Chaucer does inform us, in the words of the teller of the Tale, that the Sultan receives permission to wed his Christian bride through the Pope, the Church and "al the chivalrye"; and later King Alla is spoken of as possessing the "gentil herte," "fulfild of pitee," which is so much prized in fourteenth-century knighthood. And there is mention of the medieval custom of a knight's defending a lady by "ordeal of battle" [II (B) 631-632]. Again, the significance for us lies in that there is any chivalric reference at all in a narrative devoted to the religious and philosophical aspects of fortitude.

The Manciple, who is far below both the Monk and the Man of Law in "degree," might not be expected by us today to be sufficiently interested in chivalric virtues to mention them in his Tale, yet the fourteenth-century audience surely found his praise of Phoebus, the knight of the Tale, wholly natural, for all classes knew what a good knight should be like. In all the world, the Manciple declares, no one else is so "faire on lyve" as Phoebus—he is "fulfild of gentilesse, / Of honour, and of parfit worthynesse." Phoebus is the "flour of bachilrie, / As wel in fredom as in chivalrie" [IX (H) 123-126]. The subject of the *Manciple's Tale* itself is, of course, not chivalric in any way, but Chaucer's world caused the brief inclusion of the formalized, chivalric phrases.

One might easily anticipate that the *Squire's Tale* would be deeply concerned with everything pertaining to knighthood, but Chaucer creates the Squire in the *General Prologue* as being only twenty years old and as being very much in love with love. The Squire's natural interest, therefore, is in romance, rather than in the more philosophic aspects of knighthood, and he has gone on his Flemish crusade primarily "in hope to stonden in his lady grace," a motive far different from that of his father, the Knight, when embarking on any "religious" war. As a matter of fact, Chaucer could never have depicted a "parfit gentil knyght" as having a share in the so-called "crusade" in Flanders, for that expedition was backed entirely by political and commercial interests, not by any pious zeal. But the Squire's youthful impetuosity and his eagerness to show his current lady his prowess in battle would both serve in everyone's mind as instant and valid excuse for the Squire's presence "in Flaundres, in Artoys, and Picardie"— especially since he has borne himself well in the fighting.

Of course the Squire does not entirely neglect chivalric matters in his Tale. When she talks with Canacee, the lady-falcon speaks the words which Chaucer writes four times in the *Canterbury Tales:* "pitee renneth soone in gentil herte" (see above, p. 25); further, she says that the gentle heart displays "gentilesse" [V (F) 479, 483]. She describes the faithless tercelet as seeming to be the "welle of alle gentilesse"; his actual treason and falseness is so hidden by his outward bearing of humility and "trouthe" that no one could be aware of his true nature. The lady-falcon, who now has become in our eyes a betrayed human lady of the court, says: " 'His manere was an hevene for to see . . . And I so loved hym for his obeisaunce, and for the trouthe I demed in his herte' " [V (F) 558, 562-563]; the lady has assumed— again in the pattern of "good" courtly love—that only an affair of some sort of honor would take her lover away, for he is "gentil born, and fressh . . . and humble and free." Thus through the negation of the tenets of courtly love, there is at least some emphasis on one department of chivalry.

If Chaucer had completed the Tale, there might have been considerable emphasis on prowess in battle as well: the poet makes the promise of an account of the deeds of Cambyuskan, of the perils Algarsif encounters for the sake of Theodora, and of how Cambalo fights in the lists for Canacee. We must observe, however, that with the exception of Cambyuskan's winning of cities, all the events are in some way connected with love.

The Canon's Yeoman's Tale, swift and "contemporaneous" and colloquial though it is—but perhaps, too, because of those characteristics—has some chivalric reference. The rascally, lying canon of the Tale, assures his intended victim that "trouthe" is something he will guard as long as he lives, and he says that he will match the unsuspecting priest's "gentilesse" with his own. And when the foolish priest would have the "receite" for the alchemic miracle, his eagerness is compared to that of a "knyght in armes" desirous of performing a valiant feat in order "to stonden in grace of his lady deere."

From its title, one might expect the Rime of Sir Thopas to center strongly about knighthood, but the Tale (if such it can be called) is, of course, a parody of the stereotyped metrical romance of the Middle Ages, and as such can only be indirectly "chivalric." However, the setting of Thopas has to do with knighthood, for the narratives the Tale satirizes have

such settings; and—again following the pattern of the paro-
died narratives—the hero knight is described in detail, both
as to character and appearance; his accomplishments and
feats of arms are praised; his love affairs are discussed; he
rides out on an adventure, or quest. The romances provided
the escape literature of the fourteenth century, and one cannot assume that Geoffrey Chaucer did not himself enjoy their
absurdities at times, perhaps in idle moments on "a myrie
someris day," although his penetrating eye as a realist, his
enormous power to depict life in action, evidently enabled
him to assess all the grotesqueries and crudities of what he
read. To be able to compose with such remarkable success
the parody in the *Rime of Sir Thopas*, Chaucer had also to be
entirely familiar with the flesh-and-blood knight of his environment—as well as with the "perfect" knight of serious
literature: Chaucer needed to know that the human knight
varied, as other men, in appearance, that he was not always
beautiful, or clad in the most costly garments, or a titan in
strength; nor—the other face of the coin—would he look
ridiculous, as does the long-bearded Sir Thopas with "sydes
smale." Chaucer needed to know how the human knight
really conducted himself, that he would not excel equally in
every knightly sport or adventure, but that he might be better in some activities than in others. Consequently, although
Thopas parodies only a literary form, we are constantly reminded by it that Chaucer lived in a world where chivalry and
the implications of chivalry were of great and daily importance.

TWO ❖ The Influence of Chaucer's Religious and Philosophic World

IT IS NOT SURPRISING to find in the list of the Seven Cardinal Virtues* that Faith stands traditionally at the head, although Charity is called the greatest. The Middle Ages was indeed an Age of Faith, in spite of the scepticism which began early and reached a culmination in the fourteenth century. That scepticism, however, was confined in England to the philosophic thinker, rather than to the average man, no matter what his class, and may be said to be agnostic instead of atheistic in character. The medieval proverb, "where there are three physicians, there are two atheists," probably grew out of the physician's disregard of the Church's hostility to certain aspects of medical research. The "atheism" of physicians was generally not based on a denial of a triune God or of the validity of the sacraments. Fourteenth-century man might question beliefs if he were concerned with philo-

* The Seven Cardinal Virtues are Faith, Hope, and Charity, and Aristotle's "virtues" of Prudence, Temperance, Justice, and Fortitude.

sophic matters, but there was very little positive denial, and often the so-called doubters would "repent" towards the end of their lives that they had even mildly speculated, or deviated in any way from strict orthodoxy. When he complains about ecclesiastical abuses, Chaucer does so in apparent deep regret that the guardians of the Faith are sometimes unworthy of their trust, never attacking faith itself. "Orthodox" as he was, however, Chaucer wrote as his genius prompted him without regard to the Church's statement that "al that is writen is writen for oure doctrine." Yet in his Retraction, the great poet was prompted either by old age or illness to pray humbly that he might be forgiven the "sin" of his "translacions and enditynges of worldly vanitees."

The hierarchy of the medieval Church was a complicated structure, and need not be considered here except insofar as Chaucer implicitly treats of it. In the same way that secular nobles are omitted from the pilgrimage in the *Canterbury Tales*, so, too, the princes of the Church are omitted, as in actual life they would find their way to Canterbury with their own retinues. But less important ecclesiastical figures are on the pilgrimage, and Chaucer observes their "degrees" by the order in which he presents them in the *General Prologue*. The Prioress and the Monk stand at the top, for each is the head of a subordinate House of some parent Order; next—and there is a wide gap—comes the Friar, followed by the Clerk (a university student in Minor Orders), then the Parson (a parish priest, rich in good works, but humble in degree), and finally there is that pair of arch-rascals, the Summoner and the Pardoner, who are presumably on ecclesiastical business.

To understand the Prioress we should know something about nuns in general in the Middle Ages. It is true that nuns sometimes appear in the *fabliaux* and are shown in those coarse narratives to be wanton; however, in serious literature, whether historical or fictional, the nun is depicted as worthy of respect and praise. She may have her human faults, but in her capacity as a religious she acts with decorum.

In actual life, nuns were nearly always of gentle birth for a reason that was largely economic. Nearly every woman of the Middle Ages had her social "place" fixed from birth. If she belonged to the peasant or artisan class, she had little chance to remain single: her labor was her valuable dowry, and neither father nor guardian of any sort would be likely to withstand the pressure of a suitor. Indeed, a healthy girl of that social standing was a commodity, and although she might have some choice which man she wedded, the choice ended there, for her destiny was to be a married woman, not a nun. Upper-class women were in a different situation; they could not "labor," so their dowries could only be in money, or in the power of family connection. If a girl were the daughter of a rich or influential house, she would be married out of hand at an early age, sometimes even by proxy in her cradle. Marriage was a business through which a man furthered his finances or his opportunities for advancement. If she came from an impoverished family—and many knights were far from wealthy—the lady, if she wished to survive at all, became a nun. Today we are accustomed to think that the religious life is only for those who have a vocation, and we may wonder about those medieval ladies who entered convents simply because there was literally nothing else for them to do in the hard, non-fairytale world of practical matters. Were they "good" nuns? Were they happy? For the overwhelming majority, the answer must be "yes" to both questions. As a young girl, the lady herself had probably been schooled by gentle nuns who had taught her all the polite accomplishments, as well as the practical arts belonging to her station. In fact, the life of the schoolgirl in the convent was often more exciting and could be far more opulent than in her own home. Further, the nuns being medieval women, reared in the tradition of the medieval Church, would inculcate the Church's tenet that the virginal life was the "best," the one most surely to be rewarded everlastingly in the life to come. Existence, then, within the convent's walls was busy, and it was peaceful, pleasant and dignified. One did not starve there or lack shelter, one was surrounded by one's social peers, and spiritually one was upheld by the supreme knowledge that one was a bride of Christ.

With all those facts in mind, we are sure that Chaucer created his Prioress straight from his own world [I (A) 118-162]. True to type, she is essentially well-bred. But, paradoxically, that very fact also individualizes her for us as Madame Eglantine: her apparent memory of and sustained interest in her early life of refinement has led her to indulge in particular foibles and vanities which are distinctly hers, and yet which certainly belonged, either wholly or in part, to many nuns of Chaucer's time. Madame Eglantine should not "swear" at all, yet she swears by St. Eligius ("Seinte Loy"), that seventh-century courtier-turned-saint, beloved by many ladies of the nobility and gentry throughout later centuries. Madame Eglantine is depicted as having exaggeratedly good table manners (the poet draws largely here upon a very "worldly" passage from the *Roman de la Rose*) for, as Chaucer says, she always takes pains to imitate the manners of court life. Madame Eglantine speaks fluent French, and although it is not the "Frenssh of Parys," it is still French and hence aristocratic. Madame Eglantine is not always careful about obeying the injunctions of the bishop who inspects her convent: nuns were forbidden to go on pilgrimage by fourteenth-century bishops, yet they frequently did so, and here is our Prioress, albeit she is properly accompanied by another nun and a priest.

Nuns were also forbidden to keep pets of any kind (the money and attention given to those animals should be given instead to the poor), yet Madame Eglantine possesses little dogs upon whom she lavishes affection and care—she even feeds them meat and expensive white bread. Further, the Prioress is personally vain: her appearance is important to her, for she displays too much of her handsome broad forehead to the world and she cannot hide her love of jewelry— her rosary is too elaborate for a nun and the brooch she possesses "of gold ful sheene," bearing its ambiguous motto (does *amor* mean sacred or profane love?), should not be worn by anyone who has taken a vow of poverty. The Prioress again shows her fondness for precious stones in her Tale: in praising the Virgin, she says, "This gemme of chastite, this emeraude, / And eek of martirdom the ruby bright. . . ." [VII (B² 1799-1800) 609-610]. But even though Chaucer does censure Madame Eglantine for her vanities and for her disregard of the bishop's injunctions, the blame is extremely mild. The poet makes the lady charming, but sometimes her graceful femininity is too strong for the strictly religious.

Harry Bailly recognizes the Prioress' aristocratic bearing by toning down his customary rude exuberance, when he addresses her before she begins her Tale. He politely says:

'My lady Prioresse, by youre leve,
So that I wiste I sholde yow nat greve,
I wolde demen that ye tellen sholde
A tale next, if so were that ye wolde.
Now wol ye vouche sauf, my lady deere?'
    [*VII* (*B² 1636-1641*) *446-451*]

The *Prioress's Tale* is by its very nature appropriate to the teller, for the story primarily concerns a miracle wrought by the Virgin. From Madame Eglantine's own point of view, the miracle would be the only matter of importance in the Tale: mere convention provides the source for casting the Jews as villains in the plot. If Chaucer himself knew any

Jews, he must have done so on the Continent, for the Jews had been expelled from England by Edward I in 1290. The unhappy history of the expulsion, preceded by enactments of cruel laws and by massacres, thus antedates the *Canterbury Tales* by nearly one hundred years. Actually, the underlying causes of the expulsion were political and economic, not religious; but Christians, seeking reasons which to them could be more readily self-admitted, attempted to "excuse" what had taken place on the grounds of religion. In that way, from unfounded stories, the Jew—literally unknown in Chaucer's England—was unthinkingly accepted as a convenient monster when such a character was needed in a plot. Madame Eglantine's story, therefore, is solely in praise of "oure blisful Lady, Cristes mooder deere" and of the child martyr who sings his *Alma redemptoris* so sweetly in life and in death. Since the Tale is about a martyr, it is essentially tragic but the poet—mindful of the teller—makes it, for his own times, largely delicate and pathetic and decorative.

The medieval monk, not unlike the medieval nun, was most usually a man of the gentry or noble class; if he came from a lower class, he would need a generous patron to provide him with an expensive education, for monks had to be learned men. The monk's calling was "an ancient and honorable" one, and many of the great princes of the medieval Church—popes, cardinals, archbishops and bishops—were chosen from the monastic Orders.

We can put no exact date to the earliest monastic Rule, but we do know that both St. Augustine of Hippo (about the year 400) and St. Benedict (about the year 700) established Rules on which all later monastic regulations were based. The Rules required that the individual monk accept the principles of obedience, poverty—the Order itself might be of great wealth, but that wealth was in theory collective—and celibacy. To support the principles, the monk was required to remain within his cloister, to labor with his hands or to pursue the life of a scholar and teacher, to live abstemiously, to spend much of his time in praying and in glorifying God, and to give alms to the poor who lived within the precincts of the abbey. Undoubtedly, the early monastic communities of England assiduously obeyed the Rules; they reached their peak of important influence in the second half of the thirteenth century, when they had acquired wealth and power in government. The monasteries were generous in gifts to king and commoner, their schools had won renown, the copying of manuscripts by the monks kept learning alive.

In return for what they did, monastic communities received grants from the Crown, they enjoyed legacies from grateful noblemen, they were permitted to tax heavily the tenants upon their estates and to keep alive rights and monopolies which had been established in feudal days. We are aware, however, that riches and power frequently corrupt, and by the second half of the fourteenth century, in the opinion of many, monks had completely fallen from grace. No longer did the typical monk remain within his cloister, laboring or studying or teaching—worst of all, in medieval eyes, he lived in extravagant luxury. (The typical fourteenth-century monk is not censured in serious literature for lasciviousness, but for his idleness and for self-indulgence in expensive pastimes and in costly food and clothing.)

The widely accepted picture of a monk is reflected in Chaucer's portrait of Daun Piers. Although he has taken vows to uphold "the reule of Seint Maure or of Seint Beneit," Chaucer's Monk contemptuously chooses to ignore those vows. His greatest pleasure is in "huntyng for the hare." Strict disciplinarians in the Church held that hunting as a sport was wicked, even for the layman, and of course much more so for the clergy. The idea may have arisen from a faulty "syllogism": "Esau was a hunter; Esau was wicked; therefore, all hunters are wicked." The "hunting monk" was a stock figure in Chaucer's time and always the recipient of hostile criticism. Does Daun Piers labor with his hands as St. Augustine bids, or does he pore over a book in the cloister? No, indeed; he remarks scornfully, "Lat Austyn have his swynk to hym reserved!" Further, Daun Piers does not fast or deny himself costly clothing: instead, he loves a fat swan "the best of any roost"; he wears the finest gray fur in the land, an elaborate gold pin in the shape of a love-knot, and costly "souple" boots. Daun Piers is frequently an "outridere," that is, he leaves his cloister—and Chaucer reminds us that a monk outside the cloister is like a fish out of water; he owns greyhounds which are as swift as birds in flight, and in his stables are many valuable horses.

Thus, Chaucer's Monk is a lively representative of a class. On the other hand, however, Chaucer gives the portrait added vitality and strength by a few individual touches. Daun Piers has large, prominent eyes and a glistening, ruddy countenance, he is bald and stout; and his pomposity and implied resentment against the world (although he is "able" to be an abbot, he is but a prior) are manifest.

But what about the monks of the *fabliaux*, who, in addition to having the faults of the monks of serious literature, are nearly always portrayed as seducers and petty cheats? Chaucer himself writes about such a monk in the *Shipman's Tale*. A *fabliau*, it should be noted, is by definition coarsely cynical, its "realism" consisting largely in true-to-life dialogue and objective description—situations in a *fabliau* therefore sometimes go beyond the factual aspects of life in an author's desire to titillate his audience. The monk of the *Shipman's Tale* could be brother to Daun Piers in that he is also an outrider, a lover of pleasure and of rich food; that he is lecherous in no way serves to identify him as a member of a monastic Order, but is added to give the conventionally burlesque "entertainment" expected in the *fabliau*.

The Tale which Daun Piers tells on the way to Canterbury is considered by the other pilgrims to be one of great "hevynesse" and dullness. Harry Bailly, for example, informs Daun Piers that he himself would have "fallen down for sleep" during the latter's story, if it had not been for the clinking of Daun Piers' Canterbury bells! But the *Monk's Tale* is appropriate to the teller. Although Daun Piers as a typical monk is no longer interested in books, he has had an education proper to his calling: he is able to give a learned definition of tragedy to the company, and he informs them that he has a hundred tragedies in his "celle"—he is quite capable of instructing lesser folk. He says:

> I wol biwaille, in manere of tragedie,
> The harm of hem that stood in heigh degree,
> And fillen so that ther nas no remedie
> To brynge hem out of hir adversitee.
> For certein, whan that Fortune list to flee
> Ther may no man the cours of hire withholde.
> Lat no man truste on blynd prosperitee;
> Be war by thise ensamples trewe and olde.
>   [*VII* (*B*² *3181-3188*) *1991-1998*]

The Monk is here partially reverting to a type of an earlier age: he is now the didactic teacher, explaining the vicissitudes of Fortune to the uninformed laity; but he remains also the man who has himself suffered disappointment and who therefore thoroughly enjoys recounting the woes of those who have fallen from "heigh degree." Chaucer needed only to look about in the uncertain London of the fourteenth century to observe the sudden disasters overtaking many of his friends and acquaintances—or, for that matter, to observe the pleasure the semi-successful took in the tearing down of the wholly successful. Daun Piers, through being a consistent "type," becomes the more actual as an individual.

The monks, as has been observed, were often scorned by the laity because of the immense wealth of their orders and the luxury and idleness of the lives of many of the individual brothers, but, as historians have pointed out, the individual monk was nearly always looked upon with some degree of respect. The typical medieval friar, in contrast, seems to have met with no respect anywhere. Fact and fiction both condemn him as especially licentious and dishonest. Gower writes of him as pretending to be poor but, in actuality, as being as rich as a king. Friars are hypocrites, Gower continues, for they talk publicly against sin but condone it privately both in themselves and others. They will have nothing to do with anyone who will not advance them; and they wait for the husband to be absent and then have illicit relations with the wife. Friars usurp the function of others in the Church; their houses are the most costly in the land, betraying their greed and avarice to the world. And they are everywhere. [*Vox Clamantis*, Lib. IV, Cap. xvi-xxiii.]

The Lollards, that is, the followers of Wyclif, much less orthodox but in some ways more stern than Gower, are especially bitter about the friars. In every tract and sermon, the Lollards abuse the Mendicant Orders. One Lollard writes, for example, that friars are proud hypocrites, always encouraging sin: they permit the rich through flattery and false rules to live comfortably in vice; friars sell men's souls to Satan, for the absolutions of friars are false, yet friars say they have more power in confession than other clergy.

Popular literature of the fourteenth century—the so-called political songs—all condemn friars as imbued with wickedness. Here special emphasis is placed on the friars' seduction of women, for which the brothers were apparently notorious.

When Chaucer was writing, there were four major Orders

of Friars in England: the Dominicans, or Black Friars—sometimes called the Preaching Friars, sometimes the Jacobins, who settled in England in 1221; the Franciscans, or Grey Friars—sometimes called the Friars Minor, because of their supposed humility, who settled in England in 1224; the Carmelites, or White Friars, who settled in England in 1245; and the Augustinians, or Austin Friars, who settled in England in 1256. Although there were some small differences among them, the four major Orders had become, by the fourteenth century, essentially the same; consequently, if we trace the fall from grace of one Order, we have traced the fall of all. Since the Franciscan Order is perhaps the best known of the four, we shall consider that.

Founded by St. Francis in Italy in the year 1209, the Franciscan Order had a simply stated aim and very few "rules." The followers of St. Francis merely pledged to conduct themselves according to the exact teachings of Christ: they would live in absolute poverty journeying about the country, engaged in good deeds and giving an example to all men.

As long as St. Francis himself lived, his disciples were indeed an example to all; world-weary and disheartened men hastened to join the new Order, receiving comfort and hope from the joy of following the precepts of the Gospels. The Middle Ages, as has been pointed out, was an Age of Faith and also an Age of the Literal. "Go and sell all that Thou hast and give to the poor" meant exactly that; mortification of the flesh was a good, and so the members of the Order shunned all bodily comforts. The climate of Italy made it possible for the friars to exist without fixed shelter, to tramp the ancient ways unshod, to wear but one garment at all seasons. But in England? The cold and the snows of the winter demanded housing, shoes and warm clothes and, to obtain those things, friars needed money. St. Francis and his immediate disciples in the "warm South" could live in absolute poverty; furthermore, the friars who were first in the Order were strong zealots and St. Francis was among them, a living example of one who had totally accepted Christ's words: "If any man will come after Me, let him deny himself and take up his cross and follow Me." The great personal force of St. Francis was as necessary to the maintenance of the purity and aims of the Orders as physical and economic environment.

Shortly after 1226, when St. Francis died, the decay of the Franciscans began. Begging, which St. Francis had allowed only when truly necessary, became the chief money-raising device of the Order, and other Orders quickly followed that lead, which explains the epithet "Mendicant." The soliciting of alms turned out to be exceedingly profitable. The early belief that saintly followers of the inspiring leaders of the Orders could lead man to heaven died slowly: even if the individual friar was corrupt, the Order to which he belonged was holy, and medieval man was loath to miss any chance of escaping eternal damnation. Thus, many continued to give "silver to the povre freres" no matter how much those criers after worldly goods were hated and despised for living in their sumptuous edifices and for patently deceiving everyone they could. Indeed, the Mendicants were engaged in what may be called "big business" by the fourteenth century, and individual friars were allowed by their Orders to purchase the prized monopoly of begging rights in specified districts. Of course, there could be no check on the amount a friar collected; undoubtedly some proportion of what he received would go to his Order, for otherwise his privilege would be revoked, but we may be equally sure that the typical friar kept a good deal for himself—like Chaucer's Friar, his "purchas" or illegal gain would far exceed his "rente," or what he turned over to his Order.

The medieval friar had other opportunities for illicit gain. Friars were not cloistered, yet they belonged to religious Orders; hence they could be employed as ecclesiastical tax-gatherers and they could be licensed to hear confessions. Here again there could be no check against stealing and cheating, and we cannot be astonished that the Mendicant Orders attracted many unprincipled men who saw such easy money in the friar's life.

Chaucer's Brother Hubert is at once the embodiment of all friars as they were understood to be, as well as being very much himself [I (A) 207-269]. To begin with, he is a "lymy-tour," that is, he is a friar who has secured the begging rights in a specified district. He knows how to charm all the women in that district into easy giving; they will gladly pay him in money, or in food, or in a response to his "daliaunce." Obviously, Brother Hubert has a way with him: his English is "sweete upon his tonge," as he has affected a lisp; he knows all the latest songs, with which he entertains the "faire wyves" while he accompanies himself upon his "rote" (a musical instrument resembling a small harp); he "rewards" the wives with handsome presents of ornamental knives and pins; and his initial "blessing" of each house he visits is pleasantly satisfying—a few verses drawn from the first chapter of the Gospel according to St. John (beginning *"In principio . . ."*) was the usual form of such "blessings." But when Brother Hubert visits richer or more important folk, his manner changes: he is now "curteis" and "lowely of servyse"; he is only too ready to hear confessions, to give "esy" penance, and to absolve for money alone—surely his greatest sin. True absolution, of course, could not be granted without contrition; consequently Hubert's absolution is worthless, not the spiritual grace he claims it to be.

Chaucer's Friar has further faults, not as grave as the "selling" of absolution, but serious enough. He will have nothing to do with lepers, or with the poor in the towns he passes through; he will deal only with people who can advance him in some way: the wealthy, the sellers of food, the barmaids in the taverns. In that respect, Hubert is in striking contrast to St. Francis who, although lepers were extremely obnoxious to him personally, made the care of those sufferers one of his most cherished duties. Hubert also meddles in civil affairs, an act expressly forbidden in the Rules of the Mendicant Orders, for on "love-dayes"—those times set aside for out-of-court settlements of legal cases—he is much in evidence, officiating "lyk a maister or a pope," clad in his warm vestment of double worsted, his eyes twinkling like stars on a frosty night.

Is Hubert a Franciscan? We cannot say; but when the Summoner tells his Tale to spite Hubert, the friar in that Tale is described as a Franciscan, and it is unlikely that Chaucer would have the pilgrim Summoner step out of character by telling a story against a friar of an Order different from Hubert's. In fact, we suspect that the friar of the *Summoner's Tale* is intended by the Summoner to be Hubert himself or, at least, that the Summoner would have the company of pilgrims make such an identification. The Summoner states that his friar is a "lymytour," and continues the picture as follows:

> In every hous he gan to pour and prye,
> And beggeth mele and chese, or elles corn,
> His felawe hadde a staf tipped with horn,
> A peyre of tables al of yvory,
> And a poyntel polysshed fetisly,
> And wroot the names alwey, as he stood,
> Of alle folk that yaf him any good,
> Ascaunces that he wolde for hem preye.
> 'Yif us a busshel whete, malt, or reye,
> A Goddes kechyl, or a trype of chese
> Or elles what yow lyst, we may nat cheese;
> A Goddes halfpeny, or a masse peny,

Or yif us of youre brawn, if ye have eny;
A dagon of youre blanket, leeve dame,
Oure suster deere,—lo! heere I write youre name,—
Bacon or beef, or swich thyng as ye fynde.'

[*III* (*D*) *1738-1753*]

The Summoner is then careful to point out that his friar has no intention of praying for those who are foolish enough to give food or money, for the dishonest Mendicant carefully erases the names from his tablet when he leaves the houses where he has been successful in his begging. Throughout the Tale, the friar continues to conduct himself in typical fashion. He seeks out the man he knows will give him the most (as does Hubert); he flatters Thomas' wife and demands a meal of "softe breed," liver of capon, and a roasted pig's head; he then delivers a homily to the defenseless Thomas, putting great emphasis on the importance of poverty and fasting and the wickedness of anger. Chaucer's satire is, of course, obvious here: the typical friar was neither poor nor abstemious—and the friar of the *Summoner's Tale* is easily filled with vengeful anger. The friar then urges Thomas to confess and, again like Hubert, promises Thomas an easy penance and absolution through the payment of money. The Summoner is indeed successful in showing up a friar in the latter's true colors, but he is not as successful in repaying Hubert "every grot" for the *Friar's Tale,* a Tale which condemns summoners more emphatically than the *Summoner's Tale* condemns friars. (See below, pp. 69-71.)

Chaucer's Clerk is a university student who is in Minor Orders, for he is a candidate for a benefice. The word *clerk* in the Middle Ages always indicated a university student who, having received the tonsure, was entitled to certain ecclesiastical privileges; the clerk might or might not be in Minor Orders. Chaucer's Clerk is probably typical of the "good" students of the fourteenth century but as Rashdall, the great authority on medieval universities, says, "the life of the virtuous student has no annals." The life of the "bad" student on the other hand, is fully documented in legal records and in fiction: such a student is uniformly depicted as quarrelsome, lawless, frivolous and licentious. To understand Chaucer's Clerk fully therefore, we must contrast him with those he does not resemble. For example, the Oxford Coroners' Rolls of the period are filled with the accounts of deaths resulting from student brawls, brawls between one group of students with another, or between "town and gown"; a few of the killings seem to have been accidental, but the majority are adjudged to have been deliberate murders. Less serious breaches of the peace are also commonplace events, such as the breaking of regulations against gambling and inciting to riot, dancing and boisterous play and noisy singing in the various Halls. (One wonders how the serious students ever had quiet opportunity for their necessarily concentrated work in logic, rhetoric, mathematics, astronomy, philosophy and theology!)

For evidence of the loose living of the medieval clerk, we must turn to fiction, and here Chaucer himself supplies us with sufficient example. First we should note that in none of the most conspicuous analogues to the *Miller's Tale* are the wife's lovers stated to be clerks, but Chaucer elected to cast university students for the parts of the lovers. "Hende Nicholas" of the *Miller's Tale* is described as "sleigh and ful privee" (that is, sly and secretive); he has a private income, unlike Chaucer's impoverished Clerk, and hence he is able to afford a relatively luxurious room all to himself at the carpenter's house, where he can be free much of the time from university rules. Nicholas' "study" is apparently centered in the gayer aspects of astronomy, instead of in logic and philosophy, and although he goes through the motions each evening of singing a hymn to the Virgin, he immediately follows that hymn by some popular song, accompanying himself, no doubt, on the "gay sautrie" which he keeps "at his beddes heed." And, as would be expected, Nicholas is openly sensual in his affair with that attractive, amoral young woman, the carpenter's wife.

Absalom, the other clerk in the *Miller's Tale* and of much the same nature as Nicholas, also makes no bones about coveting the pert young wife; indeed, he would have pounced upon her immediately "if she hadde been a mous and he a cat," and he loses no time in attempting to win her favors. Chaucer, through the Miller's words, describes the "joly" Absalom as follows:

> Crul was his heer, and as the gold it shoon,
> And strouted as a fanne large and brode;
> Ful streight and evene lay his joly shode. . . .
> With Poules wyndow corven on his shoos,
> In hoses rede he wente fetisly.
> Yclad he was ful smal and proprely
> Al in a kirtel of a lyght waget;
> Ful faire and thikke been the poyntes set.
> And therupon he hadde a gay surplys
> As whit as is the blosme upon the rys.
> A myrie child he was, so God me save. . . .
> In twenty manere koude he trippe and daunce
> After the scole of Oxenforde tho,
> And with his legges casten to and fro,
> And pleyen songes on a smal rubible;
> Therto he song som tyme a loud quynyble;
> And as wel koude he pleye on a giterne.
> In al the toun nas brewhous ne taverne
> That he ne visited with his solas,
> Ther any gaylard tappestere was.
>
> [*I (A) 3314-3316, 3318-3325, 3328-3336*]

If we place Chaucer's Clerk [I (A) 285-308] beside Nicholas and Absalom—or beside the two Cambridge clerks of the *Reeve's Tale*, who have no qualms about casually seducing

Simkin's wife and daughter—the contrast is striking. For a long time, Chaucer's Clerk has devoted himself to the serious study of logic (logic may be said to have formed the backbone of the four to eight years required for Oxford medieval curricula), and it is not surprising that the Clerk would rather have twenty volumes of Aristotle at his "beddes heed" than any "gay sautrie" or rich clothing. The Clerk's outer coat is threadbare, for he is extremely poor—even his horse is as "leene . . . as is a rake": what money he receives from his benefactors (whom he fittingly repays by heartfelt prayers for their souls), he spends on books and learning. Unlike Absalom of the *Miller's Tale,* the Clerk never displays unseemly levity in behavior; he does not speak one word more than is necessary, and when he does speak, he is brief, to the point and always noble in his meaning. Chaucer's final line of description for his scholar—"And gladly wolde he lerne and gladly teche"—epitomizes the Clerk for us today, and perhaps provides us with a brief summing-up of what all good teaching has meant in the past and will mean in years to come. Chaucer himself must have had the privilege of coming in contact with such a teacher as the Clerk, for the poet's learning reflects instruction that was both sound and enthusiastic.

Exactly as it is necessary to contrast the Clerk with someone he in no way resembles, so is it necessary to contrast the Parson; for the good priest, like the good student, has no documented history. The literature of complaint inveighs heavily against the bad priest, however. Gower, for example, states that such priests set their flocks the example of sin only, the priests neglect their sacred mission in leading lives of worldly ease, they leave their congregations to seek more gainful occupation elsewhere, they fail to rebuke the sinner, and many of them are ignorant men who have no background for their calling. The priests who should be our guides to heaven are worse than the ordinary sinner, for the priests, when they fall from grace, are doubly at fault—the breaking of a vow is always present when the priests commit another sin [*Vox Clamantis*, Lib. III, Cap. xvi-xxviii].

The Lollards also are stern in their condemnation of priests, particularly when it comes to clerical absenteeism, evidently a serious problem in fourteenth-century rural England. If his parish were left without a priest, the medieval peasant was lost indeed, for if there were no one to administer the sacraments, there could be no hope of salvation. The Lollards also complain of priests' failure to rebuke the rich or influential sinner, yet of their only too great readiness to rebuke or even to excommunicate the poor or unimportant.

Chaucer's "povre Persoun of a Toun" furnishes us with the antithesis of the bad priest. The Parson is described [I (A) 477-528] as rich in "hooly thoght and werk," and as devoutly teaching his parishioners. He is "lerned," for he has been a university student. Many times he has proved himself to be patient, diligent and benign: he will not cruelly excommunicate a man who is genuinely unable to meet the ten per cent tax levied by the Church on every parishioner. (To be excommunicated or "cursed" meant to be cut off from all communion with the Church; if one were not reinstated, eternal damnation would result.) Chaucer's Parson knows, however, that it is his duty to collect the tithes; consequently, in cases of need, he will make up the deficit out of his own small "substaunce," or even out of the "offryng," the voluntary contributions—meager, we feel sure—which, by rights, he should spend upon his own needs.

This good man is not lazy or given to idle pleasure: on the contrary, in all kinds of weather, and even if he is troubled or ill, he visits on foot the members of his parish in their houses "fer asonder," not caring whether those he calls upon are rich or poor. But perhaps his most striking characteristic as a priest—three times specifically stressed by Chaucer—is his setting of an example before asking others to follow it. He holds to two figures: if gold rusts, iron will do far worse; and if the shepherd is soiled, the sheep cannot be clean. The Parson will not leave his parishioners "encombred in the myre," while he runs off to London in the hope of securing an easier post, such as a "chaunterie for soules." The chantry endowments, usually supported by Parish Gilds in the larger towns, offered a good deal of money and very little work to a priest. Every Christian in the Middle Ages firmly believed that it was his sacred duty to have masses said or sung for the souls of his deceased relatives, but for one individual to meet that obligation was at best a great financial burden, at worst an impossibility. If a number of persons joined together and contributed to a common fund, however, the problem could be—and was—solved. Parish Gilds, the brotherhoods which Chaucer mentions, were therefore organized, and a priest engaged, a priest whose sole duty was to say masses for the dead who had been related to the members of the Gild. The Parish Gild proved to be a great success; every townsman was eager to pay his dues, and the priest's compensation was accordingly high. Parish Gilds soon became wealthy enough to add the functions of a modern "benevolent society" to their original purpose, but that, of course, would not concern the priest employed for the chantry. For a country parish priest lacking in the strong virtue of Chaucer's Parson, there would indeed be every temptation to become a "mercenarie" in London if he had such an opportunity.

Although he is good himself, the Parson is not scornful or disdainful when dealing with repentant sinners, but, equally important, the Parson does not hesitate to berate soundly anyone who shows no repentance. Totally unlike Brother Hubert, the Parson treats those of high or low estate in exactly the same way; self-advancement never occurs to him. The picture which Chaucer draws of this "holy and humble man of heart" is extraordinarily appealing in its uncomplicated goodness. We hope that Chaucer knew the Parson in actual life, and that the character is not a mere reversal of the "bad" priests whom everyone apparently knew in fourteenth-century England.

There has been speculation among modern scholars as to the Parson's leaning towards Lollard teaching. Certainly the Host sneeringly remarks that he smells a "Lollere" in the wind, immediately after the Parson has rebuked him for swearing [II (B^1) 1170-1177). But Wyclif's injunctions prohibiting pilgrimage were especially strong and that fact—since the Parson now is very openly on the way to Canterbury —seems to be conclusive: we cannot call the Parson formally a Lollard, but he may have sympathy, as many of the highly orthodox clergy did, with some Lollard tenets. After all, while Chaucer was a young man in a royal household, Wyclif had entered the King's service; the poet-to-be may easily have then learned to admire much that the great reformer stood for; and we do know that, later, four of the six so-called Lollard Knights were intimate friends of Chaucer's. The long sermon on the Seven Deadly Sins, which the poet assigns to his Parson, is, however, completely orthodox in its didacticism.

Although they sin gravely and cannot be "excused," Chaucer's Monk and Friar are not the unmitigated rascals the poet shows his Summoner and Pardoner to be. A summoner in the Middle Ages was a lay, minor official employed by the bishop or archdeacon who presided at an ecclesiastical court. It was the business of a summoner, as the designation implies, to serve warnings to persons to appear before the ecclesiastical court to answer charges made against them; presumably the summoner's official pay was a percentage of the fines collected by the court. But what opportunities there were in that system for corruption! Even if at the outset the summoner were more or less "honest," that is, if he carried with him only summonses given him by the bishop or archdeacon, it was in his own interest to find as many delinquents as possible; summoners dealing with defenseless peasants in rural districts soon made it common practice both to spy into everyone's past for long-forgotten sins and to manufacture false charges deliberately. If a summoner's victim responded to the order to appear in the ecclesiastical court, he was nearly always fined (in his "trial" the court was both judge and jury); if the unfortunate defendant could not pay, he—sometimes she, for women were not exempt—was excommunicated forthwith and given a short time to meet the monetary obligation. At the close of that period, if the person was still unable to pay— and if payment was impossible at the beginning, there could hardly be any likelihood of its now being possible—a writ of *Significavit*, so called because of the initial word in the writ, was at once issued by the civil authorities and the victim was then imprisoned. As there was no means of earning money in prison, the sentence was very often for life.

Consequently we can easily understand how greatly all humble folk dreaded the approach of the summoner and were more than ready to bribe him either to destroy any summons, genuine or false, he might have for them, or to keep silent about what he might threaten to reveal to his masters. Thus blackmail, that most obnoxious of all crimes, became the commonplace stock in trade of the summoner in rural districts.

Chaucer's Summoner is basically wicked. The poet writes that if the Summoner finds anywhere some "good felawe" who is sinning, he will teach him to have no awe of the "ercedekenes curs" unless his soul is in his purse. "Purs is the ercedekenes helle," claims the Summoner, implying that money will set everything right. Chaucer then suggests ironically that the archdeacon's excommunication is worth exactly as much as his "assoillyng" of the soul, but he does add, probably in a more serious vein, that one should fear the *Significavit*. The Summoner also sees to it that he has all the young people of the parish under his thumb—he knows their secrets and acts as their counsel—and we can well believe that he turns them into informers against their elders. The Summoner will genially excuse a kindred soul for keeping a concubine for a year, if he is paid only a quart of wine; he is sexually immoral himself, which in turn undoubtedly also leads him to information that he should not possess.

To exchange Chaucer's "real" Summoner of the *General Prologue* for the more fictional summoner of the *Friar's Tale* is a simple matter, and probably something which the poet intended his audience to do. Brother Hubert and the Canterbury-bound Summoner are depicted in the Links as deadly enemies (professionally they are jealous rivals in the collection of money, and Chaucer portrays them also to be constantly at loggerheads for some more personal reason); each would gladly injure the other, and each venomously tries to do exactly that in the telling of his Tale. We cannot doubt that the Friar, at least, has been thoroughly successful in his abuse of summoners, for when Hubert has completed his exposé, we have the unforgettable picture of the Summoner, standing high in his stirrups, shaking in rage "lyk an aspen leef," convincing us by his over-protestation that the scorn and hatred the ordinary fourteenth-century citizen felt for summoners in general was completely justified.

In the Prologue to his Tale, the Friar says:

'I wol yow of a somonour telle a game.
Pardee, ye may wel knowe by the name
That of a somonour may no good be sayd;
I praye that noon of you be yvele apayd.
A somonour is a rennere up and doun

With mandementz for fornicacioun,
And is ybet at every townes ende.'
[*III (D) 1279-1285*]

When he opens his Tale, Hubert is even more specifically vituperative. He begins by listing the sins which an archdeacon of his acquaintance "boldely" punished: fornication, witchcraft, bawdry, adultery, defamation of character, the breaking of wills and contracts, disregard of the sacraments, usury, simony, neglect of "smale tithes." The archdeacon never fails to impose a fine for any of these sins and, to help him in his "correccioun," the Friar tells the pilgrims:

He hadde a somonour redy to his hond;
A slyer boye nas noon in Engelonde;
For subtilly he hadde his espiaille,
That taughte hym wel wher that hym myghte availle.
He koude spare of lechours oon or two,
To techen hym to foure and twenty mo.
For tho this somonour wood were as an hare,
To telle his harlotrye I wol nat spare. . . .
[*III (D) 1321-1328*]

After an infuriated interruption from the pilgrim Summoner, Brother Hubert continues his diatribe. "This false theef, this somonour," Hubert says,

Hadde alwey bawdes redy to his hond,
As any hauk to lure in Engelond,
That tolde hym al the secree that they knewe;
For hire acqueyntance was nat come of newe.
They weren his approwers prively.
He took hymself a greet profit therby;
His maister knew nat alwey what he want.
Withouten mandement a lewed man
He koude somne, on peyne of Cristes curs,
And they were glade for to fille his purs,

And make hym grete feestes atte nale.
And right as Judas hadde purses smale,
And was a theef, right swich a theef was he;
His maister hadde but half his duetee. . . .
He hadde eek wenches at his retenue,
That wheither that sir Robert or sir Huwe,
Or Jakke, or Rauf, or whoso that it were
That lay by hem, they told it in his ere.
Thus was the wenche and he of oon assent;
And he wolde fecche a feyned mandement,
And somne hem to chapitre both two,
And pile the man, and lete the wenche go.
    [*III (D) 1339-1352, 1355-1362*]

And when he begins the narrative proper of his Tale, the Friar misses no opportunity to place the summoner in an evil light. The summoner, the Friar says, dares not "for verray filthe and shame" admit his calling, so he dubs himself a "bailly" when questioned by the fiend; this summoner is as full of babble as a waryangle (shrike) is of venom, showing his lack of education, as does the pilgrim Summoner, who mouths Latin phrases without having any idea as to their meaning. But when the fiend slyly admits that he himself lives by extortion, the summoner does not hesitate to indulge in his rare psychological pleasure of telling the truth: he boasts that he, too, lives by extortion, and that he feels no remorse for so doing. It is truly inevitable that the summoner and fiend should become sworn brothers, and should agree to share the spoils. One might wonder as to why such a scoundrel as a summoner could be trusted to keep a pact, but because his new "brother" is a supernatural being in the *Friar's Tale*, there is decided implication that here the summoner is literally compelled to see the bargain through, once it is made.

After his disappointment that the fiend will not take the

carter's horses (the carter "spak oo thyng, but he thoghte another," explains the fiend, who is evidently much more fair-minded than the summoner), the summoner suggests to the fiend that they visit the old woman, Mabely, who is without vice, the summoner brazenly admits, but who may be tricked into giving them a bribe of twelve pence. Brother Hubert, as teller of the Tale, then dramatically records the summoners' bullying methods in dealing with a victim: Mabely is scarce given breath to reply to the summoner's purposefully vague and rapid accusations, but when her tormentor overshoots his mark (the summoner is not really a clever man) by taxing her with infidelity to her husband, Mabely consigns the summoner with honest and wrathful indignation to the devil. And since Mabely means her curse, the summoner is doomed, and we fancy that we hear the satisfaction in the Friar's voice when he says to the company of pilgrims that "this foule feend" caught hold of the summoner, who was obliged to go body and soul with the devil "where as that somonours han hir heritage." We can also imagine that we sense the agreement of his listeners with Brother Hubert's candidly expressed sentiments regarding summoners as a class.

The Pardoner, who is "freend" and "compeer" to the Summoner, is a fitting companion for a rogue, for he himself is also a wicked man and, like a summoner, he is tempted to sin by the nature of his calling, for he deals largely with the helpless poor and ignorant. The literature of complaint is much more vehement about pardoners than about summoners, however, probably because the pardoners did much greater harm to the soul than the summoners. The Middle Ages would, of course, consider damaging a man in his future life a far greater sin than cheating or blackmailing him in this life, a belief shared by some people today, but no longer a belief of universal acceptance.

The Pardoner's calling was originally instituted because of

the theory of indulgences, a theory which Chaucer in no way attacks. It may be explained briefly as follows: In heaven there was an inexhaustible "treasury of merits" created there by Christ, His Mother and the saints; to share in that treasury and so commute his time in purgatory, sinful man could confess and repent, and perform "extra" good deeds. But even as we today as individuals usually find it difficult to help others in distress and instead seek some charitable organization which will act for us, so medieval man asked the Church to act for him. An "indulgence," then, was in a sense a certificate issued by the Pope testifying that a person—or, sometimes, a group of persons, for example, a monastery—after proper confession and repentance, had given money to the Church for "good deeds" to be performed in his name, and that he was thus guaranteed of some remission of time in purgatory. Naturally, the Church needed officials for the distribution of indulgences, or "pardons," and as a result the office of pardoner was created. (A pardoner could be either lay or cleric.)

The demand for pardoners soon became great so that many pardoners were necessary to meet that demand and, as nearly always happened in the Middle Ages, quantity reduced quality. It was impossible for the Church to keep any sort of watch on the numbers of men who became pardoners or who merely called themselves pardoners, and one can readily see the inherent dangers. In the hands of an unscrupulous, even though legitimate, pardoner, most of the money exchanged for the pardon would find its way into his own pocket; or even if he did give the money to the Church, he might fail to insist upon confession and repentance. In either event, an innocent donor would be grievously cheated, for he could not under those circumstances receive his remission. And, as is plain, no one could receive any benefit whatever from a man masquerading as a pardoner.

The fourteenth-century pardoner added two other activities,

as a rule, to the selling of pardons: the selling of saints' relics —often not relics at all, but bones and bits of rags which the pardoner himself collected from refuse heaps—and preaching. The preaching, however, even if insincere, probably was generally eloquent, for most swindlers need to cultivate silver tongues.

As we have said, the literature of complaint is strong in censure of pardoners. The Lollards, as would be expected, are consistently outspoken in their denunciation; the pardoner either steals his pardons or forges them, he poses as having more power than Christ himself, he cheats the poor and the sick by selling false pardons and false relics merely so that he himself may live in sinful idleness, gluttony and lechery. Orthodox preachers are nearly as bitter as the Lollards; they call the pardoners subtle thieves, liars and false fiends. Pardoners plunder and seduce the people. Finally, history itself gives us a vivid idea of pardoners during Chaucer's lifetime.

In the tenth century, an Order of Augustinian Canons was founded in northern Spain. (A "canon" was similar to a monk except that he was not cloistered.) In 1229 a subordinate House of the same Order was established in England under the name of St. Mary Roncevall, situated near the present Charing Cross, and by the beginning of the fourteenth century had become a well-established religious group. The prior of St. Mary Roncevall in the early fourteenth century had a reputation as a pardoner; through his activities as such he had made a good deal of money. The prior was a prominent man, and his interest in material gain could not pass as unnoticed as that of an obscure official. There was much talk about the wealth of the prior: the other brothers of the Order followed the prior's example to such an extent that the Crown felt it necessary in 1379 to seize the convent of St. Mary Roncevall and to arrest all those collecting alms for their own use. Although the convent was eventually restored to the Order, there occurred

a further public scandal in 1387 concerning the sale of pardons. The dates are significant for Chaucer was living in London at the time of the scandals and, hence, was certainly
aware of pardoners and their doings.

Chaucer describes his Pardoner [I (A) 669-714] as being of
"Rouncivale" to begin with, but whether the poet meant that
the Pardoner was actually of the Order of St. Mary Roncevall or
that he is merely of the same dubious morals, is not clear.
Chaucer tells us that the Pardoner has come straight from the
Court of Rome and that he bears a wallet "bretful of pardoun,
commen from Rome al hoot." One at once questions the au-
thenticity of pardons about which Chaucer speaks so humorously. The Pardoner carries with him as relics a pillowcase,
which he claims to be part of Our Lady's Veil, and a piece of
cloth he says is part of the sail of St. Peter's boat. He also has a
cross of "latoun" and some pigs' bones, which we are convinced he will pass off on the public as saints' relics. He does
not hesitate to boast that he makes fools of the people and the
parish priest, and that he receives more money in one day
through his preaching than the priest receives in two months.
But the poet has to acknowledge that his Pardoner is a "noble ecclesiaste" in the pulpit—indeed it is his preaching that
makes him so materially successful. The congregation will listen spellbound to his sermons and, when the discourse is at an
end, the listeners become so bemused by the eloquence that
they will give all their silver to the preacher.

The *Pardoner's Tale* is that extraordinary *tour de force*, a
sample of one of the Pardoner's own sermons which is as dramatically self-revealing as it is paradoxically filled with good
lessons in moral conduct. In sweeping satire, Chaucer has the
Pardoner select a text that illustrates the Pardoner's own great
sin of cupidity, apparently the most prominent sin of almost
every pardoner; in the sermon other sins are touched upon—
such as gluttony, drunkenness, lechery, gambling ("the verray

mooder of lesynges and of deceite"), and swearing—all of which are sins belonging to pardoners in general. No one can believe that Chaucer did not actually know—if only by observation—such a pardoner as the one he portrays so accurately and realistically, or that the poet could omit such a familiar figure from his cross-section of the fourteenth-century human scene. The Pardoner, in spite of his distance from us of six hundred years, speaks to us as if we knew him today.

In the résumé given above of Chaucer's portrayal of some members of the ecclesiastical hierarchy, we should observe not only the fidelity of the poet to the actual life of his own time, but also the heterogeneous nature of the group, implying in turn another reflection of life as it was. For nearly everyone who could in the late Middle Ages, no matter what his position in the world, made a pilgrimage, if not many pilgrimages. Theoretically, a pilgrimage is religious in character and consequently the subject belongs in any investigation of Geoffrey Chaucer's religious world. By the time Chaucer was writing, however, the journey to a shrine had become the liveliest and most sought-after pleasure for the majority of English citizens, both lay and cleric, and a visit to St. Thomas' shrine in Canterbury—internationally venerated and marked by the Church as one of the places of "greater pilgrimage"—was especially popular. In one year alone in the early fifteenth century, more than one hundred thousand persons from all over Europe are said to have made the Canterbury Pilgrimage.

Thomas à Becket met his martyr's death in Canterbury Cathedral some two hundred years before Chaucer's day. The English Henry II, similar to Becket in temperament, both being arrogant and eager for power, had been Becket's friend, but had now become Becket's implacable enemy. In December of the year 1170, Henry received word in France, where he was then residing, that Archbishop Becket in a Christmas sermon had excommunicated three bishops, all important supporters of Henry's policies. The King at once gave way to one of his ungovernable furies: he denounced Becket as an outrageous upstart and inflamed four English knights who were present by crying out that he lacked adherents loyal enough to deliver him from "this low-born priest." Immediately the four knights hastened to perform Henry's implied bidding: crossing the Channel, they raced to Canterbury and murdered the Archbishop within the Cathedral, where Becket had taken sanctuary, thus making the death a martyrdom.

That Thomas à Becket became a saint almost as soon as he became a martyr was largely because of the curative powers thought to be in his miraculously preserved blood and in the presence of his now sacred body; but as time passed, pilgrimage to St. Thomas' shrine was claimed to bring about many other blessings besides the healing of ailments. As has been suggested, Chaucer's Knight may be making his journey to Canterbury to offer prayers of thanksgiving for a successful campaign. On the whole, however, the many among the pilgrims asked for St. Thomas' help "whan that they were seeke."

It has been said by some modern critics that Chaucer's basis for the *Canterbury Tales* may come from the idea that life is a "pilgrimage" which mankind makes to the shrine of Heaven. Certainly the idea is not one which would have been unfamiliar to Chaucer, but the flesh-and-blood character the poet gives to his pilgrims on their gay and noisy journey to Canterbury seems to nullify any figurative suggestion. It is impossible to believe that Chaucer had never been on a pilgrimage himself or that he had not fully observed the behavior of actual wayfarers—their loudness in laughter, in quarrels, in the music they played, and in the stories with which they regaled each other—as they rode along the dusty or muddy roads on their journeys to a shrine. The "ful devout corage" would not be manifest until the shrine was reached and the *Canterbury*

Tales—at least, as we know the work—concerns the actualities of a "real" journey.

Many of present-day man's religious beliefs and concepts existed in the Middle Ages, of course, but at the same time some of us find a few of the medieval ideas to be strange. Chaucer expresses a number of such religious and ethical concepts of the fourteenth century in the course of the *Canterbury Tales,* usually without "taking sides"; the poet allows the actors to state in appropriate terms what they themselves think of the ideas. For example, the poet uses satire and humor in having the Wife of Bath "argue" the relative merits of the married state and virginity. Dame Alisoun is aware that the Church teaching of her day claims virginity to be a greater good than the most virtuous of marriages. Consequently, Alisoun sets about to refute that claim as soon as she can in her "long preamble of a tale," by quoting in fine apposition from Scripture: there are no actual comments against marriage, she says, for God "putte it in oure owene juggement." St. Paul, she continues, only wished "that every wighte were swich as he." We cannot all be perfect—not every dish in the household is of gold, and surely, God meant some women to marry.

The Merchant, too, in telling his Tale, speaks in satiric scorn of January's words; for January, foolish dotard, says about marriage:

'Noon oother lyf . . . is worth a bene;
For wedlok is so esy and so clene,
That in this world it is a paradys.'
         [*IV (E) 1263-1265*]

Yet Virginia in the *Physician's Tale* exclaims, "Blissed be God, that I shall dye a mayde!" And the teller of the Tale praises Virginia as "floured in virginitee." Emily in the

Knight's Tale also praises the single life. She prays to the Goddess Diana (in spite of the pagan setting in ancient Athens, Emily is in spirit a fourteenth-century English maiden) as follows:

'Chaste goddesse, wel wostow that I
Desire to ben a mayden al my lyf,
Ne nevere wol I be no love ne wyf.'
            [*I (A) 2304-2306*]

The subject of "gentilesse" may be properly said to belong under the heading "chivalry"; at the same time there is strong philosophical content in what constitutes nobility of bearing. The Hag says in part of the sermon which she delivers to her new husband in the *Wife of Bath's Tale:*

'Looke who that is moost vertuous alway,
Pryvee and apert, and moost entendeth ay
To do the gentil dedes that he kan;
Taak hym for the grettest gentil man.
Crist wole we clayme of hym oure gentillesse,
Nat of oure eldres for hire old richesse.
For thogh they yeve us al hir heritage,
For which we clayme to been of heigh parage,
Yet may they nat biquethe, for no thyng,
To noon of us hir vertuous lyvyng,
That made hem gentil men ycalled be,
And bad us folwen hem in swich degree.
Wel kan the wise poete of Florence,
That highte Dante, speken in this sentence.
Lo, in swich maner rym is Dantes tale:
"Ful selde up riseth by his branches smale
Prowesse of man, for God, of his goodnesse,
Wole that of hym we clayme oure gentillesse";
For of oure eldres may we no thyng clayme
But temporel thyng, that man may hurte and mayme.
Eek every wight woot this as wel as I,

If gentillesse were planted natureelly
Unto a certeyn lynage doun the lyne.
Pryvee and apert, thanne wolde they nevere fyne
To doon of gentillesse the faire office:
They myghte do no vileynye or vice.
Taak fyr, and ber it in the derkeste house
Bitwix this and the mount of Kaukasous,
And lat men shette the dores and go thenne:
Yet wole the fyr as faire lye and brenne
As twenty thousand men myghte it biholde;
His office natureel ay wol it holde,
Up peril of my lyf, til that it dye.
Heere may ye se wel how that genterye
Is nat annexed to possessioun,
Sith fok ne doon hir operacioun
Alwey, as dooth the fyr, lo, in his kynde.
For, God it woot, men may wel often fynde
A lordes sone do shame and vileynye;
And he that wole han pris of his gentrye,
For he was boren of a gentil hous,
And hadde his eldres noble and vertuous,
And nel hymselven do no gentil dedis,
Ne folwen his gentil auncestre that deed is,
He nys nat gentil, be he duc or erl;
For vileyns synful dedes make a cherl.
For gentillesse nys but renomee
Of thyne auncestres, for hire heigh bountee,
Which is a strange thyng to thy persone.
Thy gentillesse cometh fro God allone.
Thanne cometh oure verray gentillesse of grace;
It was no thyng biquethe us with oure place.'
                    [*III (D) 1113-1164*]

The idea that man can not inherit "gentillesse," but that each one must win it himself by virtuous living is also presented specifically in Chaucer's short poem entitled "Gentilesse."

One may also consider other aspects of chivalry as being

religious and philosophical. The whole concept of love, for example, when thought of as "ideal," belongs in that category. The Church of the early Middle Ages taught that physical love between the sexes was of necessity devoid of the spiritual; consequently, it was necessary to transfer natural desires into the formulae of the dream world. In courtly circles, a young man who was "in love" with the young woman placed her in theory far above him: she was to be worshipped and served and, if possible, rescued from some dire peril—the ultimate in service. The knight whose original command was to serve God and his temporal Lord now strove to turn his eroticism into the channels leading to Heaven. Love between man and woman became part of the hierarchy of the Chain of Love, far below divine love and below the "platonic" love for one's fellow man, but it was still an aspect of the great moving force of the medieval universe. As we have seen, the love between Arveragus and Dorigen of the *Franklin's Tale* embodies the rarefied emotion accepted as "love" in the ideal world of the fourteenth century, an emotion widely accepted as love by the "romantic," as opposed to seriously realistic, writers up to the present—a fairy-tale formula to be generally accepted in literature, but seldom met in life.

We should note Chaucer's treatment of the summoner's curiosity concerning the physical nature of hell in the *Friar's Tale*. The summoner has been told that his new companion is from "fer in the north contree." (That hell is a cold region is an idea drawn from Teutonic mythology and employed later by Shakespeare in *Measure For Measure:* Claudio cries out in terror that death may bring him to a region of "thick-ribbed ice.") After he discovers that his new sworn brother is actually a fiend, the summoner, although at first nonplussed, hastens to improve his knowledge of the general appearance of devils. "Have you a figure 'determinat'?" he asks, to be told that, no, fiends have no shape unless they wish to take one; if

they wish to take a shape, they may appear as a man, or an
ape, or an angel—or "elles make yow seme we been shape."
When the summoner would pursue this interesting line of in-
quiry, however, the fiend silences his questioner in the following manner:

'. . . somtyme we been Goddes instrumentz,
And meenes to doon his comandementz,
Whan that hym list, upon his creatures.
In divers art and in diverse figures.
Withouten hym we have no myght, certayn,
If that hym list to stonden ther-agayn.
And somtyme, at our prayere, han we leve
Only the body and nat the soule greve; . . .
And somtyme han we myght of both two,
This is to seyn, of soule and body eke.
And somtyme be we suffred for to seke
Upon a man, and doon his soule unreste,
And nat his body, and al is for the beste.
Whan he withstandeth oure temptacioun,
It is a cause of his savacioun,
Al be it that it was nat oure entente
He sholde be sauf, but that we wolde hym hente . . .
Of elementz?' The feend answerde, 'Nay.
Somtyme we feyne, and somtyme we aryse
With dede bodyes, in ful sondry wyse,
And speke as renably and faire and wel. . . .'
[*III (D) 1483-1490, 1492-1500, 1507-1509*]

The fiend's short lecture on his role as the servant of God
comes in part from Boece [*Boece*, Bk. IV, Pr. 62-71] and
from the *Book of Job* [II, 12, 116]. One should also note
the medieval belief mentioned here that devils could occupy
the bodies of the dead, a belief which Shakespeare two hundred years later uses in *Hamlet:* is the Ghost in the play really
the spirit of the earlier Hamlet or is the Ghost a devil using
the earlier Hamlet's body?

The *Tale of Melibee,* Chaucer's translation and abridgement of the thirteenth-century Albertano of Brescia's *Liber Consolationii et Consilii,* is hardly a narrative, for it consists largely of ethical maxims and allegorical figures: one of the reasons that anger is wrong is that it leads to private vengeance or war; private vengeance in turn is a sin against the laws of God; mercy and forgiveness are great virtues. Melibee is the allegorical figure of earthly riches which destroys the teachings of Christ; the world, the flesh and the devil, "the three olde foes," wound Wisdom (Melibee's daughter, Sophie) through the five senses ("fyve mortel woundes in fyve sondry places"); Prudence (Melibee's wife) through the strength of her arguments brings about a "happy," that is, moral, conclusion.

That the *Tale of Melibee* is almost as long as the *Parson's Tale* is one indication that it would have been welcomed by the company of pilgrims. Its very length, combined with its prosy moralizing, would make it attractive to a fourteenth-century audience, and would provide them with welcome food for thought and discussion. Hence, it is obvious that Chaucer, writing in his own time as a medieval man, would include the *Tale of Melibee* in the *Canterbury Tales.* For the poet's contemporaries, the Tale would have been the exact opposite of the tedious and uninteresting composition which some twentieth-century critics find it to be.

As we know, the philosophers of the Middle Ages conceived of the universe as a finality: there could be no change in it. The perfected and all-embracing plan, existing with neither beginning nor end, had its being in the mind of God, that aspect of God which was called "Providence." God, however, was an indivisible unit, infinitely remote from man, so that the carrying out of the decrees of Providence was believed to be delegated to a force called Destiny; without "will" of its own,

Destiny merely followed the divine will. As a force, Destiny was divisible into different powers: powers of angelic (and demonic) spirits, of the configurations of the planets and the stars, of nature, and of—most commonly—a mysterious force, usually personified, called Fortune. Fortune was indifferent both to man's happiness and to his miseries; thus, Fortune capriciously controlled each man's personal life so that his successes and disasters often had the appearance of the illogical and the cruel. But man, infinitely small, could not "understand" the plan of Providence. Even though something seemed evil to him, he should have the faith to trust in the ultimate result, for God is omniscient and God is love. In fact, medieval man believed that God's love was what held in place the physical universe—the earth and the Ptolemaic spheres—and which ordinarily, in the last analysis, controlled the orderly cycles in this world, the cycles of the seasons and the tides and animate birth, growth and death.

In the philosophic aspect of the *Canterbury Tales,* Chaucer is mainly concerned with two of Destiny's agents: the force of the stars and the force of Fortune. Early in the *Knight's Tale* when he mistakenly supposes that Palamon is lamenting their imprisonment, Arcite addresses his companion as follows:

'For Goddes love, taak al in pacience
Oure prisoun, for it may noon oother be.
Fortune hath yeven us this adversitee.
Som wikke aspect or disposicioun
Of Saturne, by som constellacioun
Hath yeven us this, although we hadde it sworn;
So stood the hevene whan that we were born.
We moste endure it; this is the short and playn.'

[*I* (*A*) *1084-1091*]

We should especially note here that the power of the planet Saturn, the planet considered to be the bringer of the greatest misfortune to man, is emphasized. Saturn, personified as the heathen god, speaks himself later in the *Knight's Tale* as follows:

'My cours, that hath so wyde for to turne,
Hath moore power than woot any man.
Myn is the drenchyng in the see so wan;
Myn is the prison in the derke cote;
Myn is the stranglyng and hangyng by the throte,
The murmure and the cherles rebellyng,
The groynynge, and the pryvee empoysonyng;
I do vengeance and pleyn correccioun,
Whil I dwelle in the signe of the leoun.
Myn is the ruyne of the hye halles,
The fallynge of the toures and of the walles
Upon the mynour or the carpenter.
I slow Sampsoun, shakynge the piler;
And myne be the maladyes colde,
The derke tresons, and the castes olde;
My lookyng is the fader of pestilence.'

[*I (A) 2454-2469*]

Arcite, when he hears that he is to be ransomed, tells Palamon that Fortune has "yturned thee the dys," and speaks again of God's will:

'Allas, why pleynen folk so in commune
On purveiaunce of God, or of Fortune,
That yeveth hem ful ofte in many a gyse
Wel bettre than they kan hemself devyse?
Som man desireth for to han richesse,
That cause is of his mordre of gree siknesse;
And som man wolde out of his prisoun fayn,
That in his hous is of his meynee slayn. . . .
We seken faste after felicitee
But we goon wrong ful often, trewely.'

[*I (A) 1251-1258, 1266-1267*]

After Arcite's departure, Palamon also reflects in similar fashion, addressing Fortune as a "goddess":

'O crueel goddes that governe
This world with byndyng of youre word eterne,
And writen in the table of atthamaunt
Youre parlement and youre eterne graunt,
What is mankynde moore unto you holde
Than is the sheep that rouketh in the folde?
For slayn is man right as another beest,
And dwelleth eek in prison and arreest,
And hath siknesse and greet adversitee,
And ofte tymes giltelees, pardee.
What governance is in this prescience,
That giltelees tormenteth innocence?
And yet encresseth this al my penaunce,
That man is bounden to his observaunce,
For Goddes sake, to letten of his wille,
Ther as a beest may al his lust fulfille.
And whan a beest is deed he hath no peyne:
But man after his deeth moot wepe and pleyne,
Though in this world he have care and wo.'

[*I (A) 1303-1321*]

Note again the mention of the malefic Saturn. A number of scholars, notably Professor Walter Clyde Curry, have pointed out that the kings who support Palamon and Arcite, Emetreus and Lycurgus, are respectively personifications of the planets Mars and Saturn. Chaucer's mind is apparently running on Saturn's influence on mankind throughout the *Knight's Tale*.

Destiny also brings about Theseus' presence at the duel between Palamon and Arcite. Chaucer tells us through the words of the Knight:

The destinee, ministre general
That executeth in the world over al
The purveiaunce that God hath seyn biforn,

So strong it is that, though the world had sworn
The contrarie of a thyng by ye or nay,
Yet somtyme it shal fallen on a day
That falleth nat eft withinne a thousand year,
For certeinly, oure appetites heer,
Be it of werre, or pees, or hate, or love,
Al is this reuled by the sighte above.

[*I (A) 1663-1672*]

Thus, to carry out the decrees of Providence, the Knight explains that Theseus was filled with a strong desire to hunt and so came upon the two young knights.

At the close of the *Knight's Tale,* Theseus comments in his speech to Emily and Palamon on the wisdom of Providence, the "Firste Moevere." He says:

'The Firste Moevere of the cause above,
Whan he first made the faire cheyne of love,
Greet was th'effect, and heigh was his entente.
Wel wiste he why, and what thereof he mente;
For with that faire cheyne of love he bond
The fyr, the eyr, the water, and the lond
In certeyn boundes, that they may nat flee.
That same Prince and that Moevere, . . .
Hath stablissed in this wrecched world adoun
Certeyne dayes and duracioun
To al that is engendred in this place,
Over the whiche day they may nat pace,
Al mowe they yet tho dayes wel abregge.
Ther nedeth noght noon auctoritee t'allegge,
For it is preeved by experience,
But that me list declaren my sentence.
Thanne may men by this ordre wel discerne
That thilke Moevere stable is and eterne,
Wel may men knowe, but it be a fool,
That every part dirryveth from his hool;
For nature hath nat taken his bigynnyng

Of no partie or cantel of a thyng,
But of a thyng that parfit is and stable,
Descendynge so til it be corrumpable.
And therfore, of his wise purveiaunce,
He hath so wel biset his ordinaunce,
That speces of thynges and progressiouns
Shullen enduren by successiouns,
And nat eterne, withouten any lye.
This maystow understonde and seen at ye. . . .
Thanne is it wysdom, as it thynketh me,
To maken vertu of necessitee,
And take it weel that we may nat eschue,
And namely that to us alle is due.
And whoso gruccheth ought, he dooth folye,
And rebel is to hym that all may gye.'
      [*I (A) 2987-3016, 3041-3046*]

It was meant by wise Providence, Theseus continues, that Arcite should die at the height of his fame; we are guilty of
willfulness if we say the contrary.

Man never escapes from the ultimate plan of God but virtue—and virtue alone—could sometimes modify the machinations of Destiny's agents. In the *Man of Law's Tale* Constance's life is spared after her marriage to the Sultan because
of her prayers to Christ: she is worthy of the intervention of a
higher power.

Men myghten asken why she was nat slayn.
Eek at the feeste? who myghte hir body save?
And I answere to that demande agayn,
Who saved Danyel in the horrible cave
Ther every wight save he, maister and knave,
Was with the leon frete er he asterte?
No wight but God, that he bar in his herte.

God liste to shewe his wonderful myracle
In hire, for we sholde seen his myghte werkis;

> Crist, which that is to every harm triacle,
> By certeine meenes ofte, as knowen clerkis,
> Dooth thyng for certein ende that ful derk is
> To mannes wit, that for oure ignorance
> Ne konne noght knowe his prudent purveiance.
>
> [*II* (*B*¹) *470-483*]

Again, Constance's prayer to God and the Virgin is answered directly by a miracle in the slaying of the false accuser, for Constance is "dogthre of hooly chirche." And yet again Destiny's course is altered when Constance survives the second voyage in the rudderless ship, because of her devout supplication to "Cristes Mooder."

The *Monk's Tale*, since it is a series of tragedies, is "philosophical" almost by definition. The Monk himself somewhat condescendingly informs the company what the word *tragedy* means: "A tragedy," he says in his Prologue, "is a story of a man who stood in great prosperity and then falls out of his high position into misery, and so ends wretchedly." The Monk adds in the first stanza of his tale:

> For certin, whan that fortune list too flee,
> Ther may no man the cours of hire withholde.

In each of the seventeen tales which the Monk tells the company before being interrupted in his dolorous progress, Fortune does bring about a disaster.

The *Nun's Priest's Tale*, in delightful parody of a serious narrative, introduces comment on Destiny. Chauntecleer, in spite of the warning he has received in his dream, is nevertheless obliged to meet Fate:

> But what that God forwoot moot nedes bee,
> After the opinioun of certein clerkis
> Witnesse on hym that any parfit clerk is,
> That in scole is greet altercacioun
> In this mateere, and greet disputisoun,

And hath been of an hundred thousand men.
But I ne kan nat bulte it to the bren
As kan the hooly doctour Augustyn,
Or Boece, or the Bisshop Bradwardyn,
Wheither that Goddes worthy forwityng
Streyneth me nedely for to doon a thyng,—
'Nedely' clepe I symple necessitee;
Or elles, if free choys be graunted me
To do that same thymg, or do it noght,
Though God forwoot it er that was wroght;
Or if his willyng streyneth never a deel
But by necessitee condicioneel.

  [*VII* (*B²* 4424-4440) 3234-3250]

Here we have the problem of free will briefly introduced. If the will of Providence is fixed, has man any actual volition in his acts? Chaucer would evidently say here that over "simple necessity" (that is, the "acts" of birth and death) man has no control, but that over "conditional necessity" (all "acts" except birth and death) he has limited control. After Chauntecleer, all too susceptible to flattery, has been carried off by the fox, the teller of the tale exclaims, "O destinee, that mayst nat been eschewed!" But Fortune now takes a hand and permits Chauntecleer to escape, so that the Nun's Priest may also point out:

Lo, how Fortune turneth sodeynly.
The hope and the pryde eek of hir enemy!

The "worste" rioter in the *Pardoner's Tale* speaks of the treasure the three rioters find under the oak tree as being the gift of Fortune. And in the *Summoner's Tale,* the Summoner, unlettered as he is, is aware of the part Fortune plays in life. In his brief homily on the dangers of giving way to the sin of ire (directed, of course, against the Friar, although ironically the Summoner himself is the more enraged of the two), the Summoner gives an *exemplum* of three knights who lose through a judge's anger because "Fortune wolde that it was so" [III (D) 2020].

It is, however, not in the *Canterbury Tales,* but in *Troilus and Criseyde* that Chaucer places his greatest emphasis on the decrees of Providence and on the question of free will [See pp. 185-187].

According to medieval belief, the stars as agents of Destiny combined with Fortune as powerful determinants for a man's life. We have seen that brought out in the *Knight's Tale* and it is elsewhere illustrated in the *Canterbury Tales.* The Wife of Bath in the Prologue to her Tale blames her "constellacioun," meaning her horoscope, or the aspect of the stars at the moment of her birth, for her very nature. She says:

> I folwed ay myn inclinacioun
> By vertue of my constellacioun.

She was born, she explains, under the influence of three planets—Mercury, Venus and Mars—which appear in her zodiacal sign of Taurus, and these planets are scarcely at peace with each other:

> Mercurie loveth wysdom and science,
> And Venus loveth ryot and dispence.

Mars has also intensified and debased the influence of Venus so, although the Wife could have loved in more ladylike fashion if solely under Venus' influence, she is, because of Mars, coarse and frankly animal in her desires. Because of Mercury, she is extremely efficient and intelligent, but the sign of Taurus brings her passions to the fore. Consequently it is not only Fortune, but the stars as well, which have, through shaping her nature, brought her the five husbands and "oother compaignye in youthe"!

In the *Man of Law's Tale,* the teller states:

Paraventure in thilke large book
Which that men clepe the hevene ywriten was
With sterres, whan that he his birthe took,
That he for love sholde han his deeth, allas!
For in the sterres, clerer than is glas,
Is writen, God woot, whoso koude it rede,
The deeth of every man withouten drede.

In sterres, many a wynter therbiforn,
Was writen the deeth of Ector, Achilles,
Of Pompei, Julius, er they were born;
The strif of Thebes; and of Ercules,
Of Sampson, Turnus, and of Socrates
The deeth; but mennes wittes ben so dulle
That no wight kan wel rede it atte fulle. . . .

O firste moevyng! crueel firmament,
With thy diurnal sweigh that crowdest ay
And hurlest al from est til occident
That naturelly wolde holde another way,
Thy crowdyng set the hevene in swich array
At the bigynnyng of this fiers viage,
That crueel Mars hath slayn this mariage.

Infortunat ascendent tortuous,
Of which the lord is helplees falle, allas,
Out of his angle into the derkest hous!
O mars, o atazir, as in this cas!
O fieble moone, unhappy been thy paas!
Thou knyttest thee ther thou art nat receyved;
Ther thou were weel, from thennes artow weyved.

Imprudent Emperour of Rome, allas!
Was ther no philosophre in al thy toun?
Is no tyme bet than oother in swich cas?
Of viage is ther noon eleccioun.
Namely to folk of heigh condicioun?

Noght whan a roote is of a burthe yknowe?
Allas, we been to lewed or to slowe!
[II (B¹) 190-203, 295-315]

Finally, if we examine the description of the Physician in the *General Prologue*, we observe a marriage of philosophy and science. The belief that stars are agents of Destiny joins the Physician's portrait to the practical aspects of his profession. Many physicians in the Middle Ages were, like Chaucer's Doctor of Physic, "grounded in astronomye," although such knowledge was scoffed at by some of the more advanced practitioners. Each of the twelve signs of the zodiac was thought to control a different part of the human body; further, the physical characteristics and the temperament of each person were determined at his birth by his horoscope. Here we have the origin of the four medieval "humours," concepts which lasted well into the seventeenth century and which have left their traces in the speech of today—we still speak of someone being in a "good humor" or in a "bad humor," of a "sanguine" or a "phlegmatic" person, and so on. The "scientific" nature of these "humours" will be discussed later; here we need to note only that it was the stars that determined the extent of each "humour" in the individual.

The stars played a large part in the professional life of many physicians, particularly the so-called fashionable ones. It was the custom of those physicians always to cast the horoscope of the patient; they then thought it necessary to know the positions of the stars at the time of the outset of the illness, and at the time of the physician's visit to the patient. Those three configurations of the heavens were then "combined" so that the physician could discover what planets were favorable to the cure of the illness and what malefic or "antagonistic" planets were present, in order that he could "fortunen the ascendent"—that is, make discs of metal, bearing representations of a particular planet together with magic formulae which could be applied to the patient. Consequently, the purely medical school of the physicians was aided by the philosophical belief in the influence of the stars, those agents of Destiny, and, hence, indirectly of the Divine.

The Seven Deadly Sins were perhaps even a greater part of medieval religion than the Seven Cardinal Virtues. The Parson in his Tale speaks only of the former and although many modern critics have accused Chaucer of having "his little joke" in allowing the Parson to describe the long and serious sermon as a "myrie tale in prose," if we translate *myrie* as "pleasant to hear," the joke is nonexistent. The men and women of the Middle Ages were as fascinated by the didactic as they were by allegory. The company of pilgrims, in spite of Harry Bailly's admonition that the *Parson's Tale* should be kept "in litel space," would have enjoyed the very long treatment of Pride, Envy, Hatred, Sloth, Avarice, Gluttony and Lechery. Even in the medieval romances, the audience liked to find homilies and the lessons in moral virtue, and the examples of actual medieval sermons which we can read today, show that one of the most "popular" subjects was the Seven Deadly Sins.

THREE ✣ The Influence of Chaucer's Scientific World

THE WORD *science* in Chaucer's day usually meant "knowledge" or "wisdom," a more general meaning than the one most frequently given to the word today. Even when reference was made to a particular body of knowledge such as to "astronomye," the word covered not only systematized facts concerning the magnitude and movements of celestial bodies, but the religious and philosophic concepts surrounding those bodies as agents of Destiny—today's pseudo-science which we term astrology. What passed then for our medical, biological and zoological sciences was also linked loosely to religion and philosophy and to old wives' tales. Consequently, our consideration here of the influence of Chaucer's "scientific" environment upon his writing of the *Canterbury Tales* will be limited more or less in the case of astronomy to the physical aspects of the science; in other "sciences" the material will be enlarged to include what many people today would label as superstition.

In the late fourteenth century, the telling of the time of day by the sun was surprisingly accurate if one had access to tables. In the *Introduction to the Man of Law's Tale,* Harry Bailly, without tables, in a few seconds rightly concludes that it is ten o'clock in the morning: he has observed that the arc of the artificial day has run the "ferthe part, and half an houre and moore," he knows the date, he observes the equality of the shadow to the object which casts it, and he also knows the latitude of his position. A problem which would give trouble to some of our present college students who are not mathematically minded, is, for our Host, scarcely any effort at all, which fact is, of course, Chaucer's humorous exaggeration. It is true that medieval man, even when ignorant, needed little more than a glance to approximate time by the sun, but Harry Bailly's learned accuracy, an accuracy vouched for by modern calculations, is merely amusing. Chaucer must have had much imaginative enjoyment exercising his own mathematical knowledge in making the accurate calculation in the *Man of Law's Tale,* but it is doubtful if many members of his courtly audience would have had the necessary skill to follow his figuring, although they would have appreciated the poet's "joke" in supposing that Harry Bailly could be the calculator.

Harry Bailly mentions "the artificial day," and Chaucer himself in his *Treatise on the Astrolabe* explains the meaning of the phrase. The artificial day consisted of twelve "hours" of daylight (measured from sunrise to sunset) and twelve "hours" of darkness (measured from sunset to sunrise), "hours" which must obviously differ in length from day to day and which can contain sixty minutes each only when the total time of daylight is equal to the total time of darkness. If, for example, a calendar day consists of sixteen sixty-minute clock hours of daylight and eight clock hours of darkness, each "hour" of daylight of the corresponding artificial day will consist of eighty minutes by the clock, and each "hour" of darkness will consist of forty minutes by the clock—hence the medieval term " 'unequal' hours."

Each "hour" of the artificial day was considered to be dedicated to one of the seven planets, the Sun and Moon being considered as planets, and not as stars. Beginning with sunrise, the first hour was dedicated to the planet for which the day is named (the ingenious mathematical scheme making that possible appealed to the Middle Ages as a miracle of Providence). As partially illustrated by the table shown below (starting with Sunday), the first "hour" is dedicated to the Sun; the first on Monday to the Moon; the first on Tuesday (the French *Mardi*) to Mars; the first on Wednesday (the French *Mercredi*) to Mercury; the first on Thursday (the French *Jeudi*) to Jupiter (or Jove); the first on Friday (the French *Vendredi*) to Venus; and the first on Saturday to Saturn.

Planet *		\multicolumn{3}{c}{}

Hours, numbered from sunrise to sunrise, as dedicated to the particular planet (the table, if completed for the seven days of the week and then continued, will, of course, repeat itself):

Planet *		SUNDAY				MONDAY				TUESDAY	
Saturn		5	12	19		2	9	16	23		6
Jupiter		6	13	20		3	10	17	24		7
Mars		7	14	21		4	11	18	(1)		8
Sun	(1)	8	15	22		5	12	19		2	9
Venus	2	9	16	23		6	13	20		3	10
Mercury	3	10	17	24		7	14	21		4	11
Moon	4	11	18		(1)	8	15	22		5	12

* The planets are arranged in the order of what medieval astronomers believed to be their relative distances from the earth, beginning with Saturn, the farthest away.

If a planet were in a favorable position in one's horoscope, or if one hoped for a success in an undertaking characteristically associated with some planet—Mars, for instance, was particularly concerned with war—it was advisable to begin one's enterprises in an hour dedicated to that planet. In the *Knight's Tale*, Emily makes her petition to Diana, or Luna, the heathen Moon Goddess according to the narrative, but Chaucer skillfully "modernizes" the story here by temporarily treating the Moon as a planet and not as a heathen goddess, during the first hour of Monday morning [I (A) 2273-2274]. Palamon has preceded Emily by making his petition to Venus during the twenty-third hour on Sunday [I (A) 2209-2215]; Arcite petitions Mars during "the nexte houre of Mars" following Emily's prayer, a time which must bring him to the fourth hour of Monday's artificial day [I (A) 2367-2369].

Chaucer finds pleasure in the *Nun's Priest's Tale*, as he did in the *Man of Law's Tale*, by assigning mathematical knowledge to an incongruous figure. Chauntecleer, that extraordinarily accomplished fowl, knows the "ascencioun of the equynoxial" for the place where he has his dwelling, and every time that the angle of the elevation of the Sun increases by 15°, he crows lustily to indicate the passage of one of the "unequal" hours, that is, one-twelfth of the Sun's 180° arc— something which the abbey clock is unable to do since the hours it measures are each sixty minutes.

Alchemy is evidently a subject which interested Chaucer greatly, but we have no way of knowing whether he had genuine confidence in the "multiplication" of gold or felt that the whole science was dubious. The *Canon's Yeoman's Tale* might lead us to suppose the latter to be the case, but gold had been legitimately "increased" through the addition of other metals long before the fourteenth century, a fact of which the poet might have been aware. The *Canon's Yeoman's Tale* can be an exposé of the tricksters in the science without being an attack

on the science itself. In any event, Chaucer depicts the yeoman, through that worthy's racy conversation in a biograph-
ical Tale, as being ingenuous about the Canon's experiments
which may someday be successful, but which so far have been
dismal failures; "we blondren evere and pouren in the fir,"
complains the yeoman, although he adds, "but ay we han
good hope." After the flight of the Canon, who is afraid that
what should be kept secret will be revealed, the yeoman em-
barks upon his Tale with enthusiasm, for he has every wish to
show up the swindles his master has felt obliged to perpe-
trate because of the failures of the legitimate experiments. The
yeoman explains that an interest in alchemy is a disease
which will eventually ruin a man: he spends his all upon it
and goes from bad poverty to worse.

The yeoman asks rhetorical questions of the company:
why should he inform them of the proportions of silver, of
arsenic, of burnt bones, and of iron filings which go into the
cauldrons? Or why should he try to recite the names of all the
ingredients in the mixtures? The list the yeoman does give to
the company of the ingredients runs to more than a dozen,
showing Chaucer's own knowledge of what alchemists used in
their efforts to create or multiply gold. The yeoman talks of
"the foure spirites and the bodies sevene"; the "spirites" are
quicksilver, arsenic, crystalline salt and brimstone; the "bodies" take us back to the planets, for the gold belongs to the
Sun, the silver to the Moon, the iron to Mars, quicksilver to
Mercury, lead to Saturn, tin to Jupiter and copper to Venus.
(Chaucer's friend Gower has nearly two hundred lines in the
Confessio Amantis on the subject of alchemy; the lines
parallel Chaucer's description in essence, but they are written
not as a narrative but as a serious account [IV 2457 ff.].)

The second part of the *Canon's Yeoman's Tale* is devoted
to a description of frauds practiced by alchemists. Silver filings—the frauds deal with silver and not with gold—are

placed in a hole drilled in a piece of beechwood, and the hole is then stopped with wax; when the wood is placed on the fire, the wax melts and the silver runs out, deceiving someone who has brought a base metal into a belief that transmutation has actually taken place. Or, similarly, the alchemist stirs his mixture with a hollow rod containing silver filings and again stopped with wax. Or, simplest of all, an accomplice of the alchemist merely puts silver in the mixture when the person to be deceived is not looking. We must suppose that Chaucer was familiar with the tricks of alchemists, as well as with treatises on the subject, for the yeoman concludes his Tale with references to such treatises.

Medicine in Chaucer's time was primitive, if we compare it with modern medicine. Little was known about the constitution and the functions of the human body, about drugs, about distinguishing different kinds of diseases. Instruments were crude and treatment was often left to the mere influence of the stars. The surprising thing is that some of the physicians were, in spite of their handicaps, great and successful healers.

In describing the Doctor of Physic in the *General Prologue*, Chaucer writes with some satire of his Physician. That gentleman is something of a "fashionable" doctor, and we ask ourselves if Chaucer would have himself wanted him as an attendant in illness.

The Doctor of Physic is familiar with a long list of authorities:

We knew he the olde Esculapius,
And Deyscorides, and eek Rufus,
Olde Ypocras, Haly, and Galyen,
Serapion, Razis, and Avycen,
Averrois, Damascien, and Constantyn,
Bernard, and Gatesden, and Gilbertyn.
[*I (A) 429-434*]

Aesculapius, Dioscorides, Rufus, Hippocrates and Galen all belong to the period of classical antiquity, although the first named was merely a legendary figure. Haly, Serapio, Rasis, Avicenna, Averroës, Damascensus and Constantinus Africanus were all Moslem physicians whose works had entered Europe through translations into Latin. Gilbertus Anglicus, Bernard, and John Gaddesden were English physicians of the late thirteenth and early fourteenth centuries, the last, Gaddesden —some of whose methods are still in use today—being the most famous. Chaucer probably drew the list in large part from other authors, but that he makes a list of so many names shows an interest in and a familiarity with the treatises on medicine known to the late fourteenth century.

The physicians of Chaucer's day, as has been said, relied on material found in books, rather than on any study of practical anatomy. Hence, the current notions concerning the make-up of the human body were likely to be erroneous. Chaucer speaks, for example, of the "celle fantastik," which implies that he believed that the brain was divided into three cells, the front controlling fantasy, the middle controlling reason, and the back controlling memory; and the poet also refers to "animal" and "natural" virtues, which indicates his familiarity with the three "virtues" (or spirits) which were thought to control the life functions: the animal was thought to be seated in the brain, the natural in the liver and the vital in the heart. The human body was imagined to have four fluids or "humours" in it, although not in equal quantities, as always one of them was predominant. If blood were predominant, the person so constituted would be called "sanguine"; if phlegm were predominant, he would be called "phlegmatic"; if choler were predominant, he would be called "choleric"; and if black bile were predominant, he would be called "melancholic." Chaucer's Franklin, for example, is called "sanguine" and the Reeve is called "choleric."

Either one of those divisions not only determined the temperament of an individual, but also determined his physical make-up. The sanguine man, for instance, is depicted in the Middle Ages as stout and as having a fair skin and an excellent digestion, whereas the choleric man is usually lean with a pale complexion and exceedingly thin legs. We then come to the theory, which partially returns to the destinal character of the stars, that a man's physical make-up was determined also by his horoscope. Galen was responsible for the medieval theory of the four elements and the four qualities which had to be considered in treating a man's body. The four elements were designated as *fire, earth, air* and *water;* the four qualities were *hot, cold, dry, moist.* Each of the twelve signs of the zodiac was concerned with the elements and the qualities and with the "humours," all of which were believed partly to determine a man's predisposition to certain diseases and the most likely times for a cure.

Chaucer is also aware of the symptoms of certain diseases. In the *Knight's Tale,* Chaucer describes Arcite's condition after he has returned to Thebes from Athens and rightly concludes, according to medieval diagnostics, that the young man is suffering from the lover's malady. Arcite cannot sleep, meat and drink do not appeal to him, he becomes thin and "drye as is a shaft," his eyes are hollow, his complexion is pale and he wishes to be alone, he moans at night, he dislikes the sound of music and he weeps continually [I (A) 1361-1376]. Also in the *Knight's Tale,* when Arcite is thrown from his horse, Chaucer gives almost a physician's account of the injury which Arcite suffers.

As blak he lay as any cole or crowe,
So was the blood yronnen in his face.
Anon he was yborn out of the place,
With herte soor, to Theseus paleys.
Tho was he korven out of his harneys.

And in a bed ybrought ful fair and blyve;
For he was yet in memorie and alyve,
And alwey criynge after Emelye. . . .
Swelleth the brest of Arcite, and the soore,
Encreesseth at his herte moore and moore.
The clothered blood, for any lechecraft,
Corrupteth, and is in his bouk ylaft,
That neither veyne-blood, ne ventusynge,
Ne drynke of herbes may ben his helpynge.
The vertu expulsif, or animal,
Fro thilke vertu cleped natural
Ne may the venym voyden ne expelle.
The pipes of his longes gonne to swelle,
And every lacerte in his brest adoun
Is shent with venym and corrupcioun.
Hym gayneth neither, for to gete his lif,
Vomyt upward, ne dounward laxatif.
Al is tobrosten thilke regioun;
Nature hath now no dominacioun.
And certeinly, ther Nature wol nat wirche,
Fare wel phisik! Go ber the man to chirche!
        [*I (A) 2692-2699, 2743-2760*]

In the *General Prologue* Chaucer gives an extensive list of all
the remedies that the diseased Summoner has applied unsuc-
cessfully to the "fyr-reed cherubynnes face" of which the
children are all afraid [I (A) 624-633]; further, Chaucer is
aware that a man in the Summoner's condition should not eat
garlic, onions and leeks or drink strong red wine. Chaucer's
observation of the Cook, however, who has a "normal" on his
shin, and of the Pardoner, with his goat's voice, need not be
"medical"; any man of the fourteenth century probably would
have noted the same thing in each of those characters. In the
Nun's Priest's Tale, Pertelote, in her anxiety to believe that
Chauntecleer's dream merely comes from indigestion, gives
him a "prescription" which is based on a prescription recom-

mended for human beings in the Middle Ages, including, as most Chaucer scholars have pointed out, the use of earthworms.

Pertelote, in the *Nun's Priest's Tale,* may or may not be an expert on dreams; we suspect that she is full of wifely concern for Chauntecleer, and that prompts her to say that his warning dream has no meaning. She claims that the dream is engendered by repletion, and that the repletion has resulted in Chauntecleer's "greete superfluytee" of "rede colere." "No wonder," Pertelote cries out in an attempt to hearten her suddenly timid mate. "No wonder you have seen a reddish doglike animal in your dreams! If you had a superfluity of black bile, you would have dreamt of black bears or bulls or devils." But Chauntecleer has had a dream which truly foretells the future.

Chauntecleer is by nature one who likes to display his erudition, and he now has ample opportunity to produce evidence of his familiarity with the authorities on dream interpretation. Dionysius Cato (quoted by Pertelote in support of her diagnosis) is mistaken, maintains Chauntecleer, when he says we should take no account of dreams; Chauntecleer then tells two stories which refute Cato's statements, for the dream in each of the stories does prognosticate an actual event. Chauntecleer adds, as further proof, references to the dreams of "Seint Kenelm," of Scipio Africanus, of Daniel and Joseph and Pharaoh's Butler and Baker in the Old Testament, and finally of Andromache, who dreamt of the death of Hector. The list serves here not only as an ornament of style [see p. 137], but as an opportunity for Chaucer to show his interest in the whole matter of dream interpretation, an interest shared by most people from the earliest times to the present, even though the interpretations themselves have greatly changed color.

Chaucer himself shows that he relied for his "scientific" information about dreams largely upon the Macrobius' Commentary on *The Dream of Scipio*. The English poet discusses the theory of dreams not only in the *Nun's Priest's Tale*, where discussion is an integral part of the narrative, but also in the *House of Fame* and in *Troilus and Criseyde*.

Macrobius lists five types of dream:* the *somnium*, the *visio*, the *oraculum*, the *insomnium*, the *phantasma* or *visium*. The *somnium* is a dream that requires symbolic interpretation by an expert (for example, the Wife of Bath says that to dream of blood betokens gold [III (D) 581]). The *visio* is a dream which reveals a coming event exactly as it will be (Chauntecleer's dream of the fox mirrors exactly what is to take place). The *oraculum* is a dream in which a spirit or relative or some important person appears to the dreamer and announces what is to happen. All three of the dreams just mentioned are valid in their prophecies about the future. The *insomnium* and the *phantasma,* on the other hand, give clues only to the physical condition of the dreamer; neither has "meaning" in any other sense. The former may come from fear or worry or digestive disturbances: the latter may be considered as a kind of delusion. Chaucer makes no distinction between the three Middle English words meaning "to dream": *dremen, meten* and *sweven*. He writes a great deal about dreams in all his works and evidently was as puzzled as most of us are about such phenomena.

When Pertelote "prescribes" for Chauntecleer, the latter runs no risk in dealing with a dishonest apothecary, for Pertelote instructs him to find the ingredients as follows: "pekke hem up right as they growe and ete hem yn." Any patient of Chaucer's Doctor of Physic, however, is not so fortunate, for the Doctor has made a deal with a friend who is an apothecary, and each causes the other "for to wynne"—the charge to

---

* For this information I am indebted solely to W. C. Curry's *Chaucer and the Mediaeval Sciences* (New York, 1960 [2nd ed.]), pp. 199 ff.

compound a prescription far exceeds the cost of the drugs and electuaries to the apothecary, so he and the Physician divide the large profit. (In the *Mirour de L'Omme*, Gower speaks seriously in general terms of the deceiving of patients through the collusion of physicians and apothecaries, an indication that the practice was widespread.)

Magic is usually spoken of as an art but, as Chaucer treats it, magic savors of being a science. In the *Franklin's Tale*, Aurelius procures the services of a magician to remove the rocks from the coast of Brittany. Chaucer, through the voice of the Franklin, then describes the procedure followed by the magician. The magician takes his Toledan tables which are astronomical in character, he corrects them and calculates the changes of a planet's position in single years, or in round period of years; then, having secured the data for a given time or period, he uses his astrolabe and his tables of proportional parts, dividing the sphere into "houses" for his purposes. He continues with his elaborate computations paying strict attention, of course, to the Moon. Chaucer, in his detailed account of the magician's work, evidently follows some treatise on magic, but he calls the process "supersticious cursednesse," and he makes clear that, in any case, the rocks would not actually be removed, but that an illusion would be created that they were removed.

FOUR ❖ The Influence of
Chaucer's Everyday World

FOR CHAUCER HIMSELF, who had been a courtier, who was a man of wide learning, and who in the third division of his life (which we are now considering) was a busy civil servant and a dignified general factotum for the Crown, "everyday affairs" cover an exceedingly broad range, so broad that we can include here only matters which are conventionally considered to be routine. Chivalry—probably "everyday" in one sense to Chaucer—has already been discussed, as has been religion, philosophy and science, none of them out of the ordinary for Chaucer, although in the realm of the special for many of his contemporaries.

In fourteenth-century London, the activities of merchants were certainly "everyday affairs," and in the *General Prologue,* Chaucer draws a portrait of a merchant, a portrait which must have been at once recognized as taken from life—if not from some actual London figure, then made as a composite from many such figures. London merchants of the fourteenth century were men engaged in Big Business, in "banking" and, usually, in politics. They nearly always held, at one time or another, posts in one of the great victualling or non-victualling gilds, they controlled all expenditures in the state, and their social position was decidedly "gentry."

Two powerful general organizations of merchants existed in Chaucer's day, in distinction to the more specialized gilds, such as the Mercers, Goldsmiths, Fishmongers and so on. One of the two general groups was called the Merchant Adventurers and the other, the Merchants of the Staple: members of the former often lived on the Continent and were engaged in seeing that English cloth had a market in the foreign city where they resided; members of the latter lived at home as a rule and took care of the exportation of the "staple," or wool, which was the principal article of export. Middleburgh, one of the two towns which Chaucer mentions in connection with the Merchant, was one of the foreign headquarters of the Merchant Adventurers; Orwell, the English port across the Channel from Middleburgh, was a town often used by the Merchants of the Staple. It is, therefore, possible that Chaucer's Merchant belongs to both organizations, as many important merchants belonged to both: he is a lordly, dignified individual, who has evidently been accustomed to power, although he has not been altogether successful in his financial career—no one knows that he is in debt.

The Merchant is forever boasting about "th'encrees of his wynnyng," and about his "bargaynes," but he is not as talkative about his "chevyssaunce" [I (A) 270-284]. The term "chevyssaunce" was recognized throughout the English business world of the late Middle Ages; it was a euphemistic word for what amounted to medieval "usury." The Church forbade the taking of any interest at all on money which was loaned. The lender, in the Church's view, was doing a "good deed" for the borrower and for that good deed, the lender would be rewarded in heaven. The lender should not also, the Church said, be rewarded materialistically. From the point of view of economics, however, the Church's interdiction was bound to fail: merchants were essentially capitalists and, in any capitalistic system, surplus gains will always be used for profit. Thus, if no financial return could come from loans, loans would not be made. But, as a completion of the vicious circle, the lending of money is an integral part of a capitalistic economy. To meet that problem, a method was devised whereby a borrower ostensibly received a certain sum which he was legally obliged (both by civil and ecclesiastical law) to pay back to the lender on a specified date. The actual cash handed over to the borrower, however, would be less than the sum he had signed for in the ledgers. No conscientious medieval merchant seems to have been really happy about the arrangement, for he would know that it sidestepped a Church ruling; on the other hand, the letter of the ecclesiastical ban could be observed in such fashion, and the practice was common, even if somewhat surreptitious. In the *Shipman's Tale,* the monk, who has little "conscience," and the merchant discuss a "chevyssaunce" with some show of reluctance [VII (B² 1519 ff.) 329 ff.].

In connection with the life of a merchant, we should perhaps note here that the merchant in the *Shipman's Tale* has his counting house in his own dwelling; he passes long hours there with the door closed, investigating the state of his business:

> His bookes and his bagges many oon
> He leith biforn hym on his countyng-bord.
> [*VII (B² 1272-1273) 82-83*]

Chaucer himself, not an employer as a merchant, but as an employee of the government, was able to finish his calculations in the Custom House and was then free for the remainder of the day. The didactic eagle, speaking to the poet in the

House of Fame, gives us a delightful contemporaneous picture of Geoffrey Chaucer in the Aldgate days:

'. . . thou wolt make
A-nyght ful ofte thyn hed to ake
In thy studye, so thou writest— . . .
For when thy labour doon al ys,
And hast mad alle thy rekenynges,
In stede of reste and newe thynges,
Thou goost hom to thy hous anoon;
And, also domb as any stoon,
Thou sittest at another book
Tyl fully daswed ys thy look,
And lyvest thus as an heremyte,
Although thyn abstynence ys lyte.'

[*ll. 631-660*]

Chaucer's pilgrim Merchant deals in foreign exchange ("wel koude he in eschaunge sheeldes selle"), an obviously illegal practice, for the English government held a monopoly on the right to buy and sell foreign currency. The value of the French "sheeld" was 3s.4d. Other coins mentioned by Chaucer elsewhere include the French "noble," worth 6s.8d., equivalent to the English "florin," and the French "frank," worth 10s. An English "mark" was worth 13s.4d.*

The way one dresses is certainly an "everyday" matter but, since Chaucer is primarily interested in human nature, he elects to mention only those details about clothing which support character. As has been already pointed out [see above, p. 22], the Knight's gipon is of coarse material "bismotered"

---

* To arrive at any accurate equivalency between medieval and modern money is impossible. The best approximation which can be achieved—and that is misleading—is to equate through wages, or "willingness to work." A comparison of farm-labor wages in the late 1300's and in the 1960's gives the number 45 by which the medieval sum should be multiplied to obtain a purely "psychological" idea of the present "worth" of the medieval amount. For example, if a man received 3s.4d. for doing a piece of work in the late fourteenth century, we think of him as belonging to a group each of whose members would receive £7.10.0, or about $20, for the same work today.

("soiled") by his habergeon, indicating his modesty and piety.

Of course, the fourteenth-century audience did not need to be told what a gipon and a habergeon looked like, but today's reader does need that information if he is to visualize the Knight's appearance as that worthy man arrives at the Tabard Inn. A gipon was a tight-fitting, sleeveless tunic, laced under the arms and worn over the habergeon; on the gipon was embroidered the heraldic device, or the family "arms" of the knight, which served as identification in battle when the knight's visor would be closed and the face consequently hidden. The gipon, usually with a scalloped edge, was about an inch shorter than the habergeon. The latter garment, often called a "hauberk," or "coat of mail," was, in Chaucer's time, of chain mail; it was a tunic, sometimes sleeveless, reaching about halfway to the knee. The chest, upper back, arms, and legs of a knight were protected by plate armor; helmets and "shoes" were of steel, gauntlets either of steel or leather. A camail—made of chain mail—resembled a woman's wimple in shape; it was attached to the underside of the helmet and protected the neck. Very probably Chaucer's Knight does not wear full battle dress on the peaceful journey to Canterbury; in fact, the artist of the Ellesmere MS. depicts the Knight as a civilian, wearing the long "cote-hardie," a loose-fitting gown reaching almost to the ankles.

Chaucer gives us a fuller picture of the Squire's clothing than he does of the clothing of the Knight, undoubtedly because the details stress the younger man's gaiety, youthful zest, and innocent insouciance. Here is one of the happy young squires whom the poet must have seen almost daily in London; Westminster, the seat of the Court, was the municipality adjacent to the medieval City of London, and, usually, there was constant traffic between the two. We may also suppose that Chaucer is influenced in the Squire's portrait by the memory of the environment of Prince Lionel's household, when young Geoffrey may have been as carefree as the Squire of the *General Prologue*. The Squire wears a short gown, which has long and wide sleeves; the gown is embroidered with red-and-white flowers, so that it looks like a spring meadow. Short, embroidered gowns and long, wide sleeves were the marks of the ultrafashionable in the late fourteenth century, and pulpit complaints from the disciplinarians were frequent: short coats were denounced as "indecent"; embroidery was called unnecessarily expensive (the money so spent should be given to the poor). Long and wide sleeves were said to trail often in the mud, thus bringing about the wasteful purchase of new clothing, oɩ the costly cleaning of the old—again, indirectly diverting money from the poor. Even Chaucer's Parson, that mild-mannered and usually "understanding" soul, speaks of the "wickedness" of short coats and of "embrowdynge" [X (I) 416-429]. But when has youth paid heed to the admonishments of strict reformers? One cannot believe that Chaucer is censuring the Squire; rather, the poet is lightly satirical in reminding his audience of their own—and possibly the poet's own—disregard of some current sermons.

The Merchant, much older than the Squire, is also fashionably dressed, but his garments are more conservative than those of the younger man and hence are not described in as much detail. The Merchant's gown is of "mottelee," a parti-colored, figured cloth much in vogue among wealthy civilians, and a "Flaundryssh bever hat," a hat depicted by the artist of the Ellesmere MS. as having a turned-up brim and a tall crown. Such a hat was not a part of any Gild livery in the fourteenth century; most probably the poet's inclusion of the detail in the portrait was intended as an "identification" of the Merchant for the fourteenth-century audience, either seriously or in jest. Chaucer's unnamed Merchant wears boots that are clasped well and neatly and his beard is forked—two matters which seem at first glance to be unrelated, but which both establish him as being a very much up-to-date man of fashion: the Merchant must maintain an air of prosperity in order to conceal the fact that he is debt.

The Sergeant of the Law, in the same social class as the Merchant, is not clad quite as fashionably, for his "medlee cote" is a short one; Chaucer tells us that the Sergeant wears a girdle of silk decorated with strips of metal, and if the Sergeant were wearing a ceremonious, long gown, he would not use a girdle. If the Sergeant actually represents Pynchbek, and most scholars are agreed that he does, there is probably mild satire in Chaucer's designation of the Sergeant's garb as "homely"—it is difficult to think of Pynchbek being genuinely unpretentious in any respect.

The Franklin, who is the traveling companion of the Sergeant of the Law, is also of the gentry class, as we have seen, and the two lines the poet gives us concerning the Franklin's dress—"An anlaas and a gipser al of silk/Heeng at his girdel . . ."—confirm that fact. Only wealthy and distinguished men wore both an "anlaas" and a "gipser" at the same time. An "anlaas" was a dagger used in hunting, a large, broad-bladed instrument sharpened at both edges; a "gipser" was a pouch-like purse and the Franklin's is particularly handsome, for it is made all of silk.

The Five Gildsmen are modishly dressed as befits their station in life. Obviously their "fraternitee" must be a Parish Gild for no two are of the same craft, yet they are "clothed alle in o lyveree"—and what a resplendent livery it must be! Their clothing is new and freshly trimmed, their knives (knives were worn by everyone) are encased in silver sheaths (not the brass sheaths of the ordinary tradesman), and their girdles and pouches are the latest in handsome workmanship. Chaucer implies in the description of the Gildsmen [I (A) 361-378] that here are the merchant princes of tomorrow and their dress supports the brief picture we have of their neatness, efficiency and assuredness of purpose.

Little is said of the apparel of the Doctor of Physic, but again that little does add to our impression that the Physician is a stately man of fashion, but one who is overfond of money. He has frugally kept what he has gained in treating victims of the plague, and he has now allowed himself a beautiful gown "in sangwyn and in pers" (that is, parti-colored, in blood-red and bluish-gray), lined with rare, thin silk.

Chaucer mentions the dress of the Prioress, the Monk and the Friar in satiric vein. The Prioress shows rather too much concern over her well-pleated wimple and her modish cloak; the coral rosary gauded in green, on which hangs the bright gold brooch (etched with a "crowned A" and the words *amor vincit omnia*), might more properly belong to a lady of the court. The Monk, also, wears inappropriate clothing for a religious. The poet says:

> I seigh his sleves purfiled at the hond
> With grys, and that the fyneste of a lond;
> And, for to festne his hood under his chyn,
> He hadde of gold ywroght a ful curious pyn;
> A love-knotte in the gretter ende ther was.
> [*I (A) 193-197*]

The Friar is not like a "cloysterer" or a "povre scoler," but is dressed in a "semicope" of double worsted—the garment is "rounded as a belle out of the presse." Thus, all three of these religious are appareled unsuitably, but "typically"—evidently as Chaucer saw them in the streets of London or journeying about the English countryside.

As to the garb of the lay pilgrims of lower rank in Chaucer's company, we have again the poet's accurate observation of a world he knew. The Wife of Bath is dressed with neat efficiency. On Sundays, at home "biside Bathe," she may wear a ten-pound "coverchief" (that is, a head covering somewhat resembling a turban, worn only by the provincial in late fourteenth-century England), but on the pilgrimage the Wife wears a hat "as brood as is a bokeler or a targe," and her hair is trimly confined by a wimple worn underneath the hat. (A buckler—or a "targe"—was a small, round shield used for parrying blows, perhaps twelve to fourteen inches in diameter.) The Wife wears a protective skirt about her ample hips to guard against splashes of Kentish mud, her hose are tightly and neatly drawn, her shoes are of expensive new leather and her spurs are sharp. Indeed, we must all agree, no matter how much some of us may disapprove of her in other ways, that Alisoun's dress gives evidence of an orderly mind and of effective accomplishment.

Another pilgrim whom Chaucer depicts as strikingly efficient is the Knight's Yeoman. The Yeoman, who is a gamekeeper by profession although he is now acting as an attendant upon the Knight, wears a "cote and hood of grene," as well as a green "bawdryk" to which his horn is attached. (A bawdryk" was a band worn diagonally across the body from one shoulder down under the other arm.) The Yeoman's choice of green for a costume was traditional for a "forster," or gamekeeper, and Chaucer, who held the post of deputy forester in the royal forest of North Petherton for over seven years, must have been well acquainted with the orderly appearance of the "working" gamekeepers in the royal preserve. The Yeoman of the *General Prologue* [I (A) 101-117] keeps a sheaf of "pecok arwes, bright and kene" tidily stowed under his belt, he wears a decorated bracer on his arm (a "bracer" was a large leather guard, resembling a gauntlet, worn on the bow arm), he carries a "myghty bowe," and he wears a sword and buckler on one side and a "gay daggere" on the other. Further, the Yeoman wears "a Cristopher on his brest, of silver sheene," not only, we are convinced, because St. Christopher is the patron saint of foresters, but also because all travelers are under the special protection of that saint, and the Yeoman would protect his master every possible way on the journey to Canterbury.

The Shipman, another man among the pilgrims who thoroughly knows his job (although because of his piratical and coarse habits, he cannot be admired as the Yeoman can), wears clothing well adapted to his life at sea. He is described as wearing a knee-length "gowne" of "faldying" ("faldyng" was a heavy woolen material) which allows him plenty of action in rough weather; his dagger is suspended on a cord "aboute his nekke, under his arm adoun," which leaves his hands free most of the time.

The Plowman, a "good" peasant, wears a tabard, Chaucer tells us, and we can be very sure that the garment is stout and well made. A tabard was a loose, super-tunic without sleeves, often put on over the head. It was considered outdated in the fourteenth century, but the Plowman is not interested in fashion. We may say that the tabard was the ancestor of the laborer's smock of the nineteenth century (although different in shape), worn in England by farm workers well into the early twentieth century.

The Miller and the Reeve are from the country as much as is the Plowman, but their devious ways make them seem more sophisticated and hence more urban. The poet has little to say about the dress of the Miller—the Miller wears the white coat of his calling, but his blue hood is probably Chaucer's fanciful addition. The Miller's red beard is undoubtedly long and square cut, although the poet does not think it necessary to tell us that fact. The Reeve wears a "long surcote of pers" and a "rusty blade," both attesting his inferior social position. He has tucked up the long coat (as friars do, explains the poet) to give him more freedom of movement. The Reeve is elderly, and obviously indifferent as to his appearance.

We do not know what the Summoner is wearing, but he has set a huge garland on his head, and he is using a flat loaf of bread (a "cake") as a shield. The suggestion that he appears as an intensified, debauched Bacchus is strong. The garland, Chaucer states, is large enough for an alestake. (The alestakes of the Middle Ages advertised drinking places; they were poles projecting horizontally over the entrance to such a place. At the end of the pole, a garland of flowers or, more usually, a "bush" of ivy was fastened. Signs of that sort for taverns lasted through Shakespeare's time. Cf. the Epilogue to *As You Like It,* where Rosalind says: "If it be true that good wine needs no bush, 'tis true that a good play needs no epilogue; yet to good wine they do use good bushes. . . .")

Chaucer has not much to say, either, about the dress of the Summoner's companion, the Pardoner. The Pardoner's vices and his repellent physical characteristics receive the stress in the portrait and, consequently, his clothing is of little moment. He does not wear his hood, foolishly imagining that it is the latest fashion to use as head covering only his cap, to which he has sewed a "vernycle," a miniature copy of the handkerchief St. Veronica was thought to have given to Christ on the way to Calvary. But although little is said about the garb of the Summoner and the Pardoner, whatever Chaucer does say is chosen with care and supports our picture of the characters.

We cannot take leave of the subject of costume without examining the detailed description Chaucer gives of that "wynsynge" primrose, the amoral wife of John, the carpenter in the *Miller's Tale:*

> A ceynt she werede, barred al of silk,
> A barmclooth eek as whit as morne milk
> Upon hir lendes, ful of many a goore.
> Whit was hir smok, and broyden al bifoore
> And eek bihynde, on hir coler aboute,
> Of col-blak silk, withinne and eek withoute,

> The tapes of hir white voluper
> Were of the same suyte of hir coler;
> Hir filet brood of silk, and set ful hye. . . .
> And by hir girdel heeng a purs of lether,
> Tasseled with silk, and perled with latoun. . . .
> A brooch she baar upon hir lowe coler,
> As brood as is the boos of a bokeler.
> Hir shoes were laced on hir legges hye.
>
> [*I* (*A*) *3235-3243, 3251-3252, 3265-3267*]

We should contrast the fullness of the picture of the wife's dress with the lack of any sort of description of the dress of Emily in the *Knight's Tale,* and of Constance in the *Man of Law's Tale,* and of Dorigen in the *Franklin's Tale.* Emily, Constance and Dorigen, however, serve a double purpose: each is necessary to the respective narrative in which she has her being; but Emily also symbolizes the maidenly ideal as a courtly lover would see her, Constance is also very much the allegorical figure of Fortitude, and Dorigen also represents the "new" wife of the fourteenth century, virtuously very much in love with her husband. Chaucer's courtly audience—the "serious" narrative was primarily for the courtly audience—were not interested in the dress of the actors in the story; the audience knew how ladies and gentlemen dressed and conformity in such matters was expected.

Dress, food and drink are mentioned by Chaucer only as they serve to give color and actuality to setting and character. Food and drink, however, may seem to have slightly greater interest for Chaucer than dress, and we are able to recall with amusement the fact that Chaucer refers more than once to his own stoutness. He was evidently a man who appreciated a good dinner and the good wine which accompanied dinner. Chaucer writes with enthusiasm about the Franklin in the *General Prologue,* particularly in connection with the Franklin's delight in good food:

Wel loved he by the morwe a sop in wyn;
To lyven in delit was evere his wone,
For he was Epicurus owene sone,
That heeld opinioun that pleyn delit
Was verray felicitee parfit. . . .
Seint Julian he was in his contree.
His breed, his ale, was alweys after oon;
A bettre envyned man was nowher noon.
Without bake mete was nevere his hous
Of fissh and flessh, and that so plentevous,
It snewed in his hous of mete and drynke,
Of alle deyntees that men koude thynke.
After the sondry sesons of the yeer,
So chaunged he his mete and his soper.
Ful many a fat partrich hadde he in muwe,
And many a breem and many a luce in stuwe.
Wo was his cook but if his sauce were
Poynaunt and sharp, and redy al his geere.
His table dormant in his halle alway
Stood redy covered al the longe day.
      [*I* (*A*) *336-339, 341-354*]

(A "sop in wyn" was made with a sauce of wine, saffron, almonds, ginger, cinnamon, sugar, cloves and mace which was
poured over bread.) The Franklin's bread and ale are always
of the same good quality, his wine cellar is the best in the
country, and he is never without meat and fish or any choice
viands of which one can think. Following the seasons of the
year, the Franklin chooses his food. He keeps many fat par-
tridges in coops and many fish in his private ponds. The
Franklin's "table-dormant" is always heaped high with all
that one can wish for. (The "table-dormant" was what we
think of as a table today, with the four legs fixed in place by
the top. The usual "table" in the Middle Ages consisted of tres-
tles with boards laid across, which could be removed after

each meal, unlike the "table-dormant," which was a permanent piece of furniture.)

Appetites in the Middle Ages were prodigious from all accounts, but since dinner (usually served in Chaucer's day at the "fashionable" hour of eleven or even twelve o'clock in the morning) was the only substantial meal of the day, we cannot be surprised that some of the so-called feasts pictured in the medieval cookbooks were so tremendous. One of the books recommends a feast for a franklin to be as follows: brawn, beef, chicken, goose, pasties (stuffed with prunes, eggs, cream, marrow, dates and spices), stews made of all kinds of meats and fish, fried bread, fruit in season, bread and cheese, cakes and wafers. For the drinks, there would always be mead and a mixture of ale and honey and spices and—if one were really wealthy and urban in taste—wine from France. Such a meal, of course, would not be served as everyday fare, but any dinner would be larger than what we now are accustomed to.

The Cook is not the kind of person we should expect Chaucer to be enthusiastic about but, as the Cook is an artist in culinary pursuits, Chaucer gives him some praise in the *General Prologue*. The Cook knows how to:

> . . . boille the chiknes with the marybones,
> And poudre-marchant tart and galyngale.
> Wel koude he knowe a draughte of Londoun ale.
> He koude rooste, and sethe, and broille, and frye,
> Maken mortreux, and wel bake a pye. . . .
> [And] blankmanger, that made he with the beste.
> *[I (A) 380-384, 387]*

"Poudre-marchant" was a spice compounded by grinding together ginger, cinnamon and galingale, the powdered root of an East Indian plant. The "mortreux" were pies, either of fish or meat, in which the principal ingredient was mixed with almonds, milk, sugar and salt, the whole covered with grated bread and baked. The "blankmanger" prepared so successfully by the Cook, consisted of chicken, yolks of eggs, ale, grated bread and spices. The Cook, whose name we later learn to be Roger of Ware, is not always to be trusted. Harry Bailly accuses him of passing off bad meat in the cook-shop. (A "cook" in the Middle Ages often meant the proprietor of an eating house and this is apparently what Roger is, although on the pilgrimage he accompanies the Gildsmen merely as someone who prepares food.) Harry Bailly says that Roger's pasties are stale, for the gravy has been removed in order to keep them from day to day (they have "laten blood"); and flies have mingled with the parsley with which the geese have been stuffed [I (A) 4345-4352].

Chaucer allows the Pardoner to speak disparagingly of cooks in the *Pardoner's Tale*. The Pardoner says that cooks "stampe and streyne and grynde, and turnen substaunce into accident" [VI (C) 538-539]. Cooks, that is, change the essential core of something into outward forms inherently false. (It seems very doubtful to this writer that Chaucer can here be seriously thinking of Wyclif's denial of transubstantiation, as some scholars have maintained, although there may be a slight allusion to it. After all, the *Canterbury Tales* is a work which is distinctly topical.)

In regard to delicacies praised in the Middle Ages, the Monk loves best a fat swan and the friar of the *Summoner's Tale* asks in feigned modesty for but the liver of the capon and some "softe breed" to be followed by a "roosted pigges heed"—although he wishes, he says, that no animal be killed especially for him [III (C) 1839 ff.]. And later—for this friar's mind runs on food—he deplores the fact that when plenty of men were enjoying prized tidbits, mussels and oysters were the only food the poor brothers had. (Oysters, which seem to many of us today to be a delicacy, were decried as common fare: consider the popular medieval saying "not worth an oyster.")

The pilgrim Summoner, telling his tale about the greediness of friars, is himself far from temperate in his diet, as has been said. He is unlike both the Doctor of Physic, who is "mesurable" and avoids "superfluitee" in eating (perhaps Chaucer was thinking here of the advice meted out by his own actual physician), and the poor widow of the *Nun's Priest's Tale* whose board is served only with milk, brown bread, bacon and sometimes an egg.

Bread has always been eaten by every class in every age. In Chaucer's day there were four different grades of bread: "payndemayn," made from fine white wheat flour and mentioned by Chaucer in the *Tale of Sir Thopas;* "wastel breed," which was almost as expensive as the first grade, with which the Prioress extravagantly and regularly feeds her little dogs (animals if they were given bread were expected to eat a special "bread" made of lentils); a somewhat darker bread; and lastly, the "black" or brown bread enjoyed by Chauntecleer's owner.

Wine, ale and mixtures made of honey constituted the drink of the Middle Ages. The best wines came from France, and it was necessary to guard the shipments with considerable care. Chaucer's Master of the "Maudelayne" frequently steals drafts of French wine, using a well-known method. Wine merchants traveled on ships bearing their product to England in order to safeguard the casks, but if the journey were long, the merchants had to sleep, or if rough weather were encountered, seasickness was inevitable. The medieval trading ship had a rounded bow and a square stern, and its width was much greater in proportion to its length than is the width of a modern vessel. Consequently there was no cutting through high seas, and the motion in all directions made seasickness a genuine and serious problem. Thus merchants were often obliged to leave their casks unguarded; the crew could then tap the casks, as does the Shipman, leaving the cask "short" when it was later gauged in England. The shortage would then be ascribed to the merchant.

Adulteration probably took place after the wine arrived in England. The wholesale vintners might sometimes themselves be dishonest; the retail sellers of wine, it is to be feared, often were. The Pardoner (a dishonest rogue, dishonestly complaining about dishonesty in others) says that the wine of Spain,

> . . . crepeth subtilly
> In othere wynes, growynge faste by,
> Of which ther ryseth swich fumositee
> That whan a man hath dronken draughtes thre,
> And weneth that he be at hoom in Chepe,
> He is in Spaigne, right at the toune of Lepe,—
> Nat at the Rochele, ne at Burdeux toun. . . .
> [VI (C) 565-571]

The Pardoner, who drinks extensively himself, has much to say about the evils of drink. He advises against imbibing both the "white" and the "red," especially the "white wine of Lepe." (Lepe, a town in Spain, was noted for strong Spanish wine—Rochelle and Bordeaux were noted for delicate French wine.))

Chaucer seems generally to have a greater interest in urban and in court life than in rural life; nevertheless, in the *Canterbury Tales* there is a surprising emphasis on country surroundings in the *General Prologue*. For example, if we except the Knight, the Squire and the Yeoman, who belong to the chivalric world, more than half of the remaining pilgrims carry on their activities outside of towns and cities. After the Aldgate days, Chaucer spent a good part of his time in journeying about the countryside; also it is usually assumed that Chaucer lived in Kent from 1386 (or even possibly 1385) until 1389. In the last-named year Chaucer was appointed Clerk of the King's Works, which meant that for nearly two years he had charge of royal edifices and parks both in Westminster and farther afield. (It is interesting to note that in 1390 Chaucer had a special commission to oversee the repairs in St. George's Chapel at Windsor.)

Traveling from place to place as much as he must have done, without doubt enabled Chaucer to increase his knowledge of the lives of peasants and country artisans and the people who moved among them. Environment again playing a part in the poet's mind produced greater familiarity with friars ("limitours"), millers, reeves, summoners, pardoners, country parish-priests, the tillers of the soil, the provincial business-women, even wealthy franklins. As a boy and a young man, Chaucer, of course, traveled with Prince Lionel, but those journeys were royal progresses, and not conducive to the same degree of intimacy with ordinary folk as Chaucer's later business journeys.

What evidence does Chaucer give of his knowledge of manor and village life? The *fabliaux* nearly all have village settings and we have relevant descriptions in the *General Prologue*. We have already seen how the portraits of the good Parson, of the Franklin, of the Friar, of the Summoner and of the Pardoner reflect rural living, but a few of the pilgrims in the *General Prologue* have not yet been so examined. For example, the truest peasant of all, the most representative of the rustic, has scarcely been mentioned: the Parson's brother, the Plowman.

The Plowman [I (A) 529-541] is typical in the kind of labor in which he is engaged. He carries loads of dung, he knows how to thresh, to dig and to make ditches. (If we examine the contemporary books on husbandry, we find emphasis on those same duties; also in *Piers Plowman*, Langland has his plowman say: "I dyke and I delve . . . and sometyme I thresche" [B. Passus V. 552 f.].) Chaucer also tells us that the pilgrim Plowman lives in "pees" and "parfit charitee," that he loves God always and his neighbors as himself and

that he will always help—without payment—any poor creature in difficulties. Is the character of the Plowman as "typical" as his work? It is impossible to give a definite answer to
that question, for there are arguments on both sides. The social class to which Chaucer belonged, the upper-middle class,
friendly to the Crown, were unsympathetic to the peasants
and set the latter down as dishonest "sons of Cain," deserving
ill treatment. Chaucer, however, never writes in dispraise of
the peasant and he makes this particular peasant—the Plowman—brother to the beloved Parson. Since the Plowman
does not tell a tale, we have no guide to interpretation there.
Perhaps the Plowman of the *General Prologue* represents
Chaucer's wish as to what peasants should be in actuality, or
perhaps, like the poet's Clerk, we have an actual portrait of
one whom the poet would believe to be exceptional.

There are no similar problems in dealing with Robin the
Miller and Oswald the Reeve, however. Both Robin and
Oswald—if we can have any confidence in the literature of
the time—conform to type; Chaucer individualizes each of
them only in that pilgrim's physical make-up. (The Miller is
a "stout carl," big of brawn and of bones; the Reeve is a
"sclendre colerik man," with long, thin, calfless legs.)

A miller in the Middle Ages possessed an important monopoly, for all of the peasants under the rule of the lord of a
manor were obliged to take their grain to the miller of the
estate on which they lived. The miller's "toll" for grinding
was theoretically fixed by law, but since he controlled the use
of the only mill, he could—as does Robin—easily "tollen
thries" and steal some of the grain as well. In the *Reeve's Tale,*
Chaucer gives us a picture of a miller in action and, since the
Reeve is using the narrative to spite the Miller, his professional and personal enemy, we have a strong suspicion that
Robin and Simond, the miller of the Tale, are one. Robin
plays the bagpipes as does Simond; Robin always wins the

prize ram in wrestling and Simond also is a wrestler; Robin wears a sword and buckler and Simond wears a two-edged cutlass, a small dagger, and a Sheffield knife. (Sheffield was as well known in the fourteenth century for its cutlery as it is today.) No one dares attack Simond even though everyone knows he is a habitual sly thief of "corn and mele"; and when the manciple of the Soler Halle lies ill, Simond brazenly steals "an one hundred tyme moore than biforn"—he has stolen "curteisly" in the past, but now he is a "theef" outrageously, and boasts of it. Robin is also a cheat, a loud, scurrilous talker and a ribald jester. (Chaucer adds in humorous irony that Robin is "honest as millers go"!)

A medieval reeve was a natural rival to a miller on an estate, for both could gain personally from cheating the peasants. The office of reeve was that of an overseer or manager; the reeve's duty was to inspect everything on the estate regularly, to buy needed supplies and to impose fines on the workers who merited them. Chaucer writes of his particular Reeve as follows:

> Wel wiste he by the droghte and by the reyn
> The yeldynge of his seed and of his greyn.
> His lordes sheep, his neet, his dayerye,
> His swyn, his hors, his stoor, and his pultrye
> Was hoolly in this Reves governynge,
> And by his covenant yaf the rekenynge,
> Syn that his lord was twenty yeer of age.
> Ther koude no man brynge hym in arrerage.
>
> [*I (A) 595-602*]

If the portrait ended with the last line quoted immediately above, we could call Oswald a model reeve. He knows all that he should about the storage of grain, about when to sow and when to reap, about the condition of his lord's livestock and poultry, and he makes no visible errors in his accounts. But why are the peasants under Oswald's jurisdiction "adrayd of hym as of the deeth"? We sense at once that he is dishonest and that he is always willing to blame others for sins and errors far less grave than his own. Oswald is very richly "astored pryvely." He can purchase better than his master— skillfully he "sells" his master the master's own goods and is rewarded not only with unsuspecting congratulations, but also with a gift of a "cote and hood." And how can Oswald honestly afford his own handsome Norfolk dwelling, shaded with green trees? What the Miller obtains by loudness and barefaced stealing, the Reeve obtains by severity and meanness and the cunning manipulation of accounts.

The Wife of "biside Bath" is another pilgrim who is decidedly not urban, although she is far more traveled than her rural neighbors would be. She is not a peasant but may be said to belong to the artisan class, and she is highly skilled in her occupation:

> Of clooth-makyng she had swich an haunt
> She passed hem of Ypres and of Gaunt.
> *[I (A) 447-448]*

(Women in the rural neighborhood of Bath were noted for their skill in weaving, but Chaucer is mildly satirical in saying that Dame Alisoun surpasses the superior Flemish weavers.) The Wife's natural pride in her own skill causes her to demand first place in making the offering on Sundays, for importance in the community determined the order in which parishioners went to the altar to make their alms and oblations. (The desire to be first in line was gravely criticized by serious parish priests: the Parson in preaching against the sin of pride deplores the kind of pride which permits a person to "goon to offryng biforn his neighebor" [X (I) 407]. Dame Alisoun would be immune to that sort of criticism, we fear.)

The Wife herself describes her five matrimonial adventures in the Prologue to her Tale but, of course, she does not "explain" the poet's phrase "at chirche dore." There are two theories as to why marriages in medieval England were performed outside the church proper: either that the marriage ceremony was considered to be basically secular (the bride and the groom were actors in the rite, and the priest, the interlocutor and teacher, the sacramental character of the rite lying in the nuptial mass); or that the need for as many witnesses as possible was acute and therefore, the more public the marriage ceremony, the better.

Dame Alisoun's own account of her marriages and her long struggle for "governaunce" in them make us ask ourselves if many women in the Middle Ages felt as superior to the opposite sex as does Alisoun and, if so, were those women always successful in gaining the mastery. Many fourteenth-century preachers inveigh against women who will not be submissive to their husbands but, if we glance at the legal restrictions placed upon medieval women, we are amazed that any one of them dared raise her voice. Husbands were legally permitted to chastise their wives, for the wife was the husband's "property" —quite literally the husband was lord and master. Yet we can not entirely believe that the Griseldas or possibly the Dorigens of the Middle Ages were the rule without exception. There have always been women who have asserted themselves even under the most adverse conditions and, therefore, the period of the Middle Ages must have had its share. The "real" Margery Kempe who, though considerably younger than Chaucer, was living in his time, knew how to get exactly what she wanted and although her unhealthy, introspective, self-centered disposition sets her poles apart from the outgoing, matter-of-fact Wife of Bath (whom it is difficult to think of as "fictional"), both women, the one picturing herself, the other pictured by Chaucer, show that "governaunce" was their realized common ambition. Consider Griselda, however; when Walter proposes marriage she replies:

'Lord, undigne and unworthy
Am I to thilke honour that ye me beede,
But as ye wole youreself, right so wol I.
And heere I swere that nevere willyngly,
In werk ne thoght, I nyl yow disobeye,
For to be deed, though me were looth to deye.'

[*IV* (*E*) *359-364*]

When her daughter is to be taken from her, presumably to be slain, Griselda makes no protest and she says:

'Lord, al lyth in youre plesaunce.
My child and I, with hertely obeisaunce,
Been youres al, and ye mowe save or spille
Youre owene thyng; werketh after youre wille.

'Ther may no thyng, God so my soule save,
Liken to yow that may displese me;
Ne I desire no thyng for to have,
Ne drede for to leese, save oonly yee.
This wyl is in myn herte, and ay shal be;
No length of tyme or deeth may this deface,
Ne chaunge my corage to another place.'

[*IV* (*E*) *501-511*]

Griselda repeats the same sentiments when she is again asked to make the other sacrifices, and even if we think what she says is symbolical of submission under general adversity (as the Clerk belatedly asks the company of pilgrims to do), we find her meekness excessive for today's taste.

But is the Tale, as it seems to this writer to be, a psychological *tour de force* on Chaucer's part to show up the reactions of his gentle Clerk? In a sense that Alisoun, Wife of Bath, would use the word, the Clerk knows nothing of "life." Undoubtedly, he has been horrified by the Wife's ideas expressed in unrestrained language, ideas which run counter to the teachings of the Church fathers; the *Wife of Bath's Tale* must have been even worse than her *Prologue* in the Clerk's ears, for in her masterly fashion Alisoun presents in the Tale a good case for something that is to the Clerk really wrong. But the Clerk is shy and serious, he speaks no word that is unnecessary; he will not openly chide the Wife of Bath for her mistaken notions. We can feel justified in imagining the Clerk cudgeling his brains during the recital of the Friar's and Summoner's narratives, intent solely on trying to think of a story which will in all kindness show Alisoun the right path. Then triumphantly, perhaps at the last minute, he remembers Petrarch, "a worthy clerk," and the story of submissive Griselda. Does the Clerk falter at the end, aware of failure in his effort? This is the late fourteenth century where some may find it difficult to accept Griselda as a model; possibly the doubting gleam in the eye of a pilgrim prompts the Clerk to say hastily:

> This storie is seyd, nat for that wyves sholde
> Folwen Grisilde as in humylitee,
> For it were inportable, though they wolde;
> But for that every wight, in his degree
> Sholde be constant in adversitee
> As was Grisilde; therfore Petrak writeth
> This storie, which with heigh stile he enditeth.
>   [*IV (E) 1142-1148*]

Actuality has overcome him and he is obliged to remember Petrarch and to turn the Tale, which he has modestly hoped would show Alisoun the error of her theory, into an allegory as best he can. The *Lenvoy de Chaucer* may or may not have been intended to be spoken by the Clerk; to the present writer the satire (surely foreign to the Clerk) and change of meter would indicate that those six stanzas are meant to be the poet's interpolation.

The *Merchant's Tale* is another attempt to refute the general idea put forward by the forceful Alisoun. The Merchant prefaces his narrative by saying that his own wife is a shrew in every respect and that "we wedded men lyven in sorwe and care!" As a consequence, his Tale of January and May is meant to demonstrate how unfit women in general are to have the "gouvernaunce," but the Tale succeeds only in demonstrating that May in particular is unfit. (The Merchant probably does not think of himself as a kind of January, for the Merchant is not old and decrepit; May, however, may be his portrait of his own wife. Again Chaucer develops the character of the teller of a tale through the tale itself.)

As has been pointed out, the *Franklin's Tale* is highly chivalric and does, of course, stress the happy mean of partnership in marriage. Is the Wife of Bath convinced by it? Possibly, but not without reservations. Alisoun is an eminently sensible woman, and what works for the courtly ideal world is of doubtful value in her matter-of-fact surroundings. We can never place Alisoun in a tapestry and say that she has her being there as well as on this earthy earth. But Alisoun is aware of the chivalric world although not a part of it, and she must be content to accept the solution for the aristocrats (but not for herself), worked out by the courtly Arveragus and his wife Dorigen.

How did Chaucer's world amuse itself? We have already spoken about the wrestling matches the peasants enjoyed, and which provided the victor with a choice ram. Sir Thopas excels in wrestling, Chaucer tells us as part of his parody, for the sport was in no sense knightly; Sir Thopas is also a good archer and again he is to be laughed at, for the use of the bow was again confined to an inferior class. The bow-and-arrow was the weapon of the common soldier in medieval warfare, and the six-foot, "long bow," copied from the Welsh and perfected by the English, was deadly indeed, for it had a range of approximately two hundred and ninety yards, enabling a soldier to shoot from a distance. That "myghty bowe" was not only used in battle, but was also used in the sport of archery and the stalwart peasant took pride in demonstrating his skill.

Hunting, in spite of the disapproval of some of the ecclesiastics, was a sport in which high and low, rich and poor, delighted. The upper classes used the falcon in hunting for wild fowl, and the bird itself was considered as aristocratic as the people who owned it. In the *Squire's Tale,* for example, the falcon with whom Canacee talks is in essence a lady of the court, and the "sin" that the tercelet (that is, the male falcon who has loved her) commits in deserting her for a kite is the sin of a knight who forsakes the lady he loves for a prostitute. (The "kite" in chivalric circles was a symbol for everything base.) The well-to-do peasant as a rule used a goshawk in hunting for wild fowl, and again Sir Thopas is said humorously to bear one of those powerful, strong-winged but lower-class hawks on his wrist. The hunting for buck and hare was also a favorite and universal pastime. Chaucer's Monk, accompanied by his swift greyhounds, finds all his pleasure in "huntyng for the hare"; Sir Thopas, too, knows how to hunt "at wilde deer" as he spurs furiously through the fair forest, carpeted so incongruously with herbs belonging in the kitchen garden.

The mystery and miracle plays always provided interest for every class whenever they were shown. Dame Alisoun, dressed in her handsome red gown, has enjoyed the "pleyes of myracles"; an accomplished Absalom in the *Miller's Tale,* in vain effort to fascinate the wife of the carpenter, acts Herod upon a high scaffolding; Robin the Miller cries out in "Pilate's voice," quite as if he were used to appearing in a mystery play. We might even say that the dramatic aspects of the Church service came under the same heading as the plays. The Wife of Bath includes "vigilies" and preaching in her list of the amusements she has enjoyed while her fourth husband was in London; and the wives of the Five Gildsmen, Chaucer says, enjoy their attendance at the festive occasions held at the Church the evening before a religious celebration (in other words, at the "vigilies").

Christmas festivities are spoken of once by Chaucer. In the *Franklin's Tale*, Aurelius returns to Brittany after making his deal with the magician in December, the season of bitter frosts and sleet and rain. Then

> Janus sit by the fyr, with double berd,
> And drynketh of his bugle horn the wyn;
> Biforn hym stant brawen of the tusked swyn,
> And 'Nowel' crieth every lusty man.
> [V (F) 1252-1255]

The "simple necessities" of birth and death and the "conditional necessity" of a marriage also furnished excuses for celebrations, but Chaucer does not write of medieval festivities following birth and death. (The funeral games following Arcite's death in the *Knight's Tale* belong to classical antiquity, not to the Middle Ages.) On the other hand, Chaucer does write of the pleasures to be found after medieval marriages. The Wife of Bath mentions the delight she takes in attending the festivities following weddings [III (D) 558]; and in the *Cook's Tale,* Perkyn Revelour "wolde synge and hoppe" at every bridal feast [I (A) 4375].

When in more aristocratic surroundings, the marriage feast could assume Gargantuan proportions. Chaucer writes of the celebrations following May's marriage to January as follows:

> And at the feeste sitteth he and she
> With othere worthy folk upon the deys.
> Al ful of joye and blisse is the paleys,
> And ful of instrumentz and of vitaille,
> The mooste deyntevous of al Ytaille.
> Biforn hem stoode instrumentz of swich soun
> That Orpheus, ne of Thebes Amphioun,
> Ne maden nevere swich a melodye.

> At every cours thanne cam loud mynstralcye,
> That nevere tromped Joab for to heere,
> Nor he Theodomas, yet half so cleere,
> At Thebes, whan the citee was in doute.
> Bacus the wyn hem shynketh al aboute,
> And Venus laugheth upon every wight,
> For Januarie was bicome hir knyght,
> And wolde bothe assayen his corage
> In libertee, and eek in mariage;
> And with hire fyrbrond in hire hand aboute
> Daunceth biforn the bryde and al the route.
> And certeinly, I dar right wel seyn this,
> Ymeneus, that god of weddyng is,
> Saugh nevere his lyf so myrie a wedded man.
> Hoold thou thy pees, thou poete Marcian,
> That writest us that like weddyng murie
> Of hire Philologie and hym Mercurie,
> And of the songes that the Muses songe!
> > [*IV (E) 1710-1735*]

The merriment, in fact, waxes so boisterous that intoxicated old January cannot sustain the excitement:

> And finally he dooth al his
>   labour,
> As he best myghte, savyng
>   his honour,
> To haste hem fro the mete in
>   subtil wyse.
> > [*IV (E) 1765-1767*]

After the dinner the guests dance and "drynken faste," they place spices "al aboute the hous," and every man is full of joy and bliss; not until dark night falls, do the lusty guests return to their homes.

The Clerk in his Tale mentions the "revel," held all day following Griselda's wedding; and after Walter's final "test" of poor Griselda, when she has at last been told the truth, the feasting and merriment prepared for the supposed new "wife" are very much enjoyed. The Clerk tells us:

Thus hath this pitous day a blisful ende,
For every man and womman dooth his myght
This day in murthe and revel to dispende
Til on the welkne shoon the sterres lyght.
For moore solempne in every mannes syght
This feste was, and gretter of costage,
Than was the revel of hire marriage.
[*IV* (*E*) *1121-1127*]

In the *Man of Law's Tale,* also, there is mention of the festivity following the royal marriage, brief though that mention is. The teller of the Tale asks why he should take time to speak of the "roialtee at mariage, or which cours goeth biforn," or who plays what musical instrument. Instead the teller sums up the merriment by saying that the company ate and drank, and they danced and sang and amused themselves [II (B¹) 701-707].

The pilgrimage, as a diversion rather than as a religious journey, has already been mentioned [see above, p. 75], as have also been the decorous everyday amusements of the chivalric world [see above, pp. 26, 131 ff.]

FIVE ✻ The Influence of Chaucer's World of Literature

SINCE THE *Canterbury Tales* represents a series of stories placed in a framework, we should first inquire why Chaucer selected that form for his masterpiece. The poet must have long been familiar with the form and aware of its popularity, for the *Romance of the Seven Sages,* the *Decameron,* Sercambi's *Novelle,* and other works had preceded his own. That Chaucer selected a pilgrimage for the frame and was able to bring the pilgrims to life as three-dimensional human beings must be ascribed to his genius rather than to his literary environment. Further, Chaucer had also experimented with a framework in his unfinished *Legend of Good Women* so the method of construction was far from unknown in his own work.

As for the Tales themselves, we know that the medieval world was deeply interested in and entertained by romances, folk tales, *fabliaux,* beast fables, tragedies, saints' lives and homilies and allegories. No one cared for novelty in plot: the old stories were the popular ones and what we might think of today as a kind of plagiarism was considered to be merely complimentary. With very few exceptions, the plots of Chaucer's narratives are "borrowed," exactly as were the plots of Shakespeare's plays some two hundred years later.

We may roughly classify the tales as follows, even though almost none, thanks to Chaucer's brilliance, is only what the bare classification would make it: the *Knight's Tale*, the *Squire's Tale*, the *Franklin's Tale*, may come under the more general heading of romance, and the *Physician's Tale* (if we accept that as a part of the Matter of Rome) may also be categorized as having its base in romance; and we should perhaps here include the *Tale of Sir Thopas* which, though primarily a parody, does have the shape of a romance. The *Man of Law's Tale* (aside from its allegory), the *Wife of Bath's Tale*, the *Friar's Tale*, the *Summoner's Tale*, the *Clerk's Tale*, and the *Manciple's Tale* may all be classified as having their bases in the folk tale (the folk tale often borders on the *fabliau*); the *Miller's Tale*, the *Reeve's Tale*, the *Cook's Tale*, and the *Shipman's Tale* are decidedly in the *fabliau* class; the *Prioress's Tale* and the *Second Nun's Tale* are both based on saints' lives; the *Monk's Tale* is an example of a tragedy; the *Tale of Melibee* is combined allegory and homily; the *Parson's Tale* and the *Pardoner's Tale* are both sermons (but how much more than mere sermon is the *Pardoner's Tale!*); the *Nun's Priest's Tale* is at base—but only at base—a beast fable; and, finally, we have the *Canon's Yeoman's Tale*, which defies any formal medieval classification.

Thus, we have the greater number of tales stemming from the forms of nonserious literature, exactly what would be expected for stories told on a "real" pilgrimage of sundry folk. We may also note here the Host's rude remarks to the Monk after the tragedies have been cut short. No one wishes serious tales:

> Youre tale anoyeth all this compaignye,
> Swich talkynge is not worth a boterflye,
> For therinne is there no desport ne game.
> [*VII* (*B*² *3979-3981*) *2789-2791*]

When Chaucer was composing the *Canterbury Tales*, he had already learned to shed much of the conventional formality of serious French literature (the French *fabliau* was always informal and naturalistic). But many of the lessons that the poet had learned from the French rhetoricians remained with him throughout his life.

One of the most obvious aspects of style is the pace at which the writing progresses. In the *Knight's Tale* there is no hurry. Everything is measured and dignified. Descriptions and discourses are completed without the interruption of narrative. We should note, for example, that in the 603 lines of Part III of the *Knight's Tale*, only about 30 per cent of them are devoted to action; the remainder of them to material irrelevant to action. In the *Man of Law's Tale* we are better off proportionally for, of the 1,162 lines of the Tale, nearly 80 percent are devoted to action. On the other hand, if we examine a *fabliau* such as the *Miller's Tale* or even the beast fable, the *Nun's Priest's Tale*, about 98 percent of the lines involve action. (In the *Nun's Priest's Tale* the descriptions and references to authority combine to give us character delineation and hence—in the opinion of this writer—are not "irrelevant" to plot-action. Also much of the *Nun's Priest's Tale* is parody so that descriptions and authorities are fittingly included.)

In general, it is safe to say that "serious" Tales have dignified, unhurried movement, and that the narratives based on folk tale or *fabliau* have rapid movement, although we have a striking exception to part of that statement in the *Wife of Bath's Tale*. In the Hag's sermon on "gentilesse," there is matter which acts as a brake to the story, and is totally irrelevant to it and to the character of the teller. Rhetorical ornamentation, if the Hag's homily is such, has been many times adversely criticized as out of place in Alisoun's Tale. However, the deletion of Aurelius' address to Apollo, irrelevant to the narrative though it is, would harm the *Franklin's Tale.*

Even in modern times we expect the medieval stately narrative to be decorated by laments, by extended aphorisms and the like, by references to authorities, by elaborate descriptive matter, by "occupatio" and by lists. Chaucer had, we know, studied the French rhetoricians. (Note, for example, Chaucer's rather casual reference in the *Nun's Priest's Tale* to Geoffrey de Vinsauf, author of a work on the art of poetry [VII (B² 4537) 3347].) But even if Chaucer had not had precept in the art of writing, his own wide reading would have given him example, a method of teaching not to be ignored.

Two notable examples out of many of the long love complaint may be cited in the *Canterbury Tales.* In the *Knight's Tale,* Arcite, upon his impending release from prison, laments for 52 lines, and in the *Franklin's Tale,* after the rocks have been "removed" by the magician, Aurelius laments for 28 lines.

As to the extended aphorisms and the like, the philosophical musings cited elsewhere [see above, pp. 77 ff.] offer sufficient illustration. The great number of proverbs introduced by the poet gives evidence of the heed Chaucer paid to that form of embellishment. Not more than three of the Tales are without some reference to maxims current in the Middle Ages and most of the Tales have many more references.*

The references to authority are, like the proverbs, too numerous to mention. As we should expect, biblical authority is called upon extensively, as well as the works of the Church

* See Skeat's *Early English Proverbs* and B. J. Whiting's *Chaucer's Use of Proverbs.*

fathers; the Latin poets (especially Ovid) are also cited by Chaucer and, of course, the poet leans heavily on Aristotle. Medieval writers of all kinds, including Chaucer's admired Dante, are used not infrequently as authorities by him.

As has been pointed out, there are many descriptive passages in the *Knight's Tale*. The description of the temples in Part III could be removed without any violence done to story. (That Chaucer, in using the source of *Il Teseida*, did not choose to omit those descriptions, but even enlarged them, is a significant fact. The poet was evidently deeply aware of the need of such decoration in formal narrative.)

Chaucer frequently employs a rhetorical figure known as "occupatio," that is a deliberate omission of part of a description or of a narrative. The first example we meet of "occupatio" in the *Canterbury Tales*, is at the beginning of the *Knight's Tale*. The Knight, in a most "natural" manner, says that he must get on with his Tale which is a long one. He will, therefore, omit a section of the story so that other pilgrims may have a chance to tell their Tales [I (A) 885 ff.]. Thus the poet, who wishes for technical reasons to summarize much of the Boccaccio original, puts into the Knight's mouth the reason for omission. Such a device does not interrupt the smoothness of the narrative and contributes small additional proof of the Knight's consideration for others. Again in the *Squire's Tale*, Chaucer is able to show his Squire's diffidence in the presence of older people through the young man's apologetic omission of a description of Canacee's beauty, "It lyth nat in my tonge, n'yn my konnyng"; thus, at the same time, Chaucer is able to dispense with the usual repetitious catalogue of Canacee's physical features. In the *Man of Law's Tale*, as already has been pointed out [see p. 134], the teller omits the detailed description of the marriage festivities, because such a description is not really germane to his story of Constance's virtue.

The subject of "lists" covers some of the other literary devices mentioned. There can be lists of authorities, lists of items in description (note the list of trees given in the description of Arcite's funeral [I (A) 2921 ff.]), or conventional lists introduced solely for their own sake, as in the list of titles of medieval romances given in the *Tale of Sir Thopas*.

Chaucer's independence from his literary environment is present in the naturalistic way in which human beings speak (always apparent in the Links, folk tales and the *fabliaux*) in citing their wise saws, in describing scenes and actors in the narratives, and in the list of authorities he quotes. (The raciness of the dialogue in the *Reeve's Tale* is enhanced by the colloquial dialect which the poet has obviously heard in the everyday northern speech of his own times.) But there can be no doubt in anyone's mind that Chaucer's over-all manner of writing in the *Canterbury Tales* was directly determined by the medieval literary world—his universality lies in content alone, and it is the medieval Chaucer almost exclusively whom we find in matters of form and style.

PART III
The Love-Vision Poems

THE FRENCH LITERATURE which became a part of Chaucer during his service in Prince Lionel's household was dedicated primarily to the celebration of love. Love was looked upon—at least, from the point of view of the ideal—as a good in itself. Although love between man and woman was far below divine love (and also below the love spoken of in the second great Commandment of the New Testament), human physical love had grown to have a high place in the aristocratic man's list of virtues. To love a lady was an act of ennoblement of the spirit—love considered in such light purified man and brought him nearer to God. Thus, if we add to this fact that everyone in the Middle Ages took deep pleasure in listening to allegory and to moralizing, we cannot be astonished that the love-vision poem (which taught as well as interested) was widely demanded and hence supplied.

To many of us today such literature is lacking in vitality; we find it dull and unreal. Yet if we interpret "realism" as "truth to the observed facts of life," we must admit that the love-vision poem does reflect psychologically a stratum of the aspirations of medieval society, a society that is polite, ritualistic and devoted to symbolism. We may argue that flesh-and-blood men and women do not have their being in a flowered tapestry, and we shall be right for our own era; but French courtly life in the Middle Ages was extraordinarily polished, possessed of a ceremonious code, and given to expressing its ideas in the form of dreams and allegories. Hence, for that life, the unvarying conventions of the love-vision poems were wholly "natural."

The form is briefly as follows: the Lover (or, sometimes, a Narrator) complains of wakefulness and attributes his state to difficulties in love; he usually attempts to find solace in a book or poem which then causes him to sleep; he dreams (that is, has his "vision"); the dream has the beautiful setting of a spring garden where the Lover, often led by an animal guide, encounters many allegorical figures (frequently Venus and Amor are present); the Lover learns the true meaning of love; he awakes refreshed. The style of the poems is complementary to the form: allegory and other metaphors, similes, hyperboles, allusions to mythology and to Latin works, repetitions and "lists," and long introductions—all of those decorations are necessary to the love-vision poem. And, inevitably, young Geoffrey Chaucer wrote love-vision poems, but grew to desert the formula as his own happy inspiration developed.

ONE ✻ The *Book of the Duchess*

OF CHAUCER'S three love-vision poems—the *Book of the Duchess*, the *House of Fame*, the *Parliament of Fowls* (the *Prologue* to the *Legend of Good Women* does not truly belong in this category)—the first named shows the least divergence from the French pattern, although paradoxically it is the most "original" in that it is an elegy as well as a love-vision. Blanche, the first wife of John of Gaunt, Duke of Lancaster, died in September, 1369, and Chaucer undoubtedly composed the poem shortly afterwards as a tribute to her memory and as a compliment to the Duke.

As all good modern editions of Chaucer's works point out, Chaucer is immensely indebted in the *Book of the Duchess* to Machaut, to Froissart and to *Le Roman de la Rose,* and full references are given when line-for-line comparisons are possible. We shall be more concerned here with general matters. The form can be readily summarized: Chaucer, the Narrator, claims that he is unable to sleep [ll. 1-29]; he implies —most probably as a literary convention—that a hopeless love affair of eight years' duration is the cause of his insomnia [ll. 30-43]; he calls for a book, Ovid's *Metamorphoses* [ll. 44-61], and there reads the tale of Ceyx and Alcione, a tale which the Narrator then outlines [ll. 62-221]; Ovid's story reminds the Narrator of Morpheus, and the Narrator beseeches the god to bring sleep to him; the Narrator then sleeps and has his dream [ll. 222-1334], or "love-vision," which he says he will put into verse for the interest of others, "be processe of tyme." Obviously the French form is faithfully copied.

Another great resemblance to the much-admired French poetry lies in the emphasis on ideal love. To be sure, the love in the *Book of the Duchess* has been made highly spiritual, or "ideal," through death: the Man in Black, whom the Narrator meets in the dream, is at once both a lover and a mourner—his paean is also a requiem, so that we find Chaucer, even in this very early poem, going beyond the models and employing the form for a graceful, new purpose. We also note that the manner in which the Man in Black extols his lady closely resembles the French pattern: the physical beauty of Blanche, the "goode, faire White," is described in detail [ll. 950-960], and those details are drawn from any French romance of the period; her gentle character is also described in detail [ll. 961-1087], details which are greatly ornamented by the hyperboles recommended by the rhetoricians. Blanche has been a light for all her world and her own brilliance was never dimmed through the light she gave to others; she was a crown set with gems; her wit was totally without malice for she never wronged or deceived any creature; always she kept her word (a virtue which Chaucer praises over and over again in later works); she was the peer of all the noble women of song and story.

But here again in the set form the new appears—for this lovely lady is dead and all but the Narrator are aware of this.

A few modern critics accuse the Narrator of "stupidity," because (they contend) he fails to jump to the immediate conclusion—even in a "dream"—that Blanche is no longer living. The present writer feels that such critics have lost sight of the fact that the poem does not—could not—give a realistic account of a bereaved husband in the twentieth century; they have temporarily forgotten that the fourteenth-century "reader," or audience, would neither expect nor wish the Narrator of the poem (who, after all, serves mainly as a device) to come too soon to an "understanding" of the Duchess' death. The Man in Black must be given time to present his eulogy, a eulogy which is the more deeply moving (and which still moves us today) because of the dramatic irony involved. The very fact that the Narrator is slow to comprehend is a piece of psychological "realism" here demanded by the fourteenth-century poem itself.

A sublimation of love, then, is at the heart of the *Book of the Duchess*. But there are other features of the poem which are important, although not as great in importance. For example, Chaucer made the fitting choice that his Narrator (the "I" of the poem, but of course not to be thought of as the actual Chaucer) should read the story of Ceyx and Alcyone before falling asleep. Here we have in form the necessary "long" introduction, as well as a linking device with the main narrative: the queen cannot sleep because of her anxiety about her absent husband ("unsuccessful love"); through Morpheus she has a vision ("dream") that the king is dead; she is grief-stricken. Thus Chaucer provides a literary balance between the Ovid tale and the Narrator's dream, as well as making a natural connection for the reader between introduction and main body. Even the naturalism of the dialogue between Morpheus and Juno's messenger is paralleled by the naturalism of the conversation the Narrator imagines himself having with Morpheus. Further, the occasionally jocular tone in the introduction (a tone not always unknown to parts of a French love-vision poem) serves aesthetically in the *Book of the Duchess* as contrast to the high seriousness of the elegy proper.

There is no abrupt transition from the humorous proposal of the bribe to Morpheus—the feather-bed, "rayed with gold" and covered with black satin (young squires, who were accorded few bodily comforts in the medieval castle or manor house, would appreciate that touch, drawn from Machaut, it is true, but Chaucer chose to include it)—to the beautiful bedroom in which the Narrator finds himself at the beginning of his dream; it is a gentle, easily accepted change. There is a fresh gaiety in the melodies of the birds on the tiled roof (the "gret hep" of "smale foules," singing their blithe songs "to fetch in May"), even a kind of joyous simplicity in the glorious windows of rare, stained glass for all the elaboration of their pictured stories. So we find ourselves without effort in the Narrator's dream, sharing, with as little surprise as the Narrator himself shows, in the emperor's patrician hunt, readily accepting the dreamlike disappearance of huntsmen and hounds. All jocularity has vanished, but we have not watched it slip away.

The appearance of the little whelp in the dream may, or may not, be an echo of the animal guide of the French models. (Machaut includes a whelp in one of his love-vision poems.) By running away and by being followed by the Narrator, Chaucer's small dog does indirectly "guide" the Narrator to the Man in Black. On the other hand, Chaucer may have placed the little animal in the poem as a contrast to the fierce hunting hounds, and to prepare the heart (the "gentil herte" where pity dwells) for the sorrowful beauty which is to come: the praise and lament for Blanche, the Duchess of Lancaster, who lived in Richmond—the "walles white" of "a long castel" set on "a ryche hil."

TWO ✣ The *House of Fame*

THE *House of Fame*, unlike the *Book of the Duchess*, cannot be exactly dated as to year of composition. However, since it contains reference to Chaucer's "rekenynges" [l. 653], we may assume that the poem was written after 1374, a date which marks the beginning of Chaucer's position as Controller of the Customs. On the other hand, most critics agree that the employment of the octosyllabic couplet—used also in the *Book of the Duchess*—keeps the poem to a fairly early period. Thus we can say with some assurance that the *House of Fame* was at least begun before 1380, and may have been begun six years before that time.

Chaucer had taken his "first" Italian journey, therefore, when he composed this poem, and the influence of that experience on the poet's mind produced a work that is heterogeneous in style and content. It is true that the *House of Fame* is classified as a love-vision poem: it begins as such and it approaches an ending that is not out of keeping with that classification. The central portion of the poem, however, deserts the love-vision in style and only faintly suggests the genre in content—the eagle does emphasize "love" through what he says about Chaucer's devotion to Venus [ll. 613-668] and through his pledge to Chaucer that the purpose of the whole journey to the House of Fame is to acquaint the poet with "tydynges" of love [l. 675].

Although Book I follows the love-vision pattern on the whole, there is some deviation. We have, as in the *Book of the Duchess*, a narrator invoking the services of Morpheus, which is quite possibly an evidence of Chaucer's debt to Froissart. The "I" of the poem does talk of dreams, their causes and their meanings; but he shows himself to be more interested in "scientific" discussion than in his own wakefulness—in fact, he has no difficulty in falling asleep because, he says with considerable humor, he has become physically wearied. The setting of the dream in Book I is consonant with a love-vision pattern: the Narrator finds himself in an ornately decorated glass temple dedicated to Venus, and there on a tablet of brass are written the opening lines of the *Aeneid*, followed by the "story" of that poem, particularly the tale of Dido and her sorrows, with medieval stress on Venus and the theme of love.

Then, when the Narrator leaves the dream temple and finds himself in a large field near the great, golden eagle who has soared through the heavens, we are prepared for the animal guide of the love-vision pattern. We might now expect the majestic bird possibly borrowed in all his dignity from Virgil or Ovid (it is tempting, however, to think of Chaucer's having in mind Dante's golden eagle, *aquila nel ciel con penne d'oro* [Purgatorio, IX, 20]) to conduct the Narrator in stately fashion to some beautiful, cultivated garden or to a magnificent castle where the theme relating to love would be allegorically developed.

But Chaucer now appears to us to be frankly experimenting; the Italian influence is before him and he turns—without any real transition—to a realistic style, a style which the poet makes his own in English literature and which speaks meaningfully to us, especially in the twentieth century. Hence we find the eagle charmingly and irresistibly humorous (to borrow a phrase from the Wife of Bath, we are "tickled" at "the bottom of the heart"), for the great bird is no medieval, allegorical figure, but a satiric, three-dimensional portrait of a human being long familiar to every one of us: the pedantic lecturer, ever desirous of over-instructing a captive audience. We smile sympathetically at poor "Geffrey" (no longer a mere narrator, but an actor, perfect in an amusing role), suddenly borne aloft, for all his bulk, in the talking eagle's powerful claws.

Book II of the *House of Fame* gives us a picture of a Geoffrey Chaucer—a picture which he likes to repeat in other poems—which is not to be considered as a picture of the poet himself in sober actuality. The "fictional" Geoffrey is shy, rather bungling, without learning or any ability in self-expression; he has had love affairs in the distant past, but he is now too old and too stout—too "well shaped in the waist" —for any woman to look at him. In the *House of Fame,* this Geoffrey is indeed an easy victim for the despotic and patronizing eagle, that professor of science and *confidant* of Olympian deities, who would lecture interminably to his nervous and ignorant audience. To be sure, "love" is not entirely set aside in Book II, for the eagle does compliment Geoffrey upon his youthful and long past devotion to "faire Venus" and "Cupido," but one may say that that is the only link this book has with a love-vision poem.

To what, then, is it linked? To Dante's use of the everyday image and to Chaucer's own bent, of course, but also to Chaucer's own environmental experience as well. As a boy at his London school or as a young man studying law, Chaucer undoubtedly encountered (as who has not today?) some indefatigable and garrulous teacher, perhaps one of large authority, from whom there was no escape, one who could over-awe and deflate small boys and timid young men. Chaucer, the eager and interested student, may have himself enjoyed the instruction, but, whatever his own feeling, his imaginative eye would have observed those classmates who yawned or fidgeted or who were bewildered by the spate of words. ("Wilt thou lere of sterres ought?" asks the eagle—rhetorically, one is sure; but a firm reply comes from the pupil, wearied into defiance, that he will have no part of further instruction—"hyt is no nede!")

Book III of the *House of Fame* begins with an invocation to Apollo, but because Apollo is apostrophized as the god of science and light, and not as a god connected with love, we cannot term the invocation a true return to the love-vision pattern. However, Chaucer (not as Narrator or actor, but as poet alone) promises to kiss the laurel, Apollo's tree, if only the "lytel laste bok" may be inspired by the god so that the poet may accomplish a description of the "love tydynges" he seeks.

Then again Chaucer becomes the actor: he climbs the high rock of perishable ice (allegory is entering the poem) on which stands Fortune's castle, a castle so intricately beautiful that no poet may adequately describe it. All the men of magic and all the minstrels who have heralded the famous are there (it would take him, Chaucer says, until "domes day" to mention each of them). And in the center of the great hall is "our oune lady Fame" on her golden throne, besieged by crowds of suppliants, all asking for "larges."

The suppliants approach the goddess in nine companies, and the allegory is stressed. The first company are worthy of fame, but are nevertheless denied all remembrance; the second company, also worthy, are to be remembered only with obloquy; while the third company, again worthy, are rewarded by gaining what they request. The fourth company, much smaller in number than the other three, petition that their light be hidden from the world for they have acted solely for the glory of God, and Fame grants their request; but the fifth company, no different from the fourth in what they are and in what they ask, are illogically denied obscurity. The sixth and seventh companies claim that through laziness they have done nothing worthy of fame, yet both request renown; the sixth company's request is readily granted, but the seventh company are dubbed "masty swyn" and told that all that they deserve is hanging. Lastly come the eighth and ninth companies who are both composed of the wicked, both desiring to be remembered; the eighth, who desire a good reputation, are refused it, and the ninth, who desire an evil reputation, are granted their request.

But Chaucer, the poet, does not forget that Geoffrey, the Narrator, has been created as a character, and so there is a bystander provided to carry on conversation and thus show that Geoffrey is still himself, an actor in a "story," who declares he wants no part of Fame; he did not come here of his own volition; his only wish is to have the love tidings promised him by his guide. How refreshing for the reader of today! There is no long dissertation on the unfairness of Fame (as the fourteenth century might have welcomed), but merely an exit. For the Geoffrey of the poem goes forth and is transported, without too much "instruction" from his guide, the same eagle, to the House of Rumor. (We should note, in passing, that there are sixteen lines here [ll. 1961-1976] each beginning with the word *of,* a rhetorical "ornament" much admired by the French authors.) The poet-actor, or Narrator, is again spoken of as being without "solace"; it is said that he is suffering from "hevynesse" and that he is "disesperat of alle blisse"; for that reason Chaucer is taken to the place where he is to meet the epitome of all love tidings: the House of Rumor. From the interstices of that whirling wicker structure go out all the tales of the "shipmen and pilgrimes," and their "scrippes" so full of gross exaggerations. (Is Chaucer here recalling those tales of wonder he listened to with such avid fascination in the faraway London of his Vintry boyhood?) And thus we are prepared for the anonymous man of "great authority" and for those great love tidings.

Alas, "the rest is silence"; Chaucer did not finish (would not? could not?) the *House of Fame*. But we are left with an extraordinarily rich and decorated fabric, even though the beginning is headlong and hasty. The well-known 52-line sentence at the start of Book I conveys a sense of hurry, rather than any lack of skill; we do not think of the *House of Fame* as being as incomplete as it actually is. The suggestion of the love vision is in the poem, but so is the suggestion of the *Canterbury Tales* (that great insight into life as it is). We admire, if we are fourteenth-century-minded, the necessary conventions of the poem; yet at the same time we stretch out our minds gratefully to receive the humor and naturalism which are "innovations" of the times and which still enable us to laugh in rueful kindness at the vagaries of man.

THREE ❧ The *Parliament of Fowls*

THE *Parliament of Fowls* is usually classified as a love vision, but the poem shows modifications of pattern which demand our placing the work in Chaucer's mature period, that is, in the poet's Aldgate days. In the *Parliament* Chaucer has gone far beyond the *Book of the Duchess* and the *House of Fame,* and has used a blend of French and Italian styles coupled with what is by this time his own distinctive art and charm. Further, he has now adopted the longer, and hence more flexible, ten-syllable line, as a contrast to the too-abrupt eight-syllable line of both the earlier poems; and he is demonstrating his ease in managing the seven-line stanza with its rhyme royal. The effect of smooth casualness is a striking characteristic of the *Parliament,* a characteristic which comes in large measure from the poem's mechanical structure.

The first few stanzas—typical of the whole poem's flowing quality—serve to illustrate the point (italics indicate the linking words): the intricacies of love's "werkynge" (stanza 2), and one such *book* has occupied him for a full *day* (stanza

3), so much so that the *day* has seemed short (stanza 4); the *book* was written by Cicero, the "hero" is *Scipio* (stanza 5), and in the book *Scipio* has a dream concerning himself (stanza 6), who promises to show *Scipio* where now dwell the souls of all who in this world have loved mankind (stanza 7). But readily discernible as they are when searched for, the linking devices slip by unnoticed when the poem is read as literature; we have only the impression of extraordinary homogeneity.

The first 322 lines of the *Parliament* belong largely to the love-vision pattern. There is a Narrator, although he has become more remote and impersonal than his prototypes; he is no longer an actor in the story—in fact, the Narrator disappears from the *Parliament* once the dream is under way [l. 300], and does not return to the poem until he gives it well-rounded conclusion. The reading of a book concerning a dream is conventionally present, but the Narrator of the *Parliament* does not fall asleep over Cicero's *Somnium Scipionis;* he stops reading because "the derke nyght" has bereft him of illumination [ll. 85, 87]. Neither is he wakeful, although the problems of love have bothered him very much [ll. 1-21]; he falls asleep easily because he is weary from his "labour al the day" [l. 93]. The French pattern is followed, however, by linking the reading of the book to the Narrator's vision, for Africanus appears as guide in both Scipio's and the Narrator's dream.

The *Parliament* is, of course, devoted almost exclusively to the subject of love—the poem is evidently occasional, celebrating some courtly betrothal or wedding, but there are strong antitheses in the kinds of love considered. At the beginning of the poem, Chaucer takes Hippocrates' ancient aphorism, *ars longa, vita brevis,* and gives it special meaning: the art of *love,* he says, takes a lifetime to learn, and he has not yet mastered it—even though (as he tells us in the second stanza) he has read for years about love's "myrakles" and "crewel yre." Is Chaucer here speaking of physical love with its resulting joys and unhappinesses (certainly what we should expect to find in the love-vision of tradition, or is he contrasting the sacred with the profane? In describing Scipio's dream [ll. 36-84], Chaucer extols the spiritual love of "commune profyt," plainly indicating that the love for the commonweal is a fundamental human good and hence far above the more selfish love between man and woman. Yet the poet calls upon Venus, "thow blysful lady swete," to aid him in writing about his own dream and its setting.

In the setting itself, we are again confronted by interesting ambiguity. The gate of the green park, the park walled with mossy stone, to which the Narrator is conducted by Africanus, has engraved on it two inscriptions—the one in gold promising "hertes hele" and eternal spring to those who enter, the other in black promising barren wastes and ungraciousness (surely reminiscent of Dante's "lasciate ogni speranza . . ."). And again—for the park is to be a garden of love in the dream —are those two inscriptions a suggestion of the ideas the poet-philosopher will expound regarding different kinds of love? In any event, Africanus, showing that he has some small kinship with the eagle of the *House of Fame,* gives the Narrator, now caught with equal force between the desire to enter and the desire to flee, a no-uncertain shove through the gate, informing him at the same time that there is neither bliss nor danger for one who, like the Narrator, is merely to be an onlooker for, says Africanus, 'Thow of love hast lost they tast!" [l. 160]. Chaucer's humorous reference to his own exclusion from love affairs is again to the fore.

The garden the poet enters is allegorical in nature, perhaps suggesting the Garden of Eden which man may not now enter except in dreams; the trees which the Narrator observes are forever clad with leaves as "fresh and greene as emer-

aude"; the poet carefully catalogues the trees from the "byl-
dere oak" to the "laurer to devyne" by way of traditional rhetorical decoration. Chaucer's "blossmy bowes"—the white,
blue, yellow and red flowers; the silver and red fish in the
clear streams; the birds singing "with voys of aungel in
here armonye"; the gentle animals; the ravishing music; eternal day and eternal youth—all these suggest the purity and
innocence of love, albeit a dream of love, a picture of perfection not to be found in the everyday world.

But the garden is one of paradox, as the two opposing legends at the gate imply. Cupid, "oure lord," is present, but so
is his daughter, Will (or Voluptuousness), who "tempers"
the arrows of her father so that some victims will be slain or
sorely wounded. The personified figures of Pleasure, Dress,
Desire, Courtesy and Artfulness (who is badly disfigured)
are present, and under an oak tree stands Delight and Gen-
tleness. Naked Beauty and Youth, Foolhardiness, Flattery
and Ardor nearby, Bribery and "Messagerye" attend all those
figures, and about a temple in the vicinity, dance women
perpetually in "kertels, al dishevele," some fair by nature,
some by art. Venus' white doves perch on the temple and
before the door Dame Peace and Dame Patience sit, the latter
on a hill of sand, the sand, of course, implying insecurity.

Artful Promise weaves in and out among the throng; the
altar flames are nourished by sighs which have been engendered by Desire, fanned further by the 'bittere goddesse,
Jelosye"; Venus is then discerned in semidarkness upon her
golden bed, veiled by a thin silken covering ("a subtyl cover-
chef of Valence"). Other gods and goddesses are present—
Priapus, Bacchus and Diana the Chaste—and on the walls
are painted the stories of Callisto, Atalanta, Semiramis, Can-
dace, Hercules, Byblis, Dido, Pyramus and Thisbe, Tris-
tram and Isolde, Paris and Achilles and Helen and Cleopatra,
Troilus, Scylla, and the mother of Romulus—all victims of

love. The dream picture thus far drawn by Chaucer is strongly reminiscent of his reading: of *Somnium Scipionis* as has been noted, of Dante, of Boccaccio's *Il Teseida,* of the *Roman de la Rose.* We should also note that the abstractions which Chaucer mentioned so far are in keeping with the traditions of the love-vision poem; at the same time Chaucer does not allow those abstractions to become actors in the narrative— they are present as ornamentation alone. It is as if the poet is here partially outside his own times, and is leaning towards an abandonment of allegory in favor of his greater interest in the behavior of actual human beings. When Chaucer as Narrator leaves the temple with all its conflicts and contradictions and enters the grassy clearing "upon a hil of floures" —and incidentally disappears temporarily as Narrator—he calls specifically upon the twelfth century and Alanus' *Complaint of Nature* to aid him in his descriptions.

The goddess Nature is presiding over a gathering of all the birds, for this is St. Valentine's Day, Chaucer explains, when every bird comes to a "parliament" to choose a mate. The "estates" of birds are to be observed: the birds of prey represent the nobility; the water fowl represent the merchant princes; the worm fowl represent the lower middle class; and the seed fowl represent the peasants. (Chaucer probably took his classification of the birds from passages in Aristotle, which the poet found in Vincent of Beauvais.) The particular birds are then carefully listed in traditional manner, from the "royal egle" through the lesser degrees of eagle, to the voracious cormorant and the winter thrush (35 lines in all!), and we have the feeling that Chaucer makes the list, not only because it is a medieval literary adornment to his poem, but also because birds—which appear so often in his poems— have very special and affectionate meaning for him.

Nature, personified in the *Parliament of Fowls* as a goddess and a "noble emperesse," is, of course, an abstraction but, unlike the other abstractions, one which plays a leading part in the poem. In the philosophy of the Middle Ages, Nature was held to be one of the forces used by Destiny to carry out the decrees of Providence. Chaucer characterizes Nature in the *Parliament* as "the vikaire of the almyghty Lord," who has knit the humors and elements together [II. 379-381], an idea which may have come to the poet through Boethius [Book III, Met. 9], although no one particular work would be necessary. In the *Roman de la Rose*, a poem highly familiar to Chaucer, Nature is said to surpass all thought:

> Fair Nature's glorious paradise—
> Past thought of price. . . .
> Even God, whose glory is above
> All measurement, in bounteous love
> Created Nature he did make of her a fountain
> (Whence should break unceasingly a thousand rills)
> Of beauty, which the whole world fills.
> [*RR* (*Ellis Trans.*) *ll. 17006-17007, 17019-17024*]

In the *Parliament*, cool, beautiful Nature supersedes the hot passion of Venus, yet Nature and Venus are both part of the Chain of Love: the former is love which lasts beyond terrestrial life (and yet a love which renews itself on earth as the seasons pass); the latter is love which dies with man and is coupled often with sin and disaster.

Beautiful although the garden entered by the Narrator and the Temple of Venus are, all the lusts of the flesh are present there, and there is an underlying contrast in the gathering of the birds on St. Valentine's Day. The word *underlying* is perhaps necessary in this context, for Nature's speeches to the birds under her jurisdiction and the speeches of the birds themselves are not in a style which could be compared to the flower-like descriptions of the garden—rather, they resemble the conversations of everyday life, but each speech is appropriate to the social position of the particular

speaker. Chaucer contrives the transition from the tone of his "philosophical" vicar of the Almighty by an address which Nature, holding on her hand a gentle "formel" eagle, makes in "esy voys" to the assembled birds.
Nature says:

'Foules, tak hed of my sentence, I preye,
And for youre ese, in fortheryng of youre nede,
As faste as I may speke, I wol me speede.

'Ye knowe wel how, seynt Valentynes day,
Be my statut and thorgh my governaunce,
Ye come for to cheese—and fle youre way—
Youre makes, as I prike yow with plesaunce:
But natheles, my ryghtful ordenaunce
May I nat let for al this world to wynne,
That he that most is worthi shal begynne.

'The tersel egle, as that ye knowe wel,
The foul royal, above yow in degre,
The wyse and worthi, secre, trewe as stel,
Which I have formed, as ye may wel se,
In every part as it best liketh me—
It nedeth not his shap yow to devyse—
He shal first chese and speken in his gyse.

'And after hym by ordre shul ye chese,
After your kynde, everich as yow lyketh,
And, as youre hap is, shul ye wynne or lese.
But which of yow that love most entriketh,
God sende hym hire that sorest for hym syketh!'
And therwithal the tersel gan she calle,
And seyde, 'My sone, the choys is to the falle.

'But natheles, in this condicioun
Mot be the choys of everich that is heere,
That she agre to his eleccioun,

Whoso he be that shulde be hire feere.
This is oure usage alwey, from yer to yeere,
And whoso may at this tyme have his grace,
In blisful tyme he cam into this place!'

[*ll. 383-413*]

The most noble bird present, the royal tercelet, does not
hesitate to respond: in stately chivalric language entirely
fitting to him, he chooses the lady eagle on Nature's hand,
asking the lady that she take pity on his woe and saying that
if he is ever untrue to her he hopes to meet a horrible death.
He uses chivalric terms which, although ideal, are also paradoxically naturalistic, for the imagined and the actual are one
in the mind of medieval chivalric man. The lady eagle (who
has become "human" to us) is properly abashed. For she,
too, is of the ideal, as well as of the practical, world.

Ryght as the freshe, rede rose newe
Ayeyn the somer sonne coloured is,
Ryght so for shame al wexen gan the hewe
Of this formel, whan she herde al this:
She neyther answerde wel, ne seyde amys,
So sore abasht was she.

[*ll. 442-447*]

Two more tercelets speak for the lady's hand, the first of
them in chivalric tones nearly as stately as those of his royal
predecessor, the second somewhat more impatiently than the
other two (and by his impatience creating for the poet a
small transition for what is to follow, for the third suitor announces that the birds are crying eagerly for their turns to
choose their mates—"ye seen the lytle leyser heere," he
points out). Then some of the birds of lower degree, giving
the lady eagle no opportunity to speak, cry out, "Have don
and lat us wende!" so loudly that the trees shake. " 'Com
of!' " they chorus and add:

. . . 'Allas, ye wol us shende!
Whan shal youre cursede pletynge have an ende?
How sholde a juge eyther parti leve
For ye or nay, withouten any preve?'
                                    [*ll. 494-497*]

The goose, on behalf of the water fowl, says that the chivalric
speeches they have heard are in the present circumstances not
worth "a flye"—that he can make an easy decision fairly and
swiftly without such long debate. Whereupon the foolish
cuckoo says that he will, on behalf of the worm fowl, manage
the choosing and speed it up. The turtle dove, who shyly
claims to be one of the unworthiest of the seed fowl, then re-
bukes the cuckoo by saying that if the latter gives the permission for the choice, the speakers might as well keep silent. (We
may possibly ask here if Chaucer is commenting indirectly on
the amount of wisdom to be found in the various social classes
in the course of the debate—a question which cannot be answered, but one about which we might speculate.)

Nature now intervenes, and because she is addressing the
birds of lower degree, she speaks colloquially. "Hold youre
tonges there!" she cries and adds that she herself will soon
settle the matter—let each of the four groups elect a spokesman.

The first of the three tercelets who have spoken in rivalry
for the lady eagle is elected to represent the birds of prey, but
his argument is that the love debate has been inconclusive and
perhaps the decision should be "be batayle." The goose, having been chosen by the water fowl as their representative, intervenes quickly and states flatly that if the lady will not take
the suitor who loves her best, let that one choose another mate;
the goose is then promptly rebuked by one of the lesser birds
of prey as not understanding chivalric behavior and the humble turtle dove speaks in support of the aristocrats. (Is Chau-

cer here anticipating the good Plowman of the *Canterbury Tales?*)

The duck startles the Parliament by exclaiming:

> 'That men shulde loven alwey causeles,
> Who can a resoun fynde or wit in that?
> Daunseth he murye that is myrtheles?
> Who shulde recche of that is recheles?
> Ye quek! . . .
> "There been mo sterres, God wot, than a payre!" '
>
> [*ll. 590-595*]

Whereupon the gentle tercelet retorts:

> 'Now fy, cherl! . . .
> Out of the donghil cam that word ful right!
> Thow canst nat seen which thyng is wel beset!
> Thow farst by love as oules don by lyght:
> The day hem blent, ful wel they se by nyght.
> Thy kynde is of so low a wrechednesse
> That what love is, thow canst nat seen ne gesse.'
>
> [*ll. 596-602*]

(The medieval belief—for it was the genuine belief of many— that the peasant could not know anything of courtly love was strong.) The cuckoo also joins the duck in sentiment for he thinks the courtly-love debate only foolish; he does not care how long it goes on if he may choose his mate and get away. Nature again sharply intervenes and makes a "courtly" decision. She says that the lady should choose the tercelet who is royal. But the lady, again true to type, asks for a year's delay, a request which is granted, and the three suitors are then instructed to serve the lady as her potential lovers during that time. The *Parliament of Fowls* concludes with a graceful roundel in honor of St. Valentine, and the Narrator reappears to close the poem as a love vision:

And with the shoutyng, whan the song was do
That foules maden at here flyght awey,
I wok, and othere bokes tok me to,
To reede upon, and yit I rede alwey.
I hope, ywis, to rede so som day
That I shal mete som thyng for to fare
The bet, and thus to rede I nyl nat spare.

[*ll. 693-699*]

Yes, the *Parliament of Fowls* is a love-vision poem, primarily concerned with courtly love, but through the medium of naturalistic writing, the poem is also a brief study of the claims of Venus as opposed to those of Nature, and of the God-created hierarchy of social order. There can be no doubt that Chaucer's environment played a large part in shaping the content.

FOUR ❖ The *F(B) Prologue* to the *Legend of Good Women*

TO A LARGE EXTENT the *Prologue* to the *Legend of Good Women* follows the love-vision pattern. The poem begins with the mention of a book—or, rather, books, in this case. All things are to be found in the writings of wise men, the poet says, the wise men

> That tellen of these olde appreved stories
> Of holynesse, of regnes, of victories,
> Of love, of hate, of other sondry thynges,
> Of whiche I may not maken rehersynges.
> And yf that olde bokes were aweye,
> Yloren were of remembraunce the keye.
> Wel ought us thanne honouren and beleve
> These bokes, there we han noon other preve.
> *[F ll. 21-28]*

(We should note here medieval emphasis on "authority.") Chaucer, as Narrator, conventionally disclaims any knowledge, but he always delights in reading: there is no greater pleasure in the world. Yet, he says,

> . . . whan that the month of May
> Is comen, and that I here the foules synge,
> And that the floures gynnen for to sprynge,
> Farewel my bok, and my devocioun!
>
> [*F ll. 36-39*]

Thus, instead of a wakeful poet after a long day eventually lulled into sleep by a book, we meet a charmingly fresh Narrator, his heart stirred by the season which will have no "slogardie anyght," rejecting books and rising early to pay his respects to the flower which he loves the most: "thise floures white and rede, swiche as men callen daysyes in our toun." The "day's eye," the *marguerite* of France (and possibly Chaucer is here paying tribute to the French poets, such as Froissart, Deschamps and Machaut, who also praise that particular flower), is allied to the bright sun, and Chaucer exclaims:

> Allas, that I ne had Englyssh, ryme or prose,
> Suffisant this flour to preyse aryght!
>
> [*F ll. 66-67*]

The poet then apologizes for his lack of skill to all who have preceded him in songs of praise; and he speaks also to all lovers, whether they belong to the cult of the "Flower" or the "Leaf." *

After continued praise of the daisy, Chaucer, as Narrator, slowly introduces his "story." The first of May has arrived, al-

---

* Two rival Orders of Love existed in the fourteenth century, both in England and in France, the one Order devoted to the Flower and the other to the Leaf. In the anonymous Middle English poem, "The Flower and the Leaf," later "modernized" by Dryden, the devotees of the Flower are described as being clad in green—as Chaucer describes Alceste in the *Prologue*—and the devotees of the Leaf are described as being clad in white, a reversal of color from today's point of view.

ways the time "to ben at the resurrection of this flour." (Is the poet thinking here of the love that does not die with man on earth?) He goes at dawn to greet the new daisy, he kneels on "the smale, softe, swote gras," which is so delicately embroidered with flowers, he listens to the little birds singing their hymns of praise to the Creator or to their joyous love songs. (Chaucer is "borrowing" largely in this passage from the *Roman de la Rose*.) The Narrator then spends the whole day in the meadow in devotion to "this fresshe flour," and when he returns to his house as darkness falls, he directs that his bed be made "in a litel herber" that he owns which is "benched . . . on turves fressh ygrave."

And there he falls asleep, in all the sweetness of May, and has his "vision." The vision concerns love and, true to convention, the God of Love, Amor, is present. Amor enters the scene almost immediately (there is no "guide" in the dream); he is dressed in a silken robe, which is embroidered with green sprays and red rose petals, and his golden hair is crowned with a sun. He leads the noble Queen Alceste by the hand and the Narrator is so much enthralled by her beauty that he at once recites a ballade in celebration of "this lady fre." (We should observe here that Chaucer, mindful of the French rhetoricians, includes a "list" in the ballade by giving us the names of women who have been faithful in love.) Following Amor and Alceste come nineteen ladies in royal dress, and after them a vast number of women, every one of whom is faithful in love. Amor sees the poet and identifies him; the poet is then sternly rebuked for daring to appear in the presence of Alceste. The god says to the kneeling poet:

> . . . 'What dostow her
> So nygh myn oune floure, so boldely?
> Yt were better worthy, trewely,
> A worm to neghen ner my flour than thow. . . .

> And thou my foo, and al my folk werreyest,
> And of myn olde servauntes thow mysseyest,
> And hynderest hem with thy translacioun,
> And lettest folk from hire devocioun
> To serve me, and holdest it folye
> To serve Love.'
> [*F ll. 315-318, 322-327*]

Amor next speaks of Chaucer's sin against love in having translated the *Roman de la Rose* and in having told the story of Criseyde; he exclaims angrily that Chaucer shall repent that sin "so cruelly that it shal wel be sene"!

But gentle Alceste, in true womanly chivalric fashion, entreats Amor to show mercy to the poet. She pleads:

> '. . . ryght of youre curtesye,
> Ye moten herken yf he can replye
> Agayns al this that ye have to him meved.
> A god ne sholde nat thus be agreved,
> But of his deitee he shal be stable,
> And therto gracious and merciable.
> And yf ye nere a god, that knowen al,
> Thanne myght ye be as I yow tellen shal:
> This man to yow may falsly ben accused,
> Ther as by right him oughte ben excused. . . .
> And eke, peraunter, for this man ys nyce,
> He myghte doon yt, gessyng no malice,
> But for he useth thynges for to make;
> Hym rekketh noght of what matere he take.
> Or him was boden maken thilke tweye
> Of som persone, and durste yt nat withseye;
> Or him repenteth outrely of this.
> He ne hath nat doon so grevously amys,
> To translaten that olde clerkes writen,
> As thogh that he of malice wolde enditen
> Despit of love, and had himself yt wroght. . . .

This shoolde a ryghtwis lord have in his thoght. . . .
A kyng to kepe his liges in justice;
Withouten doute, that is his office.' *

[*F ll. 342-351, 362-373, 382-383*]

Alceste next lists some of Chaucer's other poems: the
House of Fame, the *Book of the Duchess,* the *Parliament of
Fowls* and "the love of Palamon and Arcite." Thus she proves
to Amor that Chaucer has been a true servant of Love upon a
number of occasions; and she supports for us our belief that
Geoffrey Chaucer was the author of many a hymn for love's
"halydayes"—"balades, roundels, virelayes."

Finally Queen Alceste sets Chaucer's penance in the following words:

'Thow shalt, while that thou lyvest, yer by yere,
The moste partye of thy tyme spende
In makyng of a glorious legende
Of goode wymmen, maydenes and wyves,
That weren trewe in lovyng al hire lyves;
And telle of false men that hem bytraien,
That al hir lyf ne do nat but assayen
How many women they may doon a shame;
For in youre world that is now holde a game.
And thogh the lyke nat a lovere bee,
Speke wel of love; this penaunce yive I thee.'

[*F ll. 481-491*]

The poet—or Narrator—gratefully accepts Alceste's behest
and the dream, or "vision," ends with the poet's promise that
he will faithfully follow instructions; he will begin with the
"strong peyne for love" which was Cleopatra's.

---

* Many critics have seen in this speech Joan of Kent—Richard II's mother—
pleading with a frequently unjust son but, to the present writer, the speech
may serve the purpose of a genuine "apology" on Chaucer's part. It is usually
accepted as fact that many of the ladies at court did not approve of the poet's
Troilus and Criseyde, and that Chaucer began the *Legend* at the suggestion—or
request—of Princess Joan.

And with that word my bokes gan I take,
And ryght thus on my Legende gan I make.

[*F ll. 578-579*]

As will be seen from the outline here given of the *Prologue* to the *Legend*, there is ample reason to include it among the love-vision poems. On the other hand, if we consider Alceste's charge to be a poetic and complimentary paraphrase of Princess Joan's request that the compensatory *Legend* be undertaken, we must add that the *Prologue* is also personal apologia and, as such, requires a few deviations from the conventional love-vision pattern. But, in any case, the *Legend* is strongly marked as springing from environmental influences.

There may be more than one answer as to why Chaucer did not complete the *Legend of Good Women,* but perhaps the most obvious one is that the poet had reached full artistic maturity by the late 1380's: he was able to look upon his *Troilus and Criseyde* and to find it good—very good; and his vital, naturalistic *Canterbury Tales* was well under way. Is it not safe to assume that the *Legend* was, therefore, not temporarily set aside, but literally abandoned as being monotonous and lifeless when compared to the greater works?

PART IV
Troilus and Criseyde

CHAUCER's *Troilus and Criseyde* is recognized generally as a great work: Professor Robinson speaks of the work as Chaucer's supreme example of sustained narration"; in *Geoffrey Chaucer*, John Livingston Lowes entitles his chapter on the *Troilus* "The Mastered Art"; in *The Poet Chaucer*, Professor Nevill Coghill—some sixteen years after the publication of Lowes' book—entitles his *Troilus* chapter "High Seriousness." The chapter headings are significant for the purposes of this book. Chaucer was fully mature as an artist when he undertook his *Troilus,* and the rich environmental background which had formed that maturity continued to play a large part in the creation of this extraordinarily polished and unified composition. In the *Troilus* the poet handles his material with such depth and insight that we readily accept his own description of the work as a "tragedye." We even experience the catharsis of "pity and terror" and, like Pandarus, we are left momentarily "as stille as stoon" by the catastrophe. Chaucer, taking his plot largely from Boccaccio's *Il Filostrato,* transforms a cynical narrative of courtly love into a thoughtful study of human relationship as psychologically true in fundamentals today as it was in the fourteenth century, or as it could have been more than a thousand years before that. The English poet himself says that his work is "nothyng of newe," and he adds:

> Ye knowe ek that in forme of speche is chaunge
> Withinne a thousand yeer, and wordes tho
> That hadden pris, now wonder nyce and straunge
> Us thinketh hem, and yet thei spake hem so,
> And spedde as wel in love as men now do;
> Ek for to wynnen love in sondry ages,
> In sondry londes, sondry ben usages.
>
> And forthi if it happe in any wyse,
> That here be any lovere in this place
> That herkneth, as the storie wol devise,
> How Troilus com to his lady grace,
> And thenketh, 'so nold I nat love purchace,'
> Or wondreth on his speche or his doynge,
> I noot; but it is me no wonderynge.
> [Book II 22-35]

What, then, are the specific environmental influences acting upon Geoffrey Chaucer the man which combine with his innate genius to produce the *Troilus?* The fourteenth-century concepts of love and the keen interest of the literate in Boethian philosophy play the largest parts in the work—we may almost say to the exclusion of other influences. We shall therefore concentrate here on those two aspects of the environment.

ONE ✠ The Influence of Chaucer's Chivalric World

CONCEPTS OF LOVE had become an inherent part of the larger concept of chivalry by the late Middle Ages, and, as has been said [see Part III, *passim*], "ideal" love possessed a strong reality in the imaginative, tapestried world—a reality as actual as the often-far-from-noble "realities" to be found in the workaday world. Literature especially, lagging as it sometimes does behind life, frequently centered around courtly-love conventions in Chaucer's day. (The stricter among the clergy still maintained that passionate love in marriage had to be equated with "lust." Chaucer, of course, emphatically denies that love in marriage is sinful—in fact, he indicates that it is a virtue by his *Franklin's Tale*.) Hence we may say that Chaucer's selection of a story concerning courtly love is an immediate outgrowth of environment: the taste of the chivalric audience "demanded" such a plot.

The two great tenets of courtly love (tenets which made the system wholly "respectable" in the mind of medieval man) are stressed throughout the *Troilus:* the need for complete se-

crecy in the relationship between the lovers and the absolute
fidelity of the lovers.

Criseyde, in one of her early conversations with Pandarus,
speaks of the disgrace that would come to her if Troilus' love
were suspected by anyone [Book II 459 ff.]; and later Troilus
decides that he can in no way interfere in the exchange of
Antenor for Criseyde, because his dear love would then by
necessity become his "fo":

'And seyn that thorugh thy medlynge is iblowe
Youre bother love, ther it was erst unknowe.'
[*Book IV 167-168*]

Again, as the love affair progresses through the consummation
to the tragic end, both Criseyde and Troilus are always aware
of the imperative need for secrecy. The exigencies of the plot
obviously demand that Pandarus be privy to the whole affair,
for he is the principal mover: Chaucer makes Pandarus far
more than the mere literary device of a *confidant*. Pandarus is
well aware of the need for secrecy in love; he tells his friend
Troilus early in the narrative that no man shall know of the
latter's love and "so we may ben gladed alle thre" [Book I
998 f.].

As the whole plot of the *Troilus* turns on Criseyde's un-
faithfulness, the emphasis on that matter is obvious. From the
medieval point of view, Criseyde's sin is great, and Chaucer,
as her medieval creator, cannot excuse her; but Chaucer, the
"timeless" man of the understanding heart, feels deep pity for
her lack of strength. The poet writes:

Ne me ne list this sely womman chyde
Forther than the storye wol devyse.
Hire name, allas! is punysshed so wide,
That for hire gilt it oughte ynough suffise.
And if I myghte excuse hire any wise,
For she so sory was for hire untrouthe,

Iwis, I wolde excuse hire yet for routhe.
[*Book V 1093-1099*]

Criseyde, as Chaucer portrays her, does suffer; she is wholly aware of her weakness and fights against it. But she is a woman who needs to be loved, and the "chivalrous" Diomede is there while Troilus is far away. We are constrained to echo the poet in saying alas, alas! that Criseyde, with all her beauty and grace and tenderness, surrenders to her need and becomes "slydynge of corage." Perhaps we would also forgive her if we "might."

The ennobling effects of love on a chivalric man—effects many times stressed in the late Middle Ages—are also brought out in the *Troilus*. When Troilus first falls in love with Criseyde, Chaucer says that the young prince

. . . bicom the frendlieste wight,
The gentilest, and ek the mooste fre,
The thriftiest and oon the beste knyght,
That in his tyme was or myghte be.
Dede were his japes and his cruelte,
His heighe port and his manere estraunge,
And ecch of tho gan for a vertu chaunge.
[*Book I 1079-1085*]

Pandarus also remarks that Troilus has been "converted out of wickednesse" by love [Book I 999].

Later in the story, when Fortune is briefly smiling on Criseyde and "this kinges sone of Troie," Troilus is again changed and purified by love. Chaucer tells us that

In suffisaunce, in blisse, and in singynges,
This Troilus gan al his lif to lede.
He spendeth, jousteth, maketh festeynges;
He yeveth frely ofte, and chaungeth wede,
And held aboute hym alwey, out of drede,
A world of folk, as com hym wel of kynde,
The fresshest and the beste he koude fynde;

That swich a vois was of hym and a stevene
Thorughout the world, of honour and largesse,
That it up rong unto the yate of hevene.
[*Book III 1716-1725*]

Troilus also sings very often to Pandarus as follows:

'Love, that of erthe and se hath governaunce,
Love, that his hestes hath in hevenes hye,
Love, that with an holsom alliaunce
Halt peples joyned, as hym lest hem gye,
Love, that knetteth lawe of compaignie,
And couples doth in vertu for to dwelle,
Bynd this acord, that I have told and telle.'
[*Book III 1744-1750*]

But there Troilus is identifying the emotion he feels for his lady with divine love, an instance of not uncommon fourteenth-century hyperbole. (In Boethian philosophy, passionate human love is made a link in the Great Chain of Being [*Boece*, Book II, met. 8], but it is not identified with divine love.)

Criseyde's niece Antigone, when she sings her "Troian song" to Love, expresses a medieval courtly attitude. After praising the god of love, Antigone sings:

And whoso seith that for to love is vice,
Or thraldom, though he feele in it destresse,
He outher is envyous, or right nyce,
Or is unmyght, for his shrewednesse,
To loven; for swich manere folk, I gesse,
Defamen Love, as nothing of him knowe.
Thei speken, but thei benten nevere his bowe!
[*Book II 855-861*]

The folly of scorning love is made as clear as is the ennobling effect of the passion. Early in the narrative, Chaucer gives serious advice to the audience, or reader:

Forthy ensample taketh of this man,
Ye wise, proude, and worthi folkes alle,
To scornen Love, which that so soone kan
The fredom of youre hertes to hym thralle;
For evere it was, and evere it shal byfalle,
That Love is he that alle thing may bynde,
For may no man fordon the lawe of kynde.

That this be soth, hath preved and doth yit,
For this trowe I ye knowen alle or some,
Men reden nat that folk han gretter wit
Than they that han be most with love ynome;
And strengest folk ben therwith overcome,
The worthiest and grettest of degree:
This was, and is, and yet men shal it see.

And trewelich it sit wel to be so.
For alderwisest han therwith ben plesed;
And they that han ben aldermost in wo,
With love han ben comforted moost and esed;
And ofte it hath the cruel herte apesed,
And worthi folk maad worthier of name,
And causeth moost to dreden vice and shame.

Now sith it may nat goodly ben withstonde,
And is a thing so vertuous in kynde,
Refuseth nat to Love for to ben bonde,
Syn, as hymselven liste, he may yow bynde.
The yerde is bet that bowen wole and wynde
Than that that brest; and therfore I yow rede
To folowen hym that so wel kan yow lede.

[*Book I 232-259*]

And Pandarus, in his usual witty and urbane manner, chides
Troilus for having disdained love in the past. Pandarus says:

'But wel is me that evere that I was born,
That thou biset art in so good a place;

For by my trouthe, in love I dorste have sworn
The sholde nevere han tid thus fayr a grace.
And wostow why? For thow were wont to chace
At Love in scorn, and for despit him calle
"Seynt Idyot, lord of thise foles alle."

'How often hastow maad thi nyce japes,
And seyd that Loves servantz everichone
Of nycete ben verray Goddes apes;
And some wolde mucche hire mete allone,
Liggyng abedde, and make hem for to grone;
And som, thow seydest, hadde a blaunche fevere,
And preydest God he sholde nevere kevere. . . .

'Yet seydestow, that for the moore part,
Thise loveres wolden speke in general,
And thoughten that it was a siker art,
For faylyng, for t'assayen overal.
Now may I jape of the, if that I shal;
But natheles, though that I sholde deye,
That thow art non of tho, I dorste saye.

'Now bet thi brest, and sey to God of Love,
"Thy grace, lord, for now I may repente,
If I mysspak, for now myself I love." '
[*Book I 904-917, 925-934*]

Other aspects of chivalry besides courtly love appear in
the *Troilus*. The portraits of Troilus and Diomede, and of
lesser figures in the narrative, are knightly in character. Hector, for example, is said by Pandarus to possess

'. . . alle trouth and alle gentilesse,
Wisdom, honour, fredom, and worthinesse. . . .
Of Ector nedeth it namore for to telle:
In al this world ther nys a bettre knyght
Than he, that is of worthynesse welle. . . .'
[*Book II 160-161, 176-178*]

Pandarus again, in his efforts to persuade Criseyde that Troilus is worthy of love, gives a picture of Troilus' prowess:

> 'For yesterday, whoso hadde with hym ben,
> He myghte han wondred upon Troilus;
> For nevere yet so thikke a swarm of been
> Ne fleigh, as Grekes fro hym gonne fleen,
> And thorugh the feld, in everi wightes eere,
> Ther nas no cry but "Troilus is there!"

> 'Now here, now ther, he hunted hem so faste,
> Ther nas but Grekes blood,—and Troilus.
> Now hym he hurte, and hym al down he caste;
> Ay wher he wente, it was arayed thus:
> He was hir deth, and sheld and lif for us;
> That, as that day, ther dorste non withstonde,
> Whil that he held his blody swerd in honde.'
>
> [*Book II 191-203*]

(We should remember here that Chaucer himself, as a young man, saw military action in France. Is the picture of Troilus in battle drawn from the poet's recollection of some actual fighting "hero"? The lines are not in *Il Filostrato*.) Pandarus continues to eulogize his friend in chivalric terms:

> '. . . the kynges deere sone,
> The goode, wise, worthi, freshe, and free.
> Which alwey for to don wel is his wone,
> The noble Troilus. . . .'
>
> [*Book II 316-319*]

Criseyde herself is described in terms which have "chivalric" coloring. Pandarus, again the spokesman, tells Troilus that Criseyde possesses "good name and wisdom and manere" and "gentilesse"; Pandarus, addressing Troilus, then continues in his praise of Criseyde:

> 'Ne I nevere saugh a more bountevous
> Of hire estat, n'a gladder, ne of speche

A frendlyer, n'a more gracious
For to do wel, ne lasse hadde nede to seche
What for to don; and al this bet to eche,
In honour, to as fer as she may strecche,
A kynges herte semeth by hyrs a wrecche. . . . .

'And also thynk, and therwith glade the,
That sith thy lady vertuous is al,
So foloweth it that there is som pitee
Amonges alle thise other in general. . . .'
[*Book I 883-889, 897-900*]

Troilus, young as he is, has already learned to display
proper knightly modesty—the same "meekness" which Chaucer assigns later to the "verray parfit gentil" Knight of the
Canterbury Tales. For when Troilus returns after an engagement with the Greeks, an engagement in which he has shown
his "heigh prowesse," and the people cry out, " 'Here cometh
oure joye, / And, next his brother, holder up of Troye!' "
Troilus waxes

. . . a litel reed for shame,
Whan he the peple upon hym herde cryen,
That to byhold it was a noble game,
How sobrelich he caste down his yën.
[*Book II 645-648*]

Diomede must also be shown to possess knightly virtues for
Chaucer's Criseyde—even in her "untrouthe"—could not otherwise accept him as her lover. Chaucer describes Diomede as
"hardy, testif, strong, and chivalrous" [Book V 468]; Diomede is as "fressh as braunch in May."

TWO ❖ The Influence of Chaucer's Philosophic World

IN THE *Troilus*, Chaucer is noticeably affected by the London of his times; that is, by the turmoil and confusions of the political background of the England of the late fourteenth century. As a partial result, the smooth simplicity of the plot of *Il Filostrato* is lacking in the English poem. Unrest in environment breeds questioning in many departments of life, and philosophical concepts even slightly and momentarily shaken become matters calling for rethinking and reaffirmations. Chaucer (equating, as he did, "Troy" to medieval London) could not have considered that the inclusion of philosophic problems would be irrelevant to a story of courtly love. On the contrary, such inclusion would lend verisimilitude to the narrative, for the contemporary audience would "expect" Troilus to be absorbed in the questions of predestination and of the place of earthly love in the Great Chain of Being. And, indeed, Troilus does have a great deal to say on the subject of predestination.

As Chaucer depicts him, Troilus is a fourteenth-century

chivalric knight who, in his woe, would learn more surely why
his disasters have come about. "Is there such a thing as Destiny?" he asks himself and proceeds as best he can, in sometimes confused argument, to answer his own question. (The
majority of Chaucer's court audience were probably as "confused" as Troilus about such matters; thus Chaucer, as usual,
is giving us a true-to-life picture in the 126 lines of Troilus'
appropriate discourse.) Troilus at first states firmly that "'al
that comth, comth by necessitee'" [Book IV 958]. But immediately he objects to his own premise for, he maintains,
many clerks deny that any such matter as "of necessity" exists. Whom shall he believe? Is God's foreknowledge that
which makes an event occur, or is the necessity for the occur-
rence that which makes the foreknowledge? Has man no free
choice? But, it is plain to see, Troilus thinks (he is presumably addressing Pandarus, but his long speech has an air of
being spoken to himself alone):

> 'For other thought, nor other dede also,
> Myghte nevere ben, but swich as purveyaunce,
> Which may nat ben deceyved nevere mo,
> Hath feled byforn, without ignoraunce.
> For yf ther myghte ben a variaunce
> To writhen out fro Goddis purveyinge,
> Ther nere no prescience of thyng comynge,
>
> 'But it were rather an opynyoun
> Uncerteyn, and no stedfast forseynge,
> And certes, that were an abusioun,
> That God sholde han no parfit cler wytynge
> More than we men that han doutous wenynge.
> But swich an errour upon God to gesse
> Were fals and foul, and wikked corsednesse.'
>   [*Book IV 981-994*]

Troilus then decides he will no longer endeavor to show how "the ordre of causes stant"; he will attempt only to make his own ideas more clear. But, alas, that Troilus cannot quite succeed in doing, although he does come to a "sensible" conclusion:

'And over al this, yet sey I more herto,
That right as whan I wot ther is a thyng,
Iwys, that thyng moot nedfully be so;
Ek right so, whan I woot a thyng comyng,
So mot it com; and thus the bifallyng
Of thynges that ben wist bifore the tyde
They mowe nat ben eschued on no syde.'
[*Book IV 1072-1078*]

Troilus is also concerned over the machinations of Fortune [see above, p. 90]. The young man complains early in the narrative that "Fortune is my fo" [Book I 837]; whereupon Pandarus, in an effort to comfort his friend, says:

. . . 'Than blamestow Fortune
For thow art wroth; ye, now at erst I see.
Woost thow nat wel that Fortune is comune
To everi manere wight in som degree?
And yet thow hast this comfort, lo, parde,
That, as hire joies moten overgon,
So mote hire sorwes passen everechon,

'For if hire whiel stynte any thyng to torne,
Than cessed she Fortune anon to be.'
[*Book I 841-849*]

(We should remember here that Chaucer had expressed many ideas concerning Fortune in the earlier *House of Fame*.) Chaucer himself—not one of the characters in the story—comments on Fortune in the *Troilus:*

> But O Fortune, executrice of wyrdes,
> O influences of thise hevenes hye!
> So this, that under God ye ben oure hierdes
> Though to us bestes ben the causes wrie.
> [*Book III 617-620*]

The *prohemium* to Book IV also blames Fortune for her beguilement of mankind. Further, the Fall of Troy is laid to the "permutacioun" of Fortune [Book V 1541 ff.].

The influence of the planets in shaping man's fate is also brought out in the *Troilus*, but to a lesser degree than is the influence of Fortune. For example, Pandarus is aware in true medieval fashion that the moon must be in a favorable position if he is to persuade his niece to listen to Troilus' pleas. He "caste" before his visit "and knew in good plit was the moone to doon viage" [Book II 74 f.]. And when, much later, Criseyde must depart for the Greek camp, she cries out that the positions of the stars at her birth have been responsible for the disaster [Book IV 745].

If we join the Middle Ages in weighing earthly love, particularly passionate love, against divine love, we must agree philosophically with Troilus who, after his death on earth, looks down from the "holughnesse of the eighthe spere" upon "this litel spot of erthe" in scorn of man's pursuit of the "blynde lust, the which that may nat laste." Chaucer then tells us to learn from Troilus' life: the love of God far transcends the love of man for woman and the poet admonishes as follows all who have heard the story:

> O yonge, fresshe folkes, he or she,
> In which that love upgroweth with youre age,
> Repeyreth hom fro worldly vanyte,
> And of youre herte up casteth the visage
> To thilke God that after his ymage
> Yow made, and thynketh al nys but a faire
> This world, that passeth soone as floures faire.

And loveth hym, the which that right for love
Upon a crois, oure soules for to beye,
First starf, and roos, and sit in hevene above;
For he nyl falsen no wight, dar I seye,
That wol his herte al holly on hym leye.
And syn he best to love is, and most meke,
What nedeth feynede loves for to seke?
[*Book V 1835-1848*]

Whatever our present ideas may be, we cannot doubt the sincerity of the medieval Chaucer in writing the two stanzas quoted immediately above; nor can we think that the beliefs expressed were not generally held—as "beliefs," at least—in Chaucer's world. The religious and philosophical environment is here paramount.

THREE ✣ Minor Influences

CHAUCER'S INTEREST in the dream lore of his time, prominent in some of the tales of the *Canterbury Tales,* appears more than once in the *Troilus.*

Criseyde has her dream of the eagle, "fethered whit as bon," after the nightingale's love song has put her to sleep [Book II 918 ff.]—a prophetic *somnium* [see above, p. 104] if ever there were one! Troilus sees his own death foreshadowed in his dreams [Book V 316 ff.], although he scoffs outwardly at "swich ordure" (that is, at such rubbish) [Book V 385]; and, after Criseyde's departure for the Greek camp, Troilus has another, and highly disturbing, dream of a wild boar [Book V 1238 ff.], at which Pandarus scoffs, perhaps thereby whistling to keep up his courage (we are reminded of Pertelote in the *Nun's Priest's Tale,* who nobly pretends that Chaunticleer's dream is meaningless). Pandarus declares:

> . . . 'Allas the while
> That I was born! Have I nat seyd er this,
> That dremes many a maner man bigile?

And whi? For folk expounden hem amys.
How darstow seyn that fals thy lady ys,
For any drem? . . .'
    [*Book V 1275-1280*]

But Troilus, more medieval maybe than Pandarus, cannot forget his dream and Cassandra, in 48 lines of dire prophecy, finally confirms the fact that here indeed is another genuine *somnium* [Book V 1457-1533].

A great many of the small details of the *Troilus* are taken from the poet's own immediate social and physical surroundings. For example, Chaucer's charming pictures of domestic scenes are unquestionably from the polite world of the late fourteenth century. When Pandarus arrives at Criseyde's house at the beginning of the story, he finds his niece and two other ladies sitting within a "paved parlour": the three are listening to a maiden who reads the story of the siege of Thebes. Pandarus speaks lightly and affectionately to the ladies and there is the wholly natural give-and-take of delicately matter-of-fact conversation:

So after this, with many wordes glade,
And frendly tales, and with merie chiere,
Of this and that they pleide, and gonnen wade
In many an unkouth glad and dep matere,
As frendes doon whan thei ben mette yfere. . . .
        [*Book II 148-152*]

May we not through that see Geoffrey Chaucer himself calling upon some ladies of his acquaintance?

Criseyde is later spoken of as going down the stairs and into the garden with her three nieces. The garden has railed walks and it is shaded with "blosmy bowes grene" [Book II 813 ff.], obviously an English fourteenth-century garden, far from ancient Troy in both time and space.

As further example, the brief account of the shutting of the city gates gives us a picture of the closing of one of London's gates—perhaps Aldgate, over which Chaucer had his dwelling.

> The warden of the yates gan to calle
> The folk which that withoute the yates were,
> And bad hem dryven in hire bestes alle,
> Or al the nyght they moste bleven there.
>
> [*Book V 1177-1180*]

And when Pandarus and Troilus stand on the walls of Troy, they might truly be standing on the walls of London, watching those who approach the city. Criseyde's "paleis," where every window is shut "as frost" and the doors "spered alle," shows us a poignantly deserted London house. " 'O paleys desolat!' " cries Troilus and adds:

> 'Yet, syn I may no bet, fayn wolde I kisse
> Thy colde dores. . . .'
>
> [*Book V 551-552*]

FOUR ❧ The Influence of Chaucer's World of Literature

THE *Troilus* owes much to Chaucer's earlier devotion to the French rhetoricians; there is also evidence of Italian influence. In general, however, Chaucer is now beginning to make his work distinctly his own, especially in the manner in which he develops the characters of Criseyde and Pandarus.

Criseyde, for example, when she is engaged seriously in her love affair is decorously formal: she has stepped from a French romance, obeying all the rituals of courtly love in her manner, a lady from the illuminations of a medieval manuscript. On the other hand, often when she is talking to her uncle, Criseyde takes on the naturalistic style of that down-to-earth figure. Contrast, for example, Criseyde's despairing promises to Troilus (when she knows that she must leave Troy) with an early light-hearted exchange she has with Pandarus.

Criseyde addresses Troilus:

> 'Myn herte and ek the woful goost therinne
> Byquethe I, with youre spirit to compleyne
> Eternaly, for they shal nevere twynne.

For though in erthe ytwynned be we tweyne,
Yet in the feld of pite, out of peyne,
That highte Elisos, shal we been yfeere,
As Orpheus with Erudice, his fere.'
                    [*Book IV 785-791*]

(The stately nature of the speech should be noted, as well as the rhetorical ornamentation of the allusion to the story of Orpheus and Eurydice.)

Now Pandarus speaks to Criseyde:

'Do wey youre book, rys up, and lat us daunce,
And lat us don to May som observaunce.'

'I? God forbede!' quod she, 'be ye mad?
Is that a widewes lif, so God yow save?
By God, ye maken me ryght soore adrad!
Ye ben so wylde, it semeth as ye rave.
It sate me wel bet ay in a cave
To bidde and rede on holy seyntes lyves;
Lat maydens gon to daunce, and yonge wyves.'
                    [*Book II 111-119*]

(Here is the quick informality of everyday speech: indeed, we might suppose that Pandarus, instead of Criseyde, were talking.) The contrasting pictures of Criseyde do not disturb us, however, for the very differences serve as a blending force to help make the *Troilus* a unified whole.

Pandarus as a character is abrupt, witty, ever ready to manage the lives of his friend and his niece—always naturalistic in style. He is not troubled by the dichotomy of the medieval world, for he is consistently the pragmatist and a firm believer in the end justifying the means. Yet he has the welfare of both Troilus and Criseyde truly at heart, and he is overwhelmed by the disaster of Criseyde's "untrouthe": his sudden and complete silence is deeply moving. Stylistically,

Pandarus belongs to the *Canterbury Tales,* yet he is curiously not out of place in the *Troilus.*

Troilus himself stays wholly in the style of the literary world of courtly romance. (Once more it must be emphasized that to the medieval mind the ideal had strong "reality"; Troilus at first glance may seem to the modern reader to be stereotyped, and hence, lifeless, but for Chaucer's contemporaries Troilus must have had a genuine vitality.) Even in conversations with Pandarus, Troilus never steps out of the literary setting in which Chaucer placed him; in fact, in one respect, Troilus' rhetorical style effects that of Pandarus.

Fourteenth-century French rhetoricians recommended long, uninterrupted speeches in literary compositions, and there are many such formal discourses in the *Troilus.* Troilus gives us the most notable examples of those, and his own "orations" fittingly call forth equally long speeches from the person he addresses. Thus Pandarus stylistically diverges from his "natural" brief speech upon occasion. Most of the long speeches occur in Books III, IV and V of the *Troilus:* roughly, Troilus, Criseyde and Pandarus share in more than 300 lines in Book III; the same three, in more than 650 lines in Book IV; the first two, in more than 200 lines in Book V. It is perhaps in the long speeches—many of them antiphonal in character— that we see in the *Troilus* the plainest evidence of the influence of Chaucer's literary environment.

Selected Glossary

The following abbreviations are used in the Glossary: ME, for Middle English; MnE, for Modern English; CT, for the Canterbury Tales; *Tr, for* Troilus and Criseyde; *HF, for the* House of Fame. *(Line numbering follows the Robinson conventions throughout.)*

ANGLE *is a technical term in astrology. The whole zodiacal circle was divided into twelve equal parts, or "houses." Four of the houses were termed "angles." See* CT, *II (B¹) 304.*

ANON *means "immediately"—not to be confused with the MnE meaning of "soon," or "after a short time."*

AP(P)ALLEN *means "to make pale"—not to be confused with the MnE meaning of "to dismay."*

APPROWERS *means "agents," or "those who look after the interests of someone." See* CT, *III (D) 1343.*

ASCAUNCES *means "as if," or "as though"—not to be confused with MnE askance.*

ATAZIR *is a technical term in astrology meaning "evil influence." See* CT, *II (B¹) 295.*

ATTE NALE *is a phrase meaning "at the ale(-house)." See* CT, *III (D) 1349.*

AVENTURE *usually means "chance," or "accident," although MnE*

*"adventure," or "hazardous risk," will occasionally trans-
late the word. But Chaucer's common phrase* by aventure
(a)s *should always be translated as MnE "by chance
or hap."*

AVYSEN *means "to consider," or "to deliberate"—not to be confused
with MnE* advise *meaning "to give advice to someone."*

BARM CLOOTH *is an apron.*

BETEN *frequently means "to ornament," or "to hammer out" (cf.
MnE " 'beaten' gold") as in* CT, I (A) *979, where the
past participle* ybete *is used; but the word can also have
the MnE meaning of "to beat," or "to scourge" as in* CT,
III (D) *1285, where again the past participle* ybete *is
used.*

BLAUNCH FEVER *literally means "white fever." Young men suffering
from the "fever" of Hereos, or the lover's malady, were
supposed to turn "white," or pale. See* Tr I *925.*

BOOS *means the protuberance, or "boss," on a shield.*

BOY *means a "rascal"—not to be confused with the MnE meaning
of "male child." Cf.* knave.

BOYDEKIN *means a "dagger"—not to be confused with MnE* bodkin
*meaning a small, blunt needle used for drawing tape
through eyelets.*

BOYSTOUS *means "rough," or "rude." See* boy. *And cf. MnE* boisterous.

BROWDYNGE *means "embroidery." But Chaucer's* browded, *the
past participle of* breyden, *besides meaning "embroidered," can also mean MnE* snatched, *or* bestirred!

BRYBEN *means "to steal," or "to rob"—not to be confused with
MnE* to bribe.

BUXOM *means "submissive"—not to be confused with the MnE
meaning of "rosy and plump."*

BY AND BY *means "side by side"—not to be confused with the MnE
meaning of "a future time."*

CANTEL *means a "portion." See* CT, I (A) *3008.*

CAREFUL *means "anxious," or "full of cares"—not to be confused
with the MnE meaning of "exercising watchful attention." Note other words used by Chaucer which end in
"-ful."*

CAS (or CAAS) *usually means "accident," or "chance." See* aventure.
But the word can mean, as in MnE, a "container," as in

CT, *I (A) 2358; or it can mean, also as in MnE, a "situation," as in Tr II 758 in cas if that me leste, which may be translated into MnE as "in the 'case' [or situation] where that pleases me."*

CELLE *may mean a religious house subordinate to a parent abbey, as in CT, I (A) 172; but the word can also mean MnE cell, as in CT, VII (B² 3162) 1972, or even MnE sill as in CT, I (A) 3822.*

CERIOUSLY *means "minutely"—not to be confused with MnE curiously or MnE seriously.*

CHE(E)RE *usually means "appearance," or "behavior," as in CT, I (A) 139 and in Tr I 14; but the word can also mean MnE cheer, as in Tr I 879.*

CHILD *can mean, as in MnE, a "young human being between infancy and youth," but it can also mean a "young man," as in CT, I (A) 3318.*

CLARIOUN *is an instrument like a trumpet.*

COLD *has the meaning of MnE cold, but the word can sometimes mean "disastrous," as in CT, VII (B² 4446) 3256.*

COMPLECCIOUN (or COMPLEXIOUN) *means "temperament," that is, the temperament created by the proportionate mixture of the four "humours" (blood, choler, phlegm and black bile) in the human body.*

COTE ARMURES *or "coat of arms," means either the armorial bearings of a person, or the identifying surcoat, embroidered with such bearings.*

COUNTREFETEN *means "to imitate," but without any derogatory implication.*

CROP *means "top," or "new sprouts"—word not to be confused with the MnE meaning "harvest." We do have, however, the MnE expression: "The sheep 'crop' the grass." (That is, "The sheep bite the 'tops' off the grass.")*

CROWDYNG *means "pushing."*

CRUL *means "curly"—not to be confused with MnE cruel.*

CURAT *means "parish priest," that is, a "priest in charge of a cure of souls." The word is not to be confused with MnE curate, meaning an "assistant clergyman."*

CURE *has three principal meanings: "remedy," as in Tr I 469; "heed," as in HF 464; and "occupation(s)" as in CT, IV (E) 82.*

CURIOUS   *usually means "delicately made," although it can also mean "heedfully."*

CURSEN   *may mean "to curse," as in* Tr *III 896; but it may also mean "to excommunicate," as in* CT, *I* (A) *486.*

CURTEISIE   *sometimes means "compassion," sometimes mere "politeness."*

DAGON   *means a "small piece."*

DAUNGER   *means "imperiousness," or sometimes "disdain." In connection with a description of a lady, the word means "the quality of being difficult to please."*

DEER   *means either "animal," or "animals," instead of the MnE meaning of "one or more of a family of antlered ruminants."*

DEF(F)ENDEN   *means both "to defend" and "to forbid." (The context usually makes clear which interpretation is to be given the word.)*

DISESE   *means "discomfort," or "grief," as a rule, but the word can mean "disease" (that is, an "illness") as in MnE.*

DOOM   *usually means "judgment," or "court sentence."*

DOUTE   *means "fear," as a rule, but occasionally means "doubt."*

DREDFUL   *means "full of fears."*

DRENCHEN   *means "to drown"—not to be confused with MnE to drench.*

DYS   *means "dice"—not to be confused with ME word dees, meaning a "dais."*

EEK (or EKE)   *means "moreover," or "also."*

ELECTION   *when used in connection with astrology, means a "choice of a favorable time."*

ENTRYKEN   *means "to entrap," or "to ensnare."*

FE(E)RE   *has three meanings: "companion," as in* Tr *I 13; "fear," as in* Tr *II 314; and "fire," as in* Tr *III 978.*

FETIS   *means "handsome," or "well made."*

FIRSTE MOEVYNG   *means the* primum mobile *in the Ptolemaic system —that is, the ninth (or outermost) sphere, conceived as diurnally revolving from east to west and carrying the other eight spheres with it.*

FOR-   *as a prefix, is often used as an intensive. For example,* drunken *would mean "intoxicated," but* fordrunken *would mean "excessively intoxicated."*

FOREWARD *usually means "agreement"—not to be confused with MnE forward.*

FORMEL *means "mate"—said only of birds.*

FOYNEN *means "to thrust."*

FRE and **FREDOM** *are words which, when used in connection with courtly behavior, always mean respectively "materially generous" and the "state of being materially generous." Note, for example, CT, I (A) 46 and VII (B² 4104) 2914. But in other contexts* fre(e) *can mean "unrestricted," as in* CT, I (A) 852.

GAYLARD *is an adjective meaning "lively."*

GENTILESSE *usually means all the moral qualities which combine to make perfection in a Christian. Mortal man could only approach, not attain, true gentilesse.*

GERL *can mean a "young female," as in CT, I (A) 3769, but also can mean a "young person of either sex," as in CT, I (A) 664.*

GESTE *means "exploit," or "tale," or "romance." Although MnE* jest *is derived from the same source as ME* geste, *the implication of banter in* jest *is not in* geste.

GIGGYNGE OF SHEELDES *means the fitting of shields with straps. (Note that, in pronunciation, all the g's in* giggynge *are "hard.")*

GIPON *is the name of a sleeveless tunic, made of heavy (but often expensive) material, worn over the coat of mail, extending halfway between knee and thigh, and embroidered with the armorial bearings of the wearer. (The gipon served as identification for the wearer when the visor of his helmet covered his face.)*

GITERNE *is a medieval musical instrument of the lute class, resembling a modern guitar.*

GLADLY *usually means "willingly," as in MnE, but sometimes the word means "habitually," as in CT, V (F) 376 and VII (B² 4414) 3224.*

GOON (vb.) *has a variety of meanings similar to those of MnE to go. But* goon, *as Chaucer uses the word, can also mean "to walk," or "to roam." Cf.* wenden *and* yede(n).

GROYNYNGE *means "murmuring," or "complaining."*

GRYS *is the name of a costly gray fur in Chaucer's day.*

HABERGEON *is the name of the tunic of chain mail worn by the* *knights of Chaucer's day. The habergeon extended about an inch below the gipon, and was the only part of late fourteenth-century armor which was of chain mail. (Plate armor was gradually replacing the chain armor of earlier times.) See* hauberk.

HARLOT means a *"low rascal,"* or *"thief,"* and may be either male or female—not to be confused with MnE harlot.

HARLOTRYE means *"wickedness"* in a general sense.

HAUBERK is a synonym for habergeon.

HAUNT means either *"skill,"* as in CT, I (A) 447; or *"district,"* as in CT, I (A) 252b. The word is not to be confused with MnE haunt, meaning *"to frequent as a specter."*

HELEN means *"to heal,"* but it can also mean *"to hide,"* as in CT, III (D) 950.

HERTE-SPOON means the concave (*"heart-shaped"*) part of the breastbone where the ribs unite.

HONEST means *"worthy,"* or *"respectable,"* or *"fitting for one's place in life"*—not to be confused with MnE honest meaning *"free from fraud."*

HOSTILER means *"innkeeper,"* or, sometimes a (general) servant at an inn—not to be confused with MnE hostler meaning a *"stable groom."*

HUMBLYNGE means a *"low growl,"* or *"murmur"*—not connected with the MnE word humble.

JOLIF can mean *"jolly"* as in MnE, but the word sometimes means *"pretty,"* or *"attractive."* Note particularly Chaucer's Pardoner—CT, I (A) 680—who wears no hood for *"jolitee,"* that is, for the sake of being attractive.

JUWISE means *"justice,"* or *"verdict,"* as in CT, I (A) 1739.

KECHYL means a small *"cake,"* as in CT, III (D) 1746.

KEPEN can mean *"to keep,"* or *"to retain,"* as in MnE; but in Chaucer's day the word frequently meant *"to guard,"* or *"to tend."*

KIND as a noun means *"nature,"* or *"species."* As an adjective the word usually means *"natural,"* but it can also mean *"benign."* Note that in CT, I (A) 647, Chaucer speaks ironically of the Summoner as being *"kinde,"* or benign.

KNAVE means a *"boy,"* or, sometimes, a *"peasant"*—not to be confused with the MnE meaning of *"rascal."* See boy(e).

LAYNERE was a thong, or strap.

LEGENDE   *means the "life of a saint, or martyr."*

LENDES   *literally means "loins"—we might loosely translate the word as "hips."*

LETTEN   *sometimes means "to let," or "to permit," as in MnE; but the word sometimes means "to hinder," or even "to cease."*

LEWED   *nearly always means "ignorant," without further bad connotation, but occasionally, as in CT, IV (E) 2149, the word can have the MnE meaning of "lascivious."*

LUST, or **LEST,** or **LIST**   *mean "pleasure," or "desire," without any bad connotation. Not to be confused with MnE lust. See luxurie.*

LUXURIE   *means "lust" in the modern sense. Not to be confused with MnE luxury. See lust.*

LYSTES   *in connection with a tournament, indicates the arena in which the tournament takes place. Note that the word is plural in form but singular in meaning.*

MANDEMENTZ   *means "summons."*

MAUGREE   *as a preposition means "in spite of." Cf. Modern French malgré.*

MESURE   *can mean "measure," but often means "moderation."*

METEN   *has three possible meanings: "to meet" in the modern sense; "to measure out" (note MnE to mete); and "to dream" (see sweven).*

MULTIPLICATIOUN   *can mean "alchemy," that is, the art of turning base metal into gold, but the word can also have the modern meaning of "multiplication," as in HF 784.*

MUWE   *means a "coop," or a "cage."*

NAILYNGE THE SPERES   *means fastening the heads of the spears to the shafts, as in CT I (A) 2503.*

NAKER   *means a "kettledrum," as in CT, I (A) 2511.*

NALE   *See atte nale.*

NAMELY   *means "especially"—not to be confused with MnE namely.*

NEET   *means "cattle," as in CT, I (A) 597.*

NYCE   *has three meanings, each of which is frequently met: "ignorant"; "foolish"; and "scrupulous."*

PAREMENTZ   *means "rich array," or "rich hangings."*

PAYEN   *as an adjective means "pagan."*

PAYNDEMAYN   *was a fine, white bread, a great delicacy in the Middle Ages.*

PHILOSOPHRE   *has three meanings: a "person versed in practical, or moral, wisdom"; an "alchemist"; and a "person versed in interpretation of the stars," as in CT, II (B¹) 310. (Note Chaucer's well-known pun in CT, I (A) 297-298 made by playing upon the first two meanings.)*

PILEN   *as a verb means "to plunder," or "to rob." But the adjective* piled *can mean "bald," that is, "robbed" of hair.*

POSITIF LAW   *means "man-made law," as opposed to natural law.*

POULES WYNDOWES   *has the literal meaning of windows in St. Paul's Cathedral. In connection with shoes, as in CT, I (A) 3318, the phrase means that the leather is cut in a design resembling the cathedral windows.*

POYNTEL   *was an instrument for writing, resembling a stylus. See CT, III (D) 1742.*

POYNTES   (in connection with Absalom's dress in the Miller's Tale) *indicates lacings finished with tags at the ends.*

PRIK(K)EN   *means "to spur," or "to incite," or "to track a hare."*

PURCHAS   *means "gain," or "acquisition," nearly always with the implication of illegality.*

PURCHASOUR   *usually means a "buyer of real estate," with some connotation of questionable means.*

PURFILED   *means "edged," or "decorated"—usually with fur or gems.*

PYNEN   *has three meanings which are obviously related: "to torture"; "to suffer pain"; and "to pine away."*

QUENE   *has two meanings: "queen" and "concubine" (cf. MnE* quean).

QUENT   *has three meanings: "strange" or "odd"; "elaborate"; and "graceful."*

QUINYBLE   *indicates a musical "part," an octave above the treble, shrill in character. See CT, I (A) 3332.*

RUBIBLE   *was a musical instrument resembling a lute. See CT, I (A) 3331.*

RYS   *means "spray," or "branch." (Nicholas in the* Miller's Tale *has a surplice that is as white as the blossom on the "rys.")*

SAD   *has a number of meanings, but by far the most usual is "serious," or "sober," as in the phrase "a sad visage," meaning "a serious face." The word rarely has the MnE meaning of "downcast."*

SAUTRIE *means a "psaltery," that is, a stringed musical instrument resembling a zither.*

SCIENCE *nearly always means "knowledge" in a general sense—rarely the specialized knowledge relative to the physical world.*

SELY *has three meanings of importance: "happy," or "blessed," as in Tr IV 503; "wretched," or "unlucky," as in CT, I (A) 3896; and "good," or "kind," as in CT, III (D) 730. The word is not to be confused with MnE* silly, *although* silly *derives from* sely.

SENTENCE *has two principal meanings: "meaning" (cf. MnE* sentence, *indicating a "meaningful" arrangement of words); and "sentence," with the MnE meaning of "decree," or "verdict."*

SHAM(E)FAST *can mean "modest," as in CT, VI (C) 55; or "ashamed," as in CT, VII (B² 2236) 1046.*

SHENDEN *has three meanings: "to destroy," as in HF 1016; "to defile," as in Tr III 1459; and "to scold," as in CT, VII (B² 1731) 541.*

SHILDEN *usually means "to shield," but it can mean "to forbid," as in the expression "God shilde that he deyde sodeynly!"*

SHODE *means a "parting of the hair," as in CT, I (A) 3316.*

SHYNKEN *means "to pour out."*

SKILE *means "reason," or "claim"—not to be confused with MnE* skill.

SKYE *means "cloud"—not to be confused with MnE* sky.

SONE *as a noun, means "son"; as an adverb, the word means "soon," or "at once."*

SOUL(E) *as a noun, means "soul"; as an adjective, the word means "sole."*

SPILLEN *can mean "to spill," as in MnE, but the word can also mean "to kill," that is, to "spill" blood.*

STERVEN *usually means simply "to die," not necessarily to die of hunger.*

STIERNE *is a variant of ME* sterne, *meaning "violent," or "stern."*

STIKEN *can mean "to pierce" (with a sword or dagger), but it can also mean "to stick fast," or "to adhere."*

STOOR *means "stock of a farm."*

STROUTEN *means "to spread," or "to fan out"—not to be confused with MnE* strut.

STUWE, or STEWE, or STYVE *has three meanings: a "(private) fish pond," as in CT, I (A) 350; a "small room," as in Tr III 601; and a "brothel," as in CT, III (D) 1332.*

SWEVEN *means "to dream."*

SWYNKEN *means "to labor," or "to toil."*

TABLES *(a plural), means the game of backgammon.*

TERCEL *means a "male eagle."*

TERCELET *means a "male falcon."*

TESTER *is the armored headpiece for either a knight or his horse.*

THEE(N) *means "to thrive." The word is most frequently used in the imprecation, "Also moote I thee!" (meaning "As I may hope to thrive!"). The word must not be confused with the second person singular pronoun* thee.

THERE(E)TO *means "besides," or "moreover."*

THO *as a pronoun, means "those"; as an adverb, the word means "then."*

THRIFT *usually means "prosperity," or "success"; but thriftily means "carefully," or "in workmanlike fashion."*

TO- *as a prefix can have a mere prepositional force, as in* to-forn *(meaning "before"); or an intensive force, as in* to-breken *(meaning "to break utterly").*

TONIGHT *can indicate not only the coming or present night, but the recently past night as well.*

TORTUOUS *when used in connection with astrology, means "like the signs of the Zodiac ascending most obliquely to the horizon."*

TOUN *besides having the MnE meaning of "town," can also mean a "farm," or a "parish."*

TRAPPURES *means the ornamental coverings of a horse (as, for one example, a saddlecloth).*

TRIACLE *means a "sovereign remedy."*

TROUTHE *nearly always means "keeping one's word." Cf. MnE* troth.

TRIPPEN *means "to dance."*

TRYPE *means a "small piece," or "morsel."*

UNKOUTH *literally means "unknown," hence "strange," or "alien" —not to be confused with MnE* uncouth *meaning "boorish."*

UPRYGHT *nearly always means "lying on the back" (cf. "right-side-*

SELECTED GLOSSARY
up")—*not to be confused with* MnE upright *meaning* "morally correct."

VERTU *nearly always means* "power," *or* "efficacy," *but it can occasionally mean* "moral practice," *as in* CT, IV (E) 216.

VIRELAY *is the term for a ballade with a return of rhyme, usually two rhymes. It is a French verse form of the Middle Ages.*

VOLUPER *is the term for a medieval form of head covering, or cap.*

WAGET *means a* "light blue." *In the* Miller's Tale, Absalom *wears a tunic of* "a light waget."

WANTOWN *can mean the MnE meaning of* "wanton," *although the word can also mean* "sportive," *without derogatory connotation.*

WENDEN *means* "to go," *or* "to wend one's way," *or* "to depart." *See* goon *and* yede.

WEYVEN *means* "to turn aside," *or* "to put aside"—*not to be confused with MnE* weave, *but note the connection with MnE* waive.

WIS (YWIS), *and* WISLY *mean* "certainly." *Not to be confused with ME* "wys." *See* wys.

WOOD *means* "mad," *or* "insane," *although sometimes the word can mean* "enraged."

WORTHY *means* "having rank," *or* "having worth," *except when used in the description of a knight. In that case, the word should be understood to mean* "brave."

WYS *may have the meaning of MnE* wise, *but if coupled with* "worthy," "wys" *means* "prudent," *and if coupled with* "war," "wys" *means* "over-shrewd."

YBET *is a past participle. See* beten.

YEDE *means* "went," *or* "walked." *See* goon *and* wenden.

YMAGINATYF *can mean* "imaginative," *but it can also mean* "suspicious," *as in* CT, V (F) 1094.

Selected Bibliography

BIBLIOGRAPHY:
"Annual Bibliography." Published by *PMLA*.
Griffith, D. D. *Bibliography of Chaucer, 1908-1953*. Seattle, 1955.

EDITIONS:
The Works of Geoffrey Chaucer. Ed. F. N. Robinson. 2nd edition. Boston, 1957.
The Complete Works of Geoffrey Chaucer. Ed. W. W. Skeat, 7 vols. Oxford, 1894-1897.
Canterbury Tales by Geoffrey Chaucer. Ed. J. M. Manly. New York, 1928.
The Book of Troilus and Criseyde by Geoffrey Chaucer. Ed. R. K. Root. Princeton, 1926.
The Parlement of Foulys. Ed. D. S. Brewer. London, 1960.

SOURCES AND REFERENCES:
Bryan, W. F. and Germaine Dempster, eds. *Sources and Analogues of Chaucer's Canterbury Tales*. Chicago, 1940.
Cummings, H. M. *The Indebtedness of Chaucer's Works to the Italian Works of Boccaccio*. Menasha, 1916.
Fansler, D. S. *Chaucer and the Roman de la Rose*. New York, 1914.

Fletcher, J. B. *Chaucer and the Consolation of Philosophy of Boethius*. Princeton, 1917.
Shannon, E. F. *Chaucer and the Roman Poets*. Cambridge, Mass., 1929.
Tatlock, J. S. P. and A. G. Kennedy. *Concordance to the Complete Works of Geoffrey Chaucer and to the Romaunt of the Rose.* Washington, 1927.

CRITICISM:
Bennett, J. A. W. *The Parlement of Foules: An Interpretation*. Oxford, 1957.
Bowden, Muriel. *A Commentary on the General Prologue to the Canterbury Tales.* New York, 1948.
Coghill, Nevill. *The Poet Chaucer*. Oxford, 1949.
Curry, W. C. *Chaucer and the Mediaeval Sciences*. 2nd edition. New York, 1960.
French, R. D. *A Chaucer Handbook*. 2nd edition. New York, 1947.
Kittredge, G. L. *Chaucer and His Poetry*. Cambridge, Mass., 1915.
Lawrence, W. W. *Chaucer and the Canterbury Tales*. New York, 1950.
Lowes, J. L. *Geoffrey Chaucer and the Development of His Genius*. Boston, 1934.
Lumiansky, R. M. *Of Sundry Folk: The Dramatic Principle in the Canterbury Tales*. Austin, 1955.
Malone, Kemp. *Chapters on Chaucer*. Baltimore, 1951.
Manly, J. M. *Some New Light on Chaucer*. New York, 1926.
Muscatine, Charles. *Chaucer and the French Tradition: A Study in Style and Meaning*. Berkeley and Los Angeles, 1957.
Patch, Howard Rollin. *On Rereading Chaucer*. Cambridge, Mass., 1939.
Root, R. K. *The Poetry of Chaucer*. 2nd edition. Boston, 1922.
Tatlock, J. S. P. *The Mind and Art of Chaucer*. Syracuse, N.Y., 1950.

SOCIAL BACKGROUNDS:
Bennett, H. S. *Life on the English Manor*. Cambridge, 1948.
Chaucer's World. Compiled by Edith Rickert. Ed. Clair C. Olsen and Martin M. Crow. New York, 1948.
Coulton, G. G. *Chaucer and His England*. 6th edition. London, 1937.
———. *Life in the Middle Ages*. 4 vols. Cambridge, 1928.

————. *Medieval Panorama.* Cambridge, 1939.

Huizinga, Johan. *The Waning of the Middle Ages.* Trans. F. Hopman. London, 1924.

Lewis, C. S. *The Allegory of Love.* London, 1951.

McKisack, May. *The Fourteenth Century, 1307-1399.* Oxford, 1959.

Owst, G. R. *Literature and Pulpit in Medieval England.* 2nd edition. Oxford, 1961.

Power, Eileen. *Mediaeval People.* London, 1924.

————. *Medieval English Nunneries, c. 1275 to 1535.* Cambridge, 1922.

Trevelyan, G. M. *England in the Age of Wycliffe.* 4th edition. London, 1909.

Unwin, George. *The Gilds and Companies of London.* London, 1938.

Workman, Herbert B. *John Wyclif.* 2 vols. Oxford, 1926.

INDEX

By title of works referred to in the text

(*Particular Tales and the* General Prologue *of the* Canterbury Tales *are listed separately.*)

ŒUVRES DE LOUIS MALLE

Aux Éditions Gallimard
LE SOUFFLE AU CŒUR
AU REVOIR, LES ENFANTS

En collaboration avec Patrick Modiano
LACOMBE LUCIEN

En collaboration avec Jean-Claude Carrière
MILOU EN MAI

AU REVOIR, LES ENFANTS

LOUIS MALLE

AU REVOIR, LES ENFANTS

scénario

GALLIMARD

1.

Gare de Lyon, 3 janvier 1944.
Une femme de quarante ans et un garçon de douze
ans se tiennent devant un wagon en bois, de ceux qui
avaient une porte par compartiment. Ils se font face,
immobiles dans le flot des voyageurs.
Il est habillé de culottes courtes, d'un chandail bleu
marine et d'une cape noire.
Elle porte un chapeau compliqué et une fourrure de
la guerre qui lui arrive aux genoux. On voit qu'elle se
maquille trop vite : une joue est plus rose que l'autre, le
rouge déborde de ses lèvres.

LA MÈRE : Julien, tu m'as promis.

JULIEN *(tête baissée)* : Je ne pleure
pas. Pas du tout même.

LA MÈRE : Je viendrai vous voir dans
trois semaines.
Et puis vous allez sortir pour le
Mardi-Gras.
Tu verras, ça va passer très vite.

Julien relève la tête. Ses yeux brillent.

> JULIEN : Pourquoi dites-vous ça ?
> Vous savez très bien que ça ne va pas
> passer vite.

> LA MÈRE : Ton père et moi nous t'écri-
> rons souvent.

> JULIEN · Papa, je m'en fous. Vous, je
> vous déteste.

I don't care

Derrière eux, deux garçons escaladent la portière
avec leurs sacs à dos.

> LES GARÇONS : Salut, Quentin... Mes
> hommages, madame...

> LA MÈRE : Bonjour, bonjour...
> Tu es quand même content de retrou-
> ver tes camarades.

> JULIEN : Ah oui, Sagard ! Quel crétin
> celui-là. Je ne peux pas le sentir.

idiot

Elle rit. Il se jette contre elle et l'étreint, éperdument.
On entend un sifflement, des appels. Le contrôleur
agite son drapeau.
Un garçon de seize ans les rejoint.

madly

10

LE GARÇON : Encore en train de vous faire des mamours.
Mon petit Julien, tu ne veux surtout pas manquer le train, un bon élève comme toi.

Il fume une dernière bouffée et jette son mégot.

LA MÈRE : François, je te défends de fumer.

le frère de Julien

FRANÇOIS : C'est pas du tabac, c'est de la barbe de maïs. Ça ne compte pas... Au revoir, maman. Soyez sage.

Il embrasse sa mère et rejoint un copain qui l'attendait.

Kneels down

La mère s'agenouille devant Julien et lui donne un baiser sur la joue.
Le rouge laisse une trace ovale bien nette.

LA MÈRE : Allez, monte.

Elle l'entraîne vers la porte du compartiment, mais il se retourne et se serre contre elle, le plus fort qu'il peut, les bras autour de son cou, le nez dans son corsage.
Elle chuchote, en lui caressant la nuque :

LA MÈRE : Et moi ? Tu ne penses pas à moi ? Tu crois que c'est drôle ? Tu me

11

manques à chaque instant. J'aimerais me déguiser en garçon et te suivre dans ton collège. Je te verrais tous les jours. Ce serait notre secret...

La voix de la mère est couverte par le sifflement d'un train en marche.

2.

La vitre du train est givrée. Une fumée noire de charbon dilue l'image par moment. On entend peiner la locomotive. Julien regarde le paysage d'hiver qui défile. Derrière lui, trois garçons de son âge se battent, grimpent sur les sièges, se suspendent aux porte-bagages comme des singes.

Julien, dans la vitre, voit la trace de rouge sur sa joue. Il l'efface, machinalement, du revers de la main. Il y a de la douceur maintenant dans son expression. Il pleure.

3.

Le vieux quartier d'une petite ville d'Île-de-France. Une quarantaine de garçons remontent la rue en désordre, chantant une chanson scoute. Ils sont tous habillés comme Julien. Les sacs à dos bourrés font une bosse sous leurs capes. Les semelles de bois de leurs bottines claquent sur le sol. Deux soldats allemands désœuvrés s'arrêtent pour les regarder passer. Un jeune moine en bure marron, rondouillard et sympathique, marche et chante avec eux. Le Père Michel, que les élèves appellent entre eux « la mère Michel », a les pieds nus dans des sandales.

> LE PÈRE MICHEL : Bonjour Julien. Vous avez passé de bonnes vacances ?

> JULIEN *(renfrogné)* : Oui. mon Père.

> LE PÈRE MICHEL : Vos parents vont bien ?

> JULIEN : Oui. mon Père.

Le garçon à côté de Julien. Babinot, zézaie :

> BABINOT : Qu'est-ce qu'ils t'ont donné pour Noël ?

13

JULIEN : Des bouquins.

BABINOT : Seulement des bouquins ?

JULIEN : Oui.

BABINOT : Les vaches.

Ils rentrent dans un portail grand ouvert sur une cour.
On lit sur une plaque : « Couvent des Carmes. Petit Collège Saint-Jean-de-la-Croix ».

4.

Le dortoir des petits était autrefois une chapelle. Chaque élève a un casier dans les placards le long des murs, où ils rangent leurs affaires. Il y a une trentaine de lits. Dans un angle se trouve une boîte en bois, où couche Moreau, un jeune surveillant sans autorité. Les élèves se moquent de lui, mais le trouvent « sympa ».
Julien, en pyjama, sort de son sac des confitures et un kilo de sucre. Il va les mettre dans son casier quand Ciron, un grand échalas, s'empare d'un pot de confitures.

CIRON *(prenant un accent allemand)* :
Ach. Marché noir, monsieur Quentin.

14

Che vous arrête. Vos confitures, che les
confisque

Julien le poursuit, le jette sur un lit et reprend son
bien.

Il passe devant quelques garçons — dont deux
jumeaux — qui se tiennent autour d'un gros poêle à
bois, le seul chauffage du dortoir. Ils regardent une
photo en chuchotant.

Julien prend la photo et y jette un coup d'œil.

JULIEN : Elle a même pas de nichons.

UNE VOIX *(près de la porte)* : Gaffe !
Babasses !

« Babasses », dans l'argot du collège, désigne les
moines.

Le Père Jean, directeur du collège, un homme de
quarante ans au visage ascétique, et le Père Hippolyte
entrent dans le dortoir avec trois garçons qui n'ont pas
l'uniforme du collège. Le plus jeune porte un manteau
beige trop petit pour lui. Le Père Jean le conduit
jusqu'au lit à côté de Julien.

Chaque élève y va de son « Bonjour, mon Père »
respectueux.

LE PÈRE JEAN : Ce lit est libre ?

MOREAU : Oui, mon Père. Depuis que
d'Éparville a eu la coqueluche.

15

LE PÈRE JEAN : Mettez-vous là, mon petit.

Mes enfants, je vous présente Jean Bonnet, votre nouveau camarade.

Dans un geste surprenant, il baise le front de Bonnet.

LE PÈRE JEAN : Monsieur Moreau, vous lui trouverez un casier.

Bonsoir, les enfants.

LES ÉLÈVES : Bonsoir, mon Père.

A la porte, le Père Jean rejoint les deux nouveaux plus âgés et le Père Hippolyte. Dès qu'ils sont sortis, Bonnet reçoit un oreiller en pleine figure, suivi de plusieurs autres. En même temps fusent les fines plaisanteries : « Bonnet de nuit, Bonnet d'âne... »

MOREAU : Fichez-lui la paix et déshabillez-vous.

Il montre un casier vide à Bonnet.

Les élèves enfilent pyjamas ou chemises de nuit. Bonnet défait son sac. Il en sort plusieurs livres qu'il pose sur son lit. Se retournant, il voit Julien qui l'observe.

BONNET : Comment tu t'appelles ?

16

Julien ne répond pas. Il prend un des livres de Bonnet.

> JULIEN *(lisant)* : « Les Aventures de Sherlock Holmes. » *(Il prononce Holmesse.)*

La lumière s'éteint brusquement. Cris, rires.

> MOREAU : C'est juste une coupure. Mettez-vous au lit.

Julien et plusieurs élèves ont des lampes de poche. Un garçon applique sa lampe sous son visage qui semble éclairé de l'intérieur. Il saute sur place et pousse des cris rauques.
Julien s'avance très près du visage de Bonnet.

> JULIEN : Je m'appelle Julien Quentin et si on me cherche on me trouve.

the responsibility for friendship is Jean's

Tout le monde se couche. Bonnet, encore habillé, regarde la grande statue de la Vierge contre le mur en face de lui.
Julien prend un livre sur la table de nuit, s'enfonce sous les draps et, s'éclairant avec sa lampe de poche, cherche sa page.

17

5.

Le matin. Les élèves font semblant de se laver. Ils se mouillent à peine les cheveux, s'ébrouent, dansent d'un pied sur l'autre.

Bonnet constate que du robinet de son lavabo, situé contre la fenêtre, pend une stalactite d'eau gelée. Il la casse et la pose délicatement sur le rebord.

Il ouvre le robinet du lavabo d'à côté. Rien ne sort pendant quelques secondes, puis un jet d'eau glacée l'éclabousse. Il saute en arrière, pousse un cri.

BONNET : Y a pas d'eau chaude ?

BOULANGER : Non, y a pas d'eau chaude.
On n'est pas des mauviettes.

Boulanger, un garçon très corpulent, prend la stalactite et la lui glisse dans le col de la chemise.

6.

Tous les élèves du collège sont debout dans les travées de la chapelle, écoutant le Père Jean qui lit l'Évangile, à l'autel, en robe d'officiant. Quelques moines se tiennent dans des stalles en bois.

Boulanger semble mal à l'aise. Il oscille, comme pris de vertige. Il porte sa main à son visage, plusieurs fois.

> VOIX DU PÈRE JEAN : En vérité, en vérité, je vous le dis, si vous ne mangez la chair du Fils de l'homme et ne buvez son sang, vous n'aurez pas de vie en vous.

Brusquement, Boulanger vacille et tombe en arrière, évanoui, une chute spectaculaire.

Moreau se précipite et, avec l'aide d'un jeune moine, le relève et l'entraîne hors de la chapelle.

Ils passent devant Bonnet assis au dernier rang avec un grand aux cheveux frisés et un rouquin. Les trois nouveaux.

François, assis à côté de Julien, commente :

> FRANÇOIS : On n'a rien à bouffer, on crève de froid, mais il faut être à jeun pour communier. Quelle boîte...

19

JULIEN : Tu vas communier ?

FRANÇOIS : Je suis pas un lèche-cul comme toi.

Le Père Jean a repris, comme si cet incident était une routine.

LE PÈRE JEAN : Qui mange ma chair et boit mon sang a la vie éternelle et je le ressusciterai au dernier jour. Car ma chair est vraiment une nourriture et mon sang vraiment une boisson. Qui mange ma chair et boit mon sang demeure en moi et moi en lui.

Un claquement de mains. Les élèves s'agenouillent et entonnent le chant d'offertoire.
Julien oscille d'un genou sur l'autre, le visage douloureux.

FRANÇOIS : Qu'est-ce que tu as ?

JULIEN : Des engelures, au genou.
frostbite

FRANÇOIS *(péremptoire)* : Il faut boire du calvados.
apple brandy

20

7

La classe de quatrième. Les élèves sont une quin-
zaine. Plusieurs, dont Julien, portent des gants de laine,
qu'ils garderont pour écrire. M. Tinchaut marche de
long en large, son manteau sur les épaules. Julien,
debout à sa place, lit, vite et très mal.

> JULIEN : « Étoile de la mer, Voici la
> lourde nappe *sheet (of water)*
> « Et la profonde houle et l'océan des blés
> « Et la mouvante écume et nos greniers *swell*
> comblés, *unstable foam*
> « Voici votre regard sur cette immense
> chape
> « Et voici votre voix sur cette lourde
> plaine
> « Et nos amis absents et nos cœurs
> dépeuplés
> « Voici le long de nous nos poings désas-
> semblés
> « Et notre lassitude et notre force pleine.
> « Étoile du matin, inaccessible reine... »

> M. TINCHAUT : Quentin, vous êtes mûr
> pour la Comédie-Française. Vous pou-
> vez nous rappeler qui était Charles
> Péguy ?

JULIEN : Il a été tué à la guerre de 14.

M. TINCHAUT : Bien. Mais vous commencez par la fin.

JULIEN : Sa mère était rempailleuse. *chair mender*
(Quelques rires.)

M. TINCHAUT : Ne riez pas bêtement. La mère de Péguy était une femme très méritante.

Il va vers Bonnet.

M. TINCHAUT : Monsieur Bonnot, vous savez quelque chose sur Charles Péguy ?

BONNET : Non, monsieur. Et je m'appelle Bonnet.

BABINOT : Comme Dubo, Dubon, Dubonnet.

Tous les autres reprennent en chœur.

M. TINCHAUT : Très spirituel, Babinot. Pour vous remettre dans le bain après les vacances, vous allez commenter les deux premières strophes du poème. Vous avez une demi-heure.

Les élèves se mettent au travail. Julien écrit quelques lignes, puis s'arrête. Tête levée, il rêve un moment. Son regard se porte sur Bonnet.

Celui-ci écrit rapidement, très concentré. Il porte sa main gauche à son oreille, plusieurs fois.

On entend une voix dehors. Bonnet lève les yeux brusquement. Julien suit son regard.

Dans la cour, un très jeune soldat allemand, tête nue, est en train de parler à un moine.

Bonnet se remet à écrire.

Julien prend son compas. Il pique le dos de sa main avec la pointe, plusieurs fois, jusqu'à ce qu'il saigne.

> BOULANGER *(son voisin)* : T'es fou.
>
> JULIEN : Ça ne fait même pas mal.

Bonnet le regarde.

8.

Grands et petits sont en récréation dans la cour du collège. Plusieurs élèves battent la semelle contre le mur en conversant. D'autres font de la barre fixe sous la direction du professeur de gymnastique.

Au milieu de la cour, une vingtaine d'élèves de tous

âges, montés sur des échasses, essaient de se faire tomber les uns les autres. En principe il y a deux camps, mais le jeu se réduit à une série de combats individuels. C'est très brutal, les chutes sont douloureuses sur le sol gelé. Le Père Michel joue avec les élèves, essayant de mettre de l'ordre, mais il vacille sur ses échasses, et Julien le fait tomber. *wavers*

> LE PÈRE MICHEL : Du calme, Quentin, du calme.

A l'abri d'un tas de bois, François et un autre grand, Pessoz, se partagent une cigarette.
Bonnet lit, une épaule appuyée *dropped* au mur. Cinq élèves de quatrième arrivent derrière lui et l'empoignent. *sieze* Deux le prennent aux jambes, deux aux bras, et le cinquième lui appuyant sur le ventre, ils lui infligent un tape-cul, rituel de bizutage. Bonnet se tortille comme un ver de terre.
Julien tourne rapidement autour d'un adversaire, feinte, charge, crochète les échasses de l'autre. Celui-ci s'écroule.
Julien, poussant des cris de triomphe, lève une échasse en l'air et sautille sur une seule jambe.

> JULIEN : Notre-Dame ! Montjoie ! Je suis Bayard, le Chevalier sans peur et sans reproche.

24

UN GRAND : Alors, le petit Quentin, on joue les terreurs ?

Il le charge et lui donne un violent coup d'épaule. Julien, sur une seule échasse, perd l'équilibre et fait une mauvaise chute.
Il reste à terre, tenant son genou égratigné.
Le visage crispé, il se retient de pleurer.

JULIEN : Salaud, Laviron.

Un garçon défie Laviron. Quatorze ans, cheveux noirs crépus, costaud, on l'avait vu aux côtés de Bonnet à la messe.

LE GARÇON : A moi, lâche, traître, félon. C'est moi Négus, le Chevalier noir, protecteur des faibles et des orphelins.

Quelques cris fusent : « Allez Négus », « Allez Laviron ».
Un cercle se forme et le combat devient une parodie de joute médiévale

LAVIRON : Arrière, moricaud. Je suis Richard Cœur de Lion, l'orgueil de la chrétienté. Je vais te bouter hors de Jérusalem. Sarazin infidèle, fils de chienne.

Négus (*prenant un accent arabe de caricature*) : Allah est Dieu et Mahomet est son prophète.
Tu trembles, monzami. Cœur de Lion, tête de lard, cul de poule, peau de vache...

Il tourne autour de Laviron, puis le charge, en hurlant.

Négus : Allah, Allah, Allah, Allah...

La faconde de Négus amuse la galerie, qui partage ses encouragements entre les deux combattants.
Julien s'est relevé. Bonnet est derrière lui.

Bonnet : Allez, Négus !

Julien : C'est son vrai nom, Négus ?

Bonnet : Qu'est-ce que tu crois ?

Julien (*agacé*) : Il a une sale gueule. Tu le connais ?

Bonnet : Il s'appelle Lafarge, et c'est mon meilleur ami.

Négus, moins solide sur ses échasses, se fait crocheter et tombe. Il se redresse aussitôt, tenant une échasse devant lui comme une lance.
Le Père Michel siffle la fin de la récréation. Les élèves se dispersent à regret.

LE PÈRE MICHEL : Babinot, dépêchez-
vous.

9.

Julien est assis sur la grande table de la cuisine.
Mme Perrin, une grosse dame très maternelle, toujours
entre deux vins, lui lave le genou et met du vinaigre sur
la plaie.
Julien pousse un hurlement.

> MME PERRIN *(elle a un accent du
> Nord)* · Ça ne fait pas mal du tout.
> Tiens-toi tranquille, que j' te mette un
> sparadrap. Vous allez vous tuer avec ces
> echasses. C'est des jeux de sauvages. Un
> de ces jours il va y avoir une jambe de
> cassée...

Julien ne l'écoute pas. Il regarde Joseph, le garçon de
cuisine, engagé dans une tractation à voix basse avec
l'un des grands.
Celui-ci lui remet une boîte de bonbons, lui arrache
un billet de banque des mains et part en courant.
Joseph lui court après en claudiquant.

27

JOSEPH : Hé, pas tout ! On avait dit quarante-cinq.

MME PERRIN : Joseph, qu'est-ce que tu manigances encore ? Retourne aux patates.

Joseph revient dans la pièce, mettant la boîte dans son tablier.

JOSEPH : Plus ils sont riches, plus ils sont voleurs.

Joseph a dix-sept ans, il est malingre, avec une jambe plus courte que l'autre. Des allures et un vocabulaire de titi parisien, effronté, beaucoup de bagout. Il sifflote constamment.
Il reprend sa place à l'épluchage.
La cuisinière se sert un grand verre de rouge.

JOSEPH : Vous buvez trop, madame Perrin.

MME PERRIN : Tais-toi, morveux. Y a pas de mal à se faire du bien.

Julien s'approche de Joseph et chuchote :

JULIEN : T'as des timbres ?

28

JOSEPH : J' fais plus d'affaires avec vous autres.

JULIEN : J'ai de la confiture.

Joseph jette un regard à Mme Perrin.

JOSEPH : Après le déjeuner. La femme du docteur, elle raffole de ta confiote. Ça lui cale les ovaires. Tu vois ce que je veux dire ?

10.

Le réfectoire. Six tables d'élèves sont alignées sur deux rangs. Moines, professeurs et surveillants mangent à une très longue table le long du mur.

Julien est assis avec des élèves de sa classe, près de la cuisine. Bonnet est en bout de table. Un plat de viande passe de mains en mains.

SAGARD : Y a de la paille dans le pain maintenant. Je vais écrire à mon père.

BOULANGER : Envoyez-moi le panier.

Il y a un panier au bout de chaque table qui contient les provisions personnelles des élèves. Boulanger y prend une grosse boîte en fer-blanc, sur laquelle son nom est écrit en gros caractères. Elle contient du beurre et des rillettes.

Le Père Jean, qui mange de bon appétit. lève les yeux. Il agite la sonnette.

> LE PÈRE JEAN : Je rappelle à ceux qui ont des provisions personnelles qu'ils doivent les partager avec leurs camarades.

> BABINOT *(zézayant)* : J'ai des sardines, mais j'ai pas de clés. Personne a une clé ?

> ROLLIN : Qui veut du saucisson ? C'est du cheval. je vous préviens.

Boulanger finit d'étaler des rillettes sur son pain, referme le pot et le remet dans le panier.

> BOULANGER : Il faut que je mange. Je fais de l'anémie.

> CIRON : Et nous alors ? T'as entendu le Père Jean ?

> BOULANGER *(la bouche pleine)* : Y en a pas assez pour tout le monde. Ils n'ont qu'à vous nourrir, vos parents.

Le plat de viande parvient à Navarre, qui est à côté de Bonnet.

NAVARRE : Y a plus qu'une tranche.

BONNET : Sers-toi.

NAVARRE : Merci. T'es chic.

La sonnette retentit. Un élève vient se placer au milieu du réfectoire et lit, dans un silence relatif :

> L'ÉLÈVE : Aujourd'hui, saint Siméon Stylite.
> « Saint Siméon Stylite avait treize ans et gardait les moutons de son père quand il entendit ce verset de l'Évangile : " Malheur à vous qui riez à présent car le jour viendra où vous pleurerez. " Il quitta ses parents, devint ermite, et vécut trente années sur une colonne. *(Rires.)* Il s'y tenait debout, sans abri, absorbé dans une prière quasi continuelle. . »

La lecture se termine dans les rires et le chahut. Julien monte sur son banc et prend une pose de statue. C'est la fin du repas. Les élèves commencent à sortir. Bonnet mange sa pomme, les yeux ailleurs.

> MOREAU *(à la cantonade)* : Biscuits vitaminés. Biscuits vitaminés.

31

Il passe de table en table, une grosse boîte à la main. Chaque élève reçoit un biscuit.

Julien tend une main derrière l'épaule, puis l'autre. Moreau, distrait, lui donne deux biscuits.

Bonnet se fait prendre son biscuit par Sagard, qui le met dans sa bouche, le lèche, puis lui rend.

> SAGARD : Tiens. C'est meilleur maintenant.

Bonnet repousse Sagard et se lève pour quitter la table. Julien lui tend un biscuit.

> JULIEN : J'en ai deux.

> BONNET : Merci. J'ai plus faim.

Il s'éloigne.

> JULIEN : Il m'énerve, ce type.

Joseph, qui ramasse les épluchures, se penche vers Julien.

> JOSEPH : T'as la confiture ?

Julien fait oui de la tête.

François passe devant eux avec des copains. Pessoz fait une clé à Joseph et le jette à terre.

JOSEPH : Arrête. J'ai des pantalons propres.

Le portefeuille de Joseph tombe à terre. Une photo s'en échappe. Pessoz la ramasse et la brandit.

PESSOZ : Joseph est amoureux, les gars.

Joseph lui arrache la photo.

PESSOZ : Elle a l'air d'une salope, ta fiancée.

JOSEPH : Et ta sœur ? Elle a l'air de quoi, ta sœur ?

Il s'éloigne en claudiquant, poursuivi par Pessoz. Visiblement. il est la tête de turc des élèves.

Julien prend son pot de confiture et court après Joseph.

11.

Julien rejoint Joseph dans une petite basse-cour où se trouvent trois cochons derrière un grillage de fortune. Joseph leur jette les épluchures. Les cochons se battent.

> JOSEPH : Dans un mois, ils seront bons à manger.

> JULIEN : Tu parles ! Ils vont les garder pour la fête du collège. Les parents diront : « Qu'est-ce que vous mangez bien ! »
> Fais voir tes timbres.

Joseph sort une enveloppe de sa poche.

> JOSEPH : Y a un Madagascar 15 centimes. Le type dit que c'est très rare.

> JULIEN : *Assez* rare.

Julien jette un coup d'œil sur le contenu de l'enveloppe et la lui rend.

> JULIEN : Pas terrible. Je crois que je vais les garder mes confitures. La bouffe est tellement dégueulasse.

34

JOSEPH : T'es un vrai juif, toi.

Il sort une deuxième enveloppe de sa poche.
Julien lui donne le pot de confitures et empoche les
deux enveloppes.

JULIEN : Alors, t'es amoureux ?

JOSEPH : Rigole pas. C'est sérieux.
T'as pas cinquante balles à me prêter ?
Les femmes, mon vieux, ça coûte cher !
Tu verras.

JULIEN : Je verrai rien du tout. Et
d'abord, t'es riche comme tout.

JOSEPH : Ah oui, avec ce qu'ils me
paient...
Si je pouvais me trouver un autre
boulot...
JULIEN *(s'éloignant)* : J'ai pas le rond.
Demande à François.

12.

M. Guibourg, le professeur de mathématiques, est au
tableau noir. Il a gardé sa canadienne, son béret et ses
gants.

M. Guibourg : Ciron, remettez du bois dans le poêle. On gèle.

Ciron se lève et claque les talons en faisant un salut militaire

M. Guibourg *(sans se retourner)* : Et ne vous croyez pas obligé de faire le pitre...

Qui peut me montrer que dans ce quadrilatère la somme des deux côtés opposés AB plus CD est égale à la somme des deux autres BC plus DA ?

Plusieurs mains se lèvent, dont celle de Bonnet.

M. Guibourg : Vous, le nouveau.

Ciron : Il s'appelle Dubonnet, monsieur.

Bonnet : Ça va. On a compris.

Bonnet va au tableau noir. Un élève avance le pied et le fait trébucher. Rires.

Bonnet : On sait que les tangentes à un cercle issues d'un point sont égales. Donc a égale a, b égale b

Et il résout le problème avec aisance.

> M. GUIBOURG : C'est très bien. Tout le
> monde a compris ?

> LES ÉLÈVES : Oui, m'sieur !

On entend une sirène lointaine, puis une autre, très
proche.

> UNE VOIX : Chouette, une alerte.

Les élèves commencent à se lever en désordre, ravis
de cette diversion.

> M. GUIBOURG : Nous allons descendre
> à l'abri.
> La classe n'est pas finie. Prenez votre
> livre.

13.

La cave du collège. Les élèves de quatrième se serrent
sur des bancs dans un long couloir qui se perd dans le
noir. Des tuyaux courent le long des murs. Un peu de
lumière vient d'une ampoule au plafond. Une voûte

ouvre sur une pièce encombrée de caisses vides, où une autre classe s'installe.

On entend le reste des élèves, mais on ne les voit pas. Le Père Michel essaie de mettre de l'ordre dans la confusion. Il tient une lampe tempête dans la main.

> UNE VOIX *(chantée)* : C'est la Mère Michel qui a perdu son chat...

> LE PÈRE MICHEL : Silence ! Boulanger, serrez-vous.
> Monsieur Guibourg, mettez-vous là.

Il avance une chaise à M. Guibourg, qui s'assied et commence à lire, éclairé par la lampe du prêtre.

> M. GUIBOURG : Quinzième leçon, page 52. Le produit de deux puissances d'un même décimal relatif...

Julien sort sa lampe de poche et la dirige sur son livre.

> BONNET : Tu m'éclaires ?

Il rapproche son livre de celui de Julien. Mais celui-ci ne suit pas le cours. Il a en main *Les Trois Mousquetaires*.

> BONNET : Lève un peu ta lampe. Je vois rien.

JULIEN : Fous-moi la paix. Tu vas me faire piquer.
Oh ! Et puis tu me fais chier.

Il s'écarte.
On entend des bruits sourds. La lumière du plafond s'éteint.
M. Guibourg s'interrompt. Les enfants s'agitent dans la pénombre.

UNE VOIX : Ils bombardent la gare.

UNE AUTRE VOIX · Mais non ! C'est la caserne d'artillerie.

LE PÈRE MICHEL . Calmez-vous. Asseyez-vous.

Il commence un « Je vous salue, Marie ».
Julien prie avec les autres. Machinalement, il promène le faisceau de sa lampe autour de lui. Des formes, des visages passent dans la lumière.
Julien s'arrête sur deux garçons blottis dans les bras l'un de l'autre. Surpris par la lumière, ils s'écartent.

UN ÉLÈVE : Les amoureux ! *(Rires.)*

LE PÈRE MICHEL : Quentin, éteignez ça.

14.

Au dortoir, les élèves agenouillés finissent la prière du soir.

Bonnet se relève sans faire le signe de croix et se glisse dans ses draps. Il essaie vainement d'enfoncer les jambes, plusieurs fois. Tous l'observent, des rires éclatent.

> LAVIRON · T'as qu'à dormir en chien de fusil !

Bonnet soulève la couverture et voit que son lit a été fait en portefeuille. Il se tourne vers Julien :

> BONNET : C'est toi qui as fait ça ?

Julien le regarde, sans répondre, et se couche.
Plus tard dans la nuit.
Julien semble faire un rêve délicieux. Il sourit, se tourne sur le côté. Ses lèvres remuent, il soupire.
Le sourire s'éteint, devient une grimace.
Il ouvre les yeux, se dresse sur son lit, glisse sa main sous les couvertures.

> JULIEN : Merde.

Il regarde à gauche et à droite : tout le monde dort. Il sort du lit, rabat les couvertures. Il y a une large tache humide au milieu du drap.

> JULIEN : Merde, merde, merde, merde, merde.

Il attrape une serviette de toilette au pied du lit et se met à frotter comme un forcené, essayant de sécher le drap. Il grelotte.
Il descend le drap vers le pied du lit autant qu'il peut, étend la serviette sur la tache, se recouche.
Il reste les yeux ouverts, toujours grelottant, essayant de trouver une position où son corps ne soit pas en contact avec la partie mouillée du drap.
Il entend un cri : « Non ! Non ! Non ! » Quelques lits plus loin, un élève se dresse, le dos arqué, et donne des coups de poing dans le vide, comme s'il se défendait contre l'homme invisible.
Bonnet se réveille en sursaut.

> BONNET : Quoi ! Qu'est-ce que c'est ?

Il voit Julien qui le regarde, se calme, se recouche.

15.

Les quatrièmes sont en gymnastique dans la cour du collège. Julien succède à Ciron à la barre fixe. Il tente une allemande et la rate.

Les autres font des tractions au sol, invectivés par le professeur, un sous-officier en retraite. Plusieurs portent des passe-montagnes. Les uns après les autres, ils s'écroulent.

> LE PROFESSEUR : Vos genoux tendus, les épaules en arrière ! Vous avez des biceps en papier mâché.

Une jeune fille attrayante rentre dans la cour sur un vélo d'homme. Un lourd cartable, accroché au guidon, la déséquilibre.

Elle passe devant la classe avec un sourire au professeur, qui la suit des yeux, oubliant ses élèves. Elle trébuche en descendant de vélo, manque de tomber. On aperçoit ses cuisses un instant. Tous les garçons regardent.

> BOULANGER : Elle le fait exprès, pour nous montrer son cul.

> CIRON : Il est mieux que le tien, son cul.

LE PROFESSEUR : Taisez-vous. Ciron, vous me ferez vingt tractions supplémentaires.

La jeune fille se dirige vers la salle de musique. François et Pessoz surgissent et entament une conversation avec elle.

16.

La salle de musique. Julien joue le *Moment musical* n° 2 de Schubert, très lentement, très mal. La jeune femme de la bicyclette, Mlle Davenne, est assise un peu en arrière du piano. Elle se fait les ongles.

Julien regarde les seins de la jeune fille, ce qui lui fait commettre une grossière erreur de doigté.

MLLE DAVENNE *(sans lever la tête)* : C'est un dièse. Tu n'entends pas que tu fais une fausse note ?

Julien recommence, à contrecœur. Mlle Davenne bâille.

MLLE DAVENNE : Tu devrais essayer le violon.

43

Julien rit. Tous deux rient.

MLLE DAVENNE : Tu détestes la musique, ou quoi ?

JULIEN : Pas du tout. C'est ma mère qui me force à faire du piano.

MLLE DAVENNE : Elle a raison. Si tu arrêtes maintenant, tu le regretteras toute ta vie. Allez, c'est l'heure. A mardi !

La porte s'ouvre. Bonnet entre. Il croise Julien, avance gauchement vers le piano.

MLLE DAVENNE : Comment tu t'appelles ?

BONNET : Jean Bonnet.

MLLE DAVENNE : Tu vas me montrer comment tu joues.

Julien sort. De l'extérieur, il entend les premières notes de son morceau.

Il se retourne, colle son nez à la porte vitrée. Mlle Davenne a le sourire. Bonnet déchiffre la pièce de Schubert avec aisance. Le tempo et les intonations sont justes.

MLLE DAVENNE : Tu te débrouilles, dis donc. Ça fait plaisir d'avoir un élève doué.

Derrière la porte, Julien grelotte. Il enroule son cache-nez autour de son cou.

JULIEN : Quel lèche-cul !

Mais il reste jusqu'à ce que Bonnet termine le morceau.

17.

Avant le dîner, en classe de quatrième, les élèves font leurs devoirs. Le Père Hippolyte, debout près du poêle, égrène son chapelet le dos tourné.

Julien est en train de trier ses nouveaux timbres.

Boulanger lui donne un coup de coude. Il lui désigne Sagard au fond de la classe, pupitre levé, visage tendu, et fait un mouvement de piston avec sa main.

JULIEN *(chuchote)* : Tu crois ?

BOULANGER *(affirmatif)* : Il paraît que ça rend idiot. Avec lui, y a pas de risques.

Julien voit Bonnet qui tourne et retourne une feuille de papier dans ses mains, le regard ailleurs. Son voisin, brusquement, la lui arrache des mains. Bonnet essaie de la lui reprendre, mais son voisin la passe derrière lui. Bonnet se lève et court après sa feuille qui passe de main en main.

> LE PÈRE HIPPOLYTE : Bonnet, retournez à votre place.

Bonnet se rassied, sans quitter la feuille des yeux. Elle parvient jusqu'à Julien. Ses coins sont écornés, ses plis marqués, comme si elle avait séjourné longtemps dans un portefeuille. Julien l'ouvre et voit une large écriture féminine aux jambages accentués.

> JULIEN *(lisant)* : « Mon petit chéri, comme tu comprends bien, il m'est très difficile de t'écrire. Monsieur D. allait à Lyon et il a bien voulu poster cette lettre. Nous sortons le moins possible ta tante et moi... »

Un élève rentre et vient parler au Père Hippolyte.

> LE PÈRE HIPPOLYTE : Julien Quentin, confesse.

46

Julien se lève. Il fait un détour pour passer près de Bonnet et laisse tomber la lettre sur son pupitre.

> JULIEN : Elle a pas la conscience tranquille, ta mère.

18.

Le bureau du Père Jean. Julien est à genoux dans la pénombre, au milieu de la pièce. Assis devant lui, le Père Jean, étole autour du cou, finit de le confesser.

> JULIEN : Ah oui, je me suis battu avec ma sœur pendant les vacances.
>
> LE PÈRE JEAN : Vous n'oubliez rien ?
>
> JULIEN : Je ne crois pas.
>
> LE PÈRE JEAN : Vous n'avez pas eu de mauvaises pensées ?

Julien le regarde.

> LE PÈRE JEAN : Vous savez très bien ce que je veux dire. Tout le monde a des mauvaises pensées.
>
> JULIEN : Même vous ?

Le Père Jean sourit.

LE PÈRE JEAN : Même moi.

Julien danse d'un genou sur l'autre, en faisant des grimaces.

LE PÈRE JEAN : Qu'est-ce que vous avez ?

JULIEN : Des engelures.

LE PÈRE JEAN : Faites voir.

Julien se redresse et lui montre son genou.

LE PÈRE JEAN : C'est le manque de vitamines. Dites à Mme Perrin de vous donner de l'huile de foie de morue.

JULIEN : C'est le froid surtout. On gèle dans le collège.

LE PÈRE JEAN : Je sais. Pensez qu'il y a des gens plus malheureux que vous.
Vous avez dit à votre mère que vous vouliez rentrer dans les ordres.

JULIEN *(surpris)* : Elle vous l'a dit ?

Le prêtre fait oui de la tête.

LE PÈRE JEAN : A mon avis, vous n'avez aucune vocation pour la prêtrise.

JULIEN : Vous croyez ?

LE PÈRE JEAN : J'en suis sûr. Et c'est un fichu métier.

Il lui donne l'absolution.
On entend la sonnerie du téléphone, stridente. Julien sursaute.
Le Père Jean se lève.

LE PÈRE JEAN . Dites trois « Je vous salue, Marie ». Vous pouvez rester debout.

Il décroche. Julien entend une voix excitée, incompréhensible, à l'autre bout de la ligne. On perçoit quelques mots : « Attention... repérés... précautions... »

LE PÈRE JEAN : D'où tenez-vous ça ?...
Méfiez-vous des rumeurs...
Qu'est-ce que vous voulez que j'y fasse...
Nous sommes entre les mains du Seigneur.

Il raccroche et reste un instant songeur comme s'il avait oublié la présence de Julien, qui termine ses « Je vous salue, Marie » en le regardant.

49

LE PÈRE JEAN : Vous vous entendez
bien avec votre nouveau camarade ?

JULIEN : Bonnet ?

LE PÈRE JEAN : Soyez très gentil avec
lui. Vous avez de l'influence sur les
autres. Je compte sur vous.

JULIEN : Pourquoi ? Il est malade ?

LE PÈRE JEAN : Mais pas du tout !
Allez, sauvez-vous...

Julien quitte la pièce. Le prêtre le regarde avec un
léger sourire.

19.

Une place de la petite ville.
Menés par le Père Michel, les quatrièmes et troisièmes
avancent dans un brouillard épais, en rangs par deux,
serviettes de toilette sous le bras.
Julien lit *Les Trois Mousquetaires* en marchant.
Derrière lui, Babinot, Sagard et Boulanger discutent
politique.

BABINOT : Si on n'avait pas Pétain, on serait dans la merde.

BOULANGER : Qu'est-ce qui dit ça ?

BABINOT : Mon père.

BOULANGER : Moi, mon père dit que Laval est vendu aux Allemands.

SAGARD *(sentencieux)* : Les juifs et les communistes sont plus dangereux que les Allemands.

CIRON *(se retournant)* : C'est ton père qui dit ça ?

SAGARD : Non, c'est moi.

Un ivrogne à bicyclette passe en zigzaguant. Rires, confusion et bousculades.

L'IVROGNE *(à tue-tête)* : *La Madelon, viens nous servir à boire...*

Bonnet marche maintenant à côté de Julien. Celui-ci cache son livre sous sa cape quand le Père Michel arrive à leur hauteur.

BONNET : C'est bien, hein ?

JULIEN : Quoi ?

51

Bonnet : *Les Trois Mousquetaires.*
Où tu en es ?

Julien : Quand ils jugent Milady.

Bonnet : Quelle salope celle-là !

Julien le dévisage.

Julien : Qu'est-ce que tu veux faire
plus tard ?

Bonnet : Je sais pas. Des maths.

Julien : Les maths, c'est chiant. Sauf
si on veut être comptable.

Bonnet : Mon père était comptable.

Ils tournent dans une petite rue et rentrent dans un établissement de bains-douches, d'aspect vieillot. Un policier français se tient devant la porte, sur laquelle on peut lire une pancarte : « Cet établissement est interdit aux juifs. »

20.

Il y a du monde dans les vestiaires des bains-douches. Quelques soldats allemands sont en train de s'habiller en chahutant et en parlant fort. Les élèves restent

debout, intimidés, mais Bonnet s'assied entre deux Allemands et délace ses bottines. Un soldat lui caresse la joue et dit à ses compagnons, en allemand : « C'est frais, c'est doux. » Gros rires.
Les Allemands s'en vont. Les élèves se déshabillent.
Babinot ramasse sous le banc une revue avec aes pnotos de femmes déshabillées. Il la cache sous ses vêtements.
Le petit Du Vallier s'assied à côté de Bonnet

DU VALLIER : C'est vrai, Bonnet, que tu fais pas ta communion solennelle ? Pourquoi ?

BONNET : Je suis protestant.

Boulanger recule en se bouchant le nez.

BOULANGER : Un parpaillot ! C'est dégueulasse.

Julien délace ses chaussures à côté de Bonnet.

JULIEN : C'est pas un nom protestant, Bonnet.

BONNET : Il faut croire que si.

Le Père Michel, en pantalon et torse nu, répartit les élèves entre les différentes douches de la salle commune. Il y a aussi quelques cabines avec des baignoires.

53

LE PÈRE MICHEL : Ciron, ici... Babinot, qu'est-ce que vous faites ?... Bonnet, prenez cette baignoire.

ROLLIN : Je peux en avoir une aussi ?

LE PÈRE MICHEL : Celle-ci.

ROLLIN : Ah non ! Elle est trop petite,
cette baignoire. J'ai les pieds qui dépas-
sent.

LE PÈRE MICHEL : Débrouillez-vous.

Plus tard.
Julien rêve dans sa baignoire, enfoncé jusqu'au cou.
Il a les mains sous l'eau et se caresse mollement. On
entend un piano — la pièce de Schubert — et la voix de
Mlle Davenne : « Tu devrais essayer le violon. »
Quelqu'un cogne à la porte.

VOIX DU PÈRE MICHEL : Dépêchez-
vous, Quentin. J'attends votre baignoire.

Julien mouille ses cheveux et les frotte avec son
savon-ersatz. Il enfonce la tête sous l'eau.
La porte de la cabine s'ouvre. Le Père Michel entre,
croit la baignoire vide, s'approche, voit Julien sous
l'eau, immobile. Il se précipite, le soulève par les
épaules. Julien éclate de rire.

54

LE PÈRE MICHEL : C'est malin ! Je vous ai dit de vous dépêcher...

Julien se dresse debout dans sa baignoire, face au Père Michel, qui détourne les yeux, gêné.

JULIEN : C'est pas de ma faute. Mon savon ne mousse pas.

21.

Un vent glacé souffle. Les élèves sortent des bains-douches, enfonçant leurs bérets sur leurs cheveux mouillés et se battant les bras contre la poitrine.

BOULANGER : Grouillez-vous, on gèle.

Derrière eux, un jeune homme sort des bains-douches, en veston. Il fait quelques pas et, tranquillement, enfile son manteau, qui porte une étoile jaune. Il s'éloigne.

BABINOT . Il a du culot, celui-là.

BOULANGER : Ta gueule, Babinot.

LE PÈRE MICHEL : Allez, vite ! On va rentrer au pas de course.

22.

Julien dort. Un son léger, persistant, lui fait ouvrir les yeux.

Bonnet a disposé deux bougies sur sa table de nuit. Debout, au pied de son lit, son béret sur la tête, il murmure.

Julien, les yeux écarquillés, regarde cette silhouette qui tremble dans la lumière des bougies, écoute cette litanie qui ne lui rappelle rien.

Il se redresse un peu, fait craquer son lit. Bonnet s'interrompt.

Julien ferme les yeux. Bonnet reprend.

23.

MOREAU : Flexion, un, deux... Les bras en arrière...

Moreau dirige le dérouillage matinal des petites classes, quand un groupe de miliciens en uniforme — vestes bleues, baudriers, bérets — pénètre dans la cour.

La file des élèves passe devant eux, au pas de course. Moreau prend la tête et entraîne les élèves vers l'autre extrémité de la cour. Il leur fait faire des flexions, son regard fixé sur les miliciens qui parlent maintenant au Père Jean, devant la cuisine. On entend des éclats de voix.

LE PÈRE JEAN : Vous n'avez pas le droit d'entrer ici.

UN MILICIEN : Nous avons des ordres.

LE PÈRE JEAN : Des ordres de qui ?

LE MILICIEN : De nos chefs.

LE PÈRE JEAN : Vous êtes ici dans une institution privée où il n'y a que des enfants et des religieux. Je me plaindrai.

LE MILICIEN : A qui ?

Les élèves commentent en faisant leurs mouvements.

BABINOT : On dirait des chasseurs alpins.

CIRON : Mais non, c'est la milice.

BOULANGER : Qu'est-ce qu'ils veulent, les collabos ?

Bonnet, arrêté, regarde les miliciens. Ceux-ci rentrent dans le bâtiment malgré les protestations du Père Jean. Moreau aussitôt interrompt le dérouillage.

MOREAU : Nous avons terminé. Vous pouvez rentrer.

Les élèves, surpris, rompent les rangs. Moreau en profite pour se glisser dans la petite cour des W.-C.
Le Père Michel remonte rapidement la file des élèves. Il prend Bonnet par le bras et l'entraîne avec lui. Ils rejoignent Moreau.
Julien rebrousse chemin et les voit tous trois disparaître par une petite porte. Il revient vers le bâtiment. Les autres élèves sont déjà rentrés.
Joseph ramène les poubelles.

JOSEPH : Ta confiote a fait un malheur. T'en as d'autres ?

JULIEN : Qu'est-ce qui se passe ? Qu'est-ce qu'ils sont venus faire, les miliciens ?

JOSEPH : Ils fouinent. *cherchent* On leur a dit qu'il y avait des réfractaires au collège. *gens refuser devoir soldats Allemand*

JULIEN : C'est quoi, des réfractaires ?

JOSEPH : Des types qui se cachent parce qu'ils veulent pas aller faire leur travail obligatoire en Allemagne. Moreau, c'en est un

JULIEN : Ah bon ?

58

JOSEPH : Ouais. C'est pas son vrai nom, Moreau. *(Il tape sur sa mauvaise jambe.)* Moi, je m'en fous, je serai réformé.

On entend la voix de Mme Perrin, venant de la cuisine.

MME PERRIN : Joseph ! Joseph !

Elle débouche de la cuisine comme un torpilleur.

JOSEPH : On vient ! *(A Julien :)* Elle est pire que l'Allemagne.

24.

En classe, M. Tinchaut donne les résultats de la composition française.

M. TINCHAUT : Rollin, c'est moyen. Neuf et demi. Bonnet... Bonnet n'est pas là ?

SAGARD : Bon débarras !

> M. Tinchaut : Quentin, treize. C'est
> intelligent, mais un tantinet prétentieux.
> Vous écrivez par exemple : « Charles
> Péguy voit la cathédrale comme un
> phare grandiose et généreux. » *(Rires.)*

Le Père Michel rentre avec Bonnet et l'envoie s'asseoir à sa place, à côté du petit Navarre.

> Navarre : Où t'étais ?

Le Père Michel chuchote quelque chose à l'oreille de Tinchaut, puis s'en va. Tinchaut enchaîne :

> M. Tinchaut : Ciron, douze. Où êtes-
> vous allé chercher qu'il y a des péniches
> au milieu de la Beauce ?

> Ciron : Le canal de la Foussarde,
> m'sieur. J'y étais en vacances.

> M. Tinchaut : Bonnet, je vous ai mis
> treize et demi. Bon travail. Sensible et
> bien écrit. Quentin, vous allez avoir de la
> compétition.

Julien ne quitte pas Bonnet des yeux. Celui-ci soutient son regard.

25.

Le déjeuner est fini, les élèves sortent du réfectoire.
Bonnet et Négus passent en discutant à voix basse.
Près de la cuisine, Julien voit Joseph glisser quelques
cigarettes à François qui les met rapidement dans sa
poche.

> FRANÇOIS : J' peux pas te payer tout de
> suite.

> JOSEPH : Tu m'as promis, Quentin.

François, s'éloignant, désigne son frère :

> FRANÇOIS : Demande au petit con, je
> suis sûr qu'il lui reste du sucre. Il est
> tellement radin.

Joseph rattrape Julien et sort des billes de sa poche.

> JOSEPH : Des agathes. Tiens, je t'en
> donne une.

Julien fait briller une agathe dans la lumière.

> UNE VOIX : Quentin. Julien Quentin.

C'est un surveillant qui distribue le courrier au pied
de l'escalier.

Julien empoche la bille et court chercher sa lettre.

JOSEPH : Attends !

Julien monte l'escalier en déchirant l'enveloppe.

26.

Julien entre dans le dortoir désert. Il va s'asseoir sur
son lit, lisant la lettre.

> VOIX DE LA MÈRE : L'appartement
> semble vide sans toi. Paris n'est pas
> drôle en ce moment. Nous sommes bom-
> bardés presque chaque nuit. Hier une
> bombe est tombée sur un immeuble
> à Boulogne-Billancourt. Huit morts.
> Charmant !
> Tes sœurs sont rentrées à Sainte-
> Marie. Sophie travaille à la Croix-Rouge
> le jeudi et le dimanche. Il y a tellement
> de malheureux !
> Ton père est à Lille. Son usine tourne
> au ralenti, il est d'une humeur de chien.

Il est vraiment temps que la guerre se termine.

Je viendrai vous sortir dimanche en huit, comme prévu. Nous irons déjeuner au Grand Cerf. Je m'en réjouis déjà et te serre sur mon cœur.

Ta maman qui t'aime.

P.-S. : Mange tes confitures. Je vous en apporterai d'autres. Prends bien soin de ta santé.

Julien replie la lettre, la porte à son visage et la renifle, puis la range dans sa table de nuit.

Il regarde autour de lui, soulève l'oreiller de Bonnet, trouve deux bougies qu'il fait tourner dans ses doigts.

Il se lève et va ouvrir son casier. Il y surprend une souris le nez dans son kilo de sucre.

JULIEN : Pousse-toi, Hortense !

Il chasse la souris, prend un morceau de sucre et le croque.

Il va ouvrir un placard un peu plus loin, fouille dans les vêtements, sort une pile de livres. Dans l'un d'entre eux il découvre une photo de Bonnet plus jeune assis entre un homme et une femme. Tous trois sourient et se tiennent par le bras devant des fortifications — le château d'If.

Il ouvre un livre, une édition illustrée de *L'Homme à*

63

l'oreille cassée, d'Edmond About. Sur la page de garde, un papier est collé. Il lit : « Lycée Jules Ferry. Année scolaire 1941-1942. Premier prix de calcul. Jean... » Le nom de famille a été raturé. Mais, sur la page opposée, l'encre de l'inscription est reproduite à l'envers.

Il approche le livre d'une glace murale et lit : « Jean Kippelstein. » Il répète à mi-voix : « Kippelstein, Kippelstein » avec différentes prononciations.

Une cloche sonne. Il entend des pas et replace vivement le livre.

Boulanger et quelques élèves rentrent dans le dortoir.

> BOULANGER : J'ai faim.

Bonnet rentre à son tour, discutant avec Navarre. Il ne voit pas Julien.

> NAVARRE : Qu'est-ce que c'est exactement, une médiatrice ?
>
> BONNET : La perpendiculaire d'un segment en son milieu.

27.

M. Florent, le professeur de grec, marche à petits pas dans la classe, cassé en deux, se frottant les mains constamment pour se réchauffer. Il dicte lentement un passage de la *Guerre du Péloponnèse,* où Thucydide raconte la mutilation des Hermès à Athènes.

Julien écrit sous la dictée, très vite. Après chaque phrase, il a un moment pour sortir *Les Trois Mousquetaires* de sous son cahier et lire avidement quelques lignes. Il en est aux dernières pages.

Bonnet ne fait pas de grec. Il dessine un avion de chasse aux cocardes tricolores, très minutieusement.

La cloche sonne. Les élèves se ruent vers la porte. Bonnet continue son dessin.

> M. FLORENT *(à Bonnet)* : Le grec est très utile, vous savez. Tous les mots scientifiques ont une racine grecque.

Il s'en va.

Bonnet lève la tête et voit Julien, accroupi près du poêle. Ils sont seuls.

Julien termine *Les Trois Mousquetaires,* soupire, referme le livre.

> JULIEN : Qui tu préfères, Athos ou d'Artagnan ?

> BONNET *(sans lever la tête)* : Aramis.

> JULIEN : Aramis ! C'est un faux-cul.

> BONNET : Oui, mais c'est le plus intelligent.

65

Julien s'avance vers Bonnet et regarde son dessin.

JULIEN : Pourquoi tu fais pas de grec ?

BONNET : Je faisais latin-moderne.

JULIEN : Où ça ?

BONNET : Au lycée. A Marseille.

JULIEN : T'es marseillais ? T'as pas l'accent.

BONNET : Je ne suis pas né à Marseille.

JULIEN : Où t'es né ?

BONNET : Si je te disais, tu saurais pas où c'est. C'est dur, le grec ?

JULIEN : Pas tellement, une fois que t'as pigé l'alphabet. Tes parents sont à Marseille ?

Bonnet se lève, range son dessin.

BONNET : Mon père est prisonnier.

JULIEN : Il s'est pas évadé ?

Bonnet met sa cape et va sortir. Julien l'attrape par l'épaule.

JULIEN : Et ta mère ? Elle est où, ta mère ?

66

Bonnet essaie de se dégager, mais Julien le coince contre un pupitre.

> JULIEN : Tu veux pas me dire où est ta mère ?

> BONNET : Elle est en zone libre.

> JULIEN : Y a plus de zone libre.

> BONNET : Je sais. Fous-moi la paix ! Je te demande rien, moi... Je sais pas où elle est. Elle m'a pas écrit depuis trois mois. Là, t'es content ?

Le Père Hippolyte est entré dans la pièce, silencieusement.

> LE PÈRE HIPPOLYTE : Qu'est-ce que vous faites là tous les deux ?

> JULIEN : Je suis enrhumé. Je tousse. *(Il tousse.)*

> LE PÈRE HIPPOLYTE : Allez, pas d'histoires. Allez en récréation.

Il sort.
Les deux garçons se regardent, aussi gênés l'un que l'autre.

JULIEN : Il est salaud, Hippo. Toujours à fouiner.

28.

Les élèves jouent au foulard. Ils ont des foulards de scouts passés dans leur ceinture, derrière leur dos, et essaient de se les arracher mutuellement.

Julien traverse le jeu, tête baissée, et va rejoindre François, à côté des cochons, en train de fumer avec Pessoz et un autre grand. Ils discutent philosophie.

FRANÇOIS : Saint Thomas, ça tient pas debout. Ses preuves de l'existence de Dieu sont foireuses.

PESSOZ : Puisque nous avons.l'idée de Dieu, Dieu existe.

FRANÇOIS : Pur sophisme... Bergson, lui au moins, il cherche la transcendance dans la science moderne. C'est moins con.

Il fait tirer une bouffée de sa cigarette à Julien, qui s'étrangle. Les autres rient.

JULIEN : Qu'est-ce que c'est fort !

FRANÇOIS : C'est du vrai, petit con. Pas de la barbe de maïs.

Les joueurs se rapprochent. Négus arrache un foulard et, poussant des cris de triomphe, le fait tourner au-dessus de sa tête.

FRANÇOIS : Allez, restons pas là, on va se faire piquer par les babasses.

Il jette son mégot et entraîne Julien par le bras.

FRANÇOIS : Rends-moi service.

JULIEN : Quoi ?

FRANÇOIS : Tu vas passer un billet à la petite Davenne, ton prof de piano.

JULIEN : T'es fou ! Je vais me faire virer.

FRANÇOIS : Mais non. Elle dira rien. Ce que t'es trouillard !

JULIEN : François, qu'est-ce que c'est un youpin ?

FRANÇOIS : Un juif.

JULIEN : Je sais ! Mais c'est quoi exactement ?

François : Quelqu'un qui ne mange pas de cochon.

Julien : Tu te fous de ma gueule.

François : Pas du tout.

Julien : Qu'est-ce qu'on leur reproche exactement ?

François : D'être plus intelligents que nous. Et aussi d'avoir crucifié Jésus-Christ.

Julien : C'est pas vrai, c'est les Romains. Et c'est pour ça qu'on leur fait porter l'étoile jaune ?

François : Mais non ! Tu donneras ma lettre à Davenne ?

Julien . Sûrement pas. Qu'est-ce que tu lui veux d'abord ?

François : T'occupes ! Allez, sois gentil, je te passerai les *Mille et Une Nuits*, pour t'apprendre à bander.

Ils entendent des cris, voient un rassemblement près de la cuisine. Joseph est à terre au milieu d'un groupe d'élèves qui se moquent de lui et le font tomber chaque fois qu'il se relève.

UN ELÈVE : Tu sens mauvais, Joseph.

LE PÈRE MICHEL : Allons ! Arrêtez tout de suite !

Joseph est enragé. Il se jette sur un élève.

JOSEPH : Il m'a traité d'enfoiré.

Moreau intervient et l'entraîne.

MOREAU : Joseph, calme-toi et rentre à la cuisine.

JOSEPH : Couché, Joseph. A la niche, Joseph. Je suis pas un chien !

Un élève se met à aboyer.

LE PÈRE MICHEL : D'Arsonval, ça suffit.

29.

Julien et Bonnet sont les plus jeunes des huit garçons du collège qui s'avancent dans un chemin forestier — l'équivalent d'une patrouille scoute. Ils portent capes et bérets, un foulard vert autour du cou, la ceinture par-dessus la cape et, dans le dos, un autre foulard passé dans la ceinture.

Ils suivent des signes de piste marqués sur les rochers, une flèche d'abord puis, plus loin, une croix.

UN GARÇON : Merde, encore une fausse piste...

Pessoz, le chef de patrouille, leur fait rebrousser chemin.

PESSOZ : Il faut revenir au croisement, vite. Et en silence. Je me demande où sont les autres.

Boulanger, Julien et Bonnet traînent derrière. Bonnet joue avec une pomme de pin. Julien est perdu dans une songerie.

JULIEN : C'est quel jour aujourd'hui ?

BOULANGER : 17 janvier 44. Jeudi.

JULIEN : Est-ce que tu réalises qu'il n'y aura plus jamais de 17 janvier 44. Jamais, jamais, jamais plus.

PESSOZ *(de loin)* : Grouillez-vous, les petits.

JULIEN : Et dans quarante ans, la moitié de ces types seront morts et enterrés

BOULANGER : Allez, viens.

Le chemin fait le tour d'un gros rocher, derrière lequel les autres disparaissent. Boulanger accélère pour les rejoindre.

> JULIEN *(à Bonnet)* : Y a que moi qui pense à la mort dans ce collège. C'est quand même incroyable.

Ils entendent des cris, se mettent à courir. Ils s'arrêtent derrière le rocher et voient les verts un peu plus loin, attaqués par une autre patrouille, les foulards rouges. Le combat est presque terminé. Pessoz se défend avec acharnement, mais tous les rouges l'encerclent et lui arrachent son foulard de ceinture.

> UN ROUGE : Vous êtes prisonniers. Suivez-nous. On va vous attacher les mains dans le dos.

> PESSOZ : Vous saviez qu'on était là ?

> UN ROUGE : On vous entendait à un kilomètre.

> D'AUTRES ROUGES : Il en manque deux... Là-bas !... C'est Quentin !

Quatre ou cinq rouges courent vers Julien et Bonnet en essayant de les encercler.

Julien et Bonnet s'enfuient à travers la futaie, le plus vite qu'ils peuvent. Bonnet perd du terrain sur ses poursuivants et se fait prendre. Julien tourne brusquement à gauche et les perd de vue.

Il continue longtemps, sans se retourner, jusqu'à ce que, épuisé, il se couche derrière un rocher.

Il reprend son souffle, la tête dans les mains et entend des appels, des voix, très proches, puis qui s'éloignent.

Le silence revient. Il marche. Sa jambe lui fait mal et le ralentit. Il se retrouve sur un chemin forestier et voit une flèche sur un arbre.

Il sourit, monte dans la direction de la flèche. Au loin, on entend encore des coups de sifflets, quelques appels. La nuit commence à tomber.

Sur un rocher, il trouve un cercle qui entoure une flèche pointée vers le sol.

Il cherche autour du rocher, voit des branches cassées en forme d'étoiles. Il fouille et extrait du sol une petite boîte en fer-blanc qui contient des biscuits vitaminés et un papier sur lequel il lit : « Vous avez gagné. Le jeu est terminé. Rentrez par le même chemin. »

Julien se dresse, triomphant, et se met à hurler, de toutes ses forces :

JULIEN : J'ai le trésor ! On a gagné !
Les verts ont gagné !

Un grand silence lui répond. Il fait nuit maintenant. Les arbres serrés de la futaie forment un mur noir qui l'encercle. Il prend la boîte et se met à descendre en claudiquant, cherchant les signes qui le ramèneront vers les autres, mais il se perd dans un dédale de rochers. Il ouvre la boîte et mange un biscuit. Il lance des appels, de temps en temps, sans conviction.

Il entend un craquement, s'arrête brusquement. Au-dessous de lui, une silhouette se cache derrière un rocher.

Julien, terrifié, recule. Il fait craquer une branche.

L'autre se lève, regarde, se cache.

Julien descend en faisant le tour des rochers, très vite. Il s'éloigne en courant quand il entend un « Julien » étouffé.

Il revient et reconnaît Bonnet, mort de froid comme lui.

JULIEN : Ils t'ont pas attrapé ?

BONNET : Si. Ils m'ont attaché à un arbre, mais je me suis déficelé.

JULIEN : Les salauds !

Julien lui tend la boîte.

JULIEN : J'ai trouvé le trésor. Tout seul.

BONNET : Y a des loups dans cette forêt ?

75

Ils marchent à travers les ronces, trébuchent dans le noir. Bonnet gémit, ou marmonne une prière, on ne sait. Julien a de grosses larmes sur les joues. Il chantonne *Maréchal, nous voilà*. Bonnet se joint à lui.

Ils entendent une cavalcade, des grognements. Ils voient un sanglier qui trotte entre les arbres, fouinant le sol. Julien claque des dents, de plus en plus vite. Bonnet le tire en arrière. Ils tombent, faisant craquer des branches. Le sanglier s'enfuit.

Ils débouchent sur une route goudronnée.

JULIEN : C'est à droite. J'en suis sûr.

BONNET : Mais non, c'est à gauche.

Ils font quelques pas, chacun de leur côté, quand ils entendent un bruit de moteur.

Deux phares viennent vers eux, deux phares de la guerre, occultés à la peinture noire. Seule une mince raie laisse passer la lumière.

Julien se met au milieu de la route, levant les bras. La voiture ralentit, s'arrête. Il entend des voix allemandes qui l'interpellent, le cliquetis de fusils qu'on arme.

Pris de panique, Bonnet se jette dans les arbres, trébuche, tombe en criant.

Deux Allemands le rattrapent, leurs Mauser pointés sur lui. Ils rient quand ils voient cet enfant à terre qui les regarde, terrorisé.

30.

Julien et Bonnet sont coincés entre deux soldats à l'arrière de la voiture allemande. Ils partagent une couverture et grelottent.

La voiture rentre en ville. Le caporal assis à côté du chauffeur se retourne. Son français est plutôt bon.

> LE CAPORAL : C'est à côté de l'Église, le grand mur ?

Julien fait oui de la tête.

> LE CAPORAL *(content de lui)* : Je connais. Les Bavarois, nous sommes catholiques.

31.

Le Père Hippolyte ouvre la porte du collège au caporal, qui pousse devant lui les deux enfants toujours blottis sous la couverture.

LE CAPORAL *(goguenard)* : Bonsoir, mon Père. Est-ce que vous avez perdu des enfants ?

LE PÈRE HIPPOLYTE : On vous a cherché partout tous les deux. Julien, tu sais l'heure qu'il est ? Il faut toujours que tu fasses l'imbécile.

JULIEN *(il explose)* : L'imbécile ! C'est trop fort. *(Il brandit la boîte en fer-blanc.)* J'ai trouvé le trésor, et après, tout le monde avait disparu, et après...

Il s'effondre en sanglots, furieux, épuisé.
Le Père Jean apparaît, suivi de quelques élèves. Il serre Julien dans ses bras.

LE PÈRE JEAN : C'est fini, mon petit. C'est fini.

UN ÉLÈVE : Qu'est-ce qui leur est arrivé ?

UN AUTRE ÉLÈVE : Ils se sont fait arrêter par les boches.

Quelqu'un fait : « Chut ! »

LE CAPORAL *(goguenard)* : Est-ce que les boches peuvent avoir leur couverture.

Le Père Jean prend la couverture et la rend à l'Allemand.

LE CAPORAL : La forêt est interdite aux civils après 20 heures. Vous n'avez pas entendu parler du couvre-feu ?

LE PÈRE JEAN *(agacé)* : Vous croyez que nous l'avons fait exprès ? Voulez-vous entrer boire quelque chose de chaud ?

LE CAPORAL : Merci. Nous sommes en patrouille.

Il salue et retourne à sa voiture.
Pessoz apparaît.

PESSOZ : Dis donc, Quentin, qu'est-ce que je me suis fait engueuler à cause de toi !

JULIEN *(il claque des dents)* : Je vous ai fait gagner, espèce de con !

LE PÈRE JEAN : Emmenez-les à l'infirmerie.

32.

L'infirmerie est située sous les combles. La plupart des lits sont inoccupés.

Bonnet, assis sur son lit, est en grande conversation avec Négus.

Un peu plus loin, Julien lit, dressé sur un coude. Il lève les yeux, agacé par les rires de Négus et Bonnet.

François rentre et tend à Julien une tartine avec du pâté.

FRANÇOIS : Ça va mieux, petit con ?

Tiens, je t'apporte un cadeau de Joseph. Et une lettre. Ta mère m'a quand même écrit.

JULIEN : *Ma* mère. C'est aussi la tienne.

FRANÇOIS : Oui, mais c'est toi le petit chéri.

Papa est tout le temps à Lille, elle doit s'envoyer en l'air.

JULIEN : Qu'est-ce qui te fait dire ça ?

FRANÇOIS : Les femmes, mon cher, c'est toutes des putes. Oh pardon, ma sœur...

Il contourne l'infirmière avec une pirouette et disparaît.

JULIEN : Quel imbécile !

Il prend la lettre de sa mère et la lit.
L'infirmière, une bonne sœur avec un grain de beauté au menton d'où sortent des poils, avance vers Julien, tenant à la main une bouteille remplie d'un liquide violet.

L'INFIRMIÈRE : C'est l'heure du badigeon.

JULIEN : Encore !

L'INFIRMIÈRE : Trois fois par jour.

Elle trempe dans la bouteille une baguette en bois dont l'extrémité est enroulée d'ouate. Julien continue de lire la lettre.

L'INFIRMIÈRE : Ouvre la bouche... Plus grand que ça.

D'une main, elle lui retient la langue avec une cuillère, et de l'autre lui enfonce vigoureusement la baguette dans la gorge, la remuant en tous sens comme si elle lui peignait le larynx.

Julien s'étouffe, tousse, proteste.
Ciron et Boulanger sont aux pieds du lit.

> BOULANGER : T'as dû avoir drôlement peur hier soir !

> JULIEN : Oh, pas tellement.

> CIRON : Il paraît que vous avez vu des sangliers ? Ils étaient nombreux ?

Julien regarde Bonnet qui est venu se joindre à eux.

> JULIEN : Une cinquantaine.

> BOULANGER : Et les Allemands ? Ils ont tiré ?

> JULIEN : Quelques rafales, c'est tout.

> CIRON : Tu parles !

Il prend le livre de Julien sur le lit.

> CIRON : Qu'est-ce que tu lis ?

> JULIEN : Les *Mille et Une Nuits*. C'est mon frère qui me l'a passé. Interdit par les babasses.

> CIRON : Pourquoi ?

> JULIEN : C'est des histoires de cul. Très chouette. Je te le prêterai.

La cloche sonne.

L'INFIRMIÈRE : La récréation est terminée.

BOULANGER : Faut qu'on aille en instruction religieuse.

JULIEN : Vous embrassez la Mère Michel pour moi.

BOULANGER : Plutôt deux fois qu'une. A demain !

Ciron et Boulanger s'en vont.
Bonnet attrape une mouche dans ses mains fermées. Il la saisit entre ses doigts et lui arrache une aile, délicatement.

JULIEN : T'es dégueulasse.

BONNET : Ça lui fait pas mal.

Julien mord la tartine de pâté. Il la coupe en deux et en tend une moitié à Bonnet.

BONNET : Non, merci. J'aime pas le pâté.

Julien essaie de lui mettre dans la bouche.

JULIEN : Allez, mange.

Bonnet repousse la tartine et se lève, en colère.

> BONNET : Non, je te dis. J'aime pas le pâté.

> JULIEN : Parce que c'est du cochon ?

> BONNET : Pourquoi tu me poses toujours des questions idiotes ?

> JULIEN *(à voix très basse)* : Parce que tu t'appelles Kippelstein, pas Bonnet. Au fait, c'est Kippelstein ou Kippelstin ?

Bonnet se jette sur lui. L'infirmière survient et les sépare.

> L'INFIRMIÈRE : Bonnet, si vous ne vous couchez pas tout de suite, je vous renvoie en étude.

Bonnet retourne dans son lit. Julien, sans le quitter des yeux, finit la tartine.

84

33.

Aux lavabos, les élèves sont en tenue du dimanche, vestes et cravates.

Julien s'ajuste devant son miroir, très soigneusement. Il se mouille les cheveux, se fait une raie, avec une touche de narcissisme.

> JULIEN *(à son voisin)* : Tes parents viennent ?

> L'AUTRE *(soupir)* : Toute la famille...

Bonnet vient se laver, habillé comme tous les jours.

> JULIEN *(gaiement)* : Tu t'habilles pas ? T'as pas de visites ?

> BONNET : Qu'est-ce que ça peut te foutre ?

34.

Les travées de la chapelle sont pleines. Tous les professeurs sont là et beaucoup de parents, aux côtés de leur progéniture. Mme Quentin est avec François et Julien.

Bonnet, Négus et Dupré sont seuls, derrière, un peu comme des parias.

Claquement de mains. Tout le monde s'assied. Le Père Jean, qui officie, s'avance vers l'assemblée.

> LE PÈRE JEAN : Aujourd'hui, je m'adresserai particulièrement aux plus jeunes d'entre vous, qui vont faire leur communion solennelle dans quelques semaines.
>
> Mes enfants, nous vivons des temps de discorde et de haine. Le mensonge est tout puissant, les chrétiens s'entre-tuent, ceux qui devraient nous guider nous trahissent. Plus que jamais, nous devons nous garder de l'égoïsme et de l'indifférence.
>
> Vous venez tous de familles aisées, parfois très aisées. Parce qu'on vous a donné beaucoup, il vous sera beaucoup demandé. Rappelez-vous la sévère parole de l'Évangile : « Il est plus facile à un chameau de passer par le chas d'une aiguille qu'à un riche d'entrer dans le Royaume du Seigneur. » Et saint Jacques : « Eh bien maintenant, les riches ! Pleurez, hurlez sur les malheurs qui vont vous arriver. Votre richesse est

pourrie, vos vêtements sont rongés par les vers... »

Les richesses matérielles corrompent les âmes et dessèchent leurs cœurs. Elles rendent les hommes méprisants, injustes, impitoyables dans leur égoïsme. Comme je comprends la colère de ceux qui n'ont rien, quand les riches banquètent avec arrogance. *party*

Cette diatribe suscite des réactions dans l'assistance.

MME QUENTIN : Il y va fort quand même !

Un monsieur bien mis se lève et quitte la chapelle.
Impassible, le Père Jean attend que l'homme soit sorti.

LE PÈRE JEAN : Je n'ai pas voulu vous choquer, mais seulement vous rappeler que le premier devoir d'un chrétien est la charité. Saint Paul nous dit dans l'Épître d'aujourd'hui : « Frères, ne vous prenez pas pour des sages. Ne rendez à personne le mal pour le mal. Si ton ennemi a faim, donne-lui à manger. S'il a soif, donne-lui à boire. »

Nous allons prier pour ceux qui souffrent, ceux qui ont faim, ceux que l'on

87

persécute. Nous allons prier pour les victimes, et aussi pour les bourreaux.

Plus tard.

Communion. Élèves et parents vont recevoir la Sainte Hostie. Julien s'avance, mains jointes, yeux baissés. Bonnet sort de son banc et vient se placer dans la file, malgré Négus qui tente de le retenir.

Il s'agenouille à côté de Julien. Le Père Jean s'avance vers eux, ciboire à la main. Il approche l'hostie de la bouche de Bonnet. Quand il le reconnaît, sa main se fige.

Rapide échange de regards entre Bonnet, Julien et le Père Jean. Celui-ci dépose l'hostie sur la langue de Julien et continue.

35.

Après la messe, parents et élèves conversent par petits groupes avec les prêtres et les professeurs dans la cour du collège. Mme Quentin discute avec le Père Jean. François est auprès de Mlle Davenne, en robe du dimanche.

Julien et quelques copains simulent des combats de boxe française, s'envoyant des coups de pied, la jambe levée très haut. Ils sont excités, parlent fort, font les malins en présence de leurs parents.

Ciron et Babinot viennent tourner autour de Bonnet, qui les observe.

> Babinot : En garde, Dubonnet, en garde.

Bonnet reçoit un coup de pied à la hanche. Furieux, il se jette sur Babinot. Ciron l'attrape par-derrière.

> Ciron : Aidez-moi, les autres. Tape-cul pour le parpaillot.

Dans la mêlée qui s'ensuit, Bonnet donne une manchette à Julien, qui l'empoigne et lui fait un croche-pied. Bonnet l'entraîne à terre avec lui et ils roulent sur le sol, se battant avec acharnement.
Mme Quentin se précipite.

> Mme Quentin : Julien, tu es complètement fou ! Ton beau costume...

Ils se relèvent. Julien frotte sa veste. Il a une manche déchirée.

> Mme Quentin : Nous aurons l'air de quoi au restaurant !

Bonnet regarde Julien, et rit. Julien se met à rire lui aussi.

MME QUENTIN : Qu'est-ce qui vous prend ? Vous trouvez ça drôle ?

Cela dégénère en un fou rire contagieux, auquel Mme Quentin ne peut résister.

Julien va parler à l'oreille de sa mère.

36.

Le Grand Cerf est le restaurant élégant de la ville. Plusieurs tables sont occupées par des officiers de la Wehrmacht. Mme Quentin est en train de commander. Avec elle sont assis François, Julien, et Bonnet qui observe les Quentin comme s'il était au théâtre.

MME QUENTIN : Qu'est-ce que vous avez comme poisson ?

LE MAÎTRE D'HÔTEL : Il y a longtemps que nous n'avons pas eu de poisson, madame. Je vous recommande le lapin chasseur. Un demi-ticket de viande par portion.

FRANÇOIS : C'est du lapin, ou du chat ?

LE MAÎTRE D'HÔTEL : Du lapin, monsieur. Avec des pommes rissolées.

MME QUENTIN : Elles sont au beurre, vos pommes de terre ?

LE MAÎTRE D'HÔTEL : A la margarine, madame. Sans ticket.

Mme Quentin regarde ses fils avec une moue comique.

MME QUENTIN : Va pour le lapin chasseur. Et une bouteille de bordeaux.

Le maître d'hôtel s'éloigne. Mme Quentin tourne la tête. Les Allemands à la table d'à côté parlent bruyamment en la regardant. L'un deux lève son verre à son intention.

MME QUENTIN *(chuchote)* : Il y a de la verdure aujourd'hui. Je croyais qu'ils étaient tous sur le front russe.

FRANÇOIS : Vous leur avez tapé dans l'œil.

MME QUENTIN *(à Bonnet)* : Vos parents n'ont pas pu venir ?

BONNET : Non, madame.

MME QUENTIN : Pauvre petit.

FRANÇOIS : Et papa, au fait ? Il avait dit qu'il viendrait.

91

MME QUENTIN : Il a été empêché. Des problèmes avec l'usine.

JULIEN : Comme d'habitude...

MME QUENTIN : Ton pauvre père a des responsabilités écrasantes en ce moment.

FRANÇOIS : Il est toujours pétainiste ?

MME QUENTIN : Personne n'est plus pétainiste !
(A Julien :) Au fait, on m'a appris ce qui t'était arrivé dans la forêt. Qu'est-ce que je n'ai pas dit au Père Jean ! Ces jeux scouts sont ridicules, avec le froid qu'il fait. Dieu sait ce qui aurait pu t'arriver, mon pauvre chou. Une balle est si vite partie !

Elle lui caresse la joue. Julien recule le visage.

FRANÇOIS : Ça lui forme le caractère.

MME QUENTIN : C'est exactement ce que le Père Jean m'a répondu. Former le caractère ! Je vous demande un peu.

JULIEN *(désignant Bonnet)* : C'est lui qui était avec moi dans la forêt.

Mme Quentin sourit à Bonnet.

MME QUENTIN : Je parie que vous êtes lyonnais. Tous les Gillet sont de Lyon et ils fabriquent tous de la soie.

JULIEN : Il s'appelle Bonnet, pas Gillet. Et il est de Marseille.

MME QUENTIN *(elle se tape la tête)* : Bien sûr !... J'ai connu une Marie-Claire Bonnet à Marseille, une cousine des Du Perron, les huiles. C'est votre mère ?

BONNET : Non, madame. Ma famille n'est pas dans les huiles.

MME QUENTIN : Tiens, ça m'étonne.

JULIEN : Le père de Bonnet est comptable.

MME QUENTIN : Ah bon !

Seul à une table, un vieux monsieur très élégant demande son addition. Le maître d'hôtel s'adresse à lui comme à un familier.

LE MAÎTRE D'HÔTEL : Tout de suite, monsieur Meyer. Vous avez bien déjeuné ?

MEYER *(sourire)* : Merci. Le lapin était acceptable.

93

Deux miliciens en uniforme sont entrés dans le restaurant et inspectent les tables. Le plus jeune s'approche de Meyer.

LE MILICIEN : Vos papiers, monsieur.

M. Meyer écrase sa cigarette, sort son portefeuille, tend sa carte d'identité. Le milicien y jette un œil.

LE MILICIEN *(très fort)* : Dis donc toi, tu ne sais pas lire ? Ce restaurant est interdit aux youtres.

Un grand silence s'est fait dans le restaurant. Julien regarde Bonnet, qui regarde Meyer.

MME QUENTIN : Qu'est-ce qu'ils ont besoin d'embêter les gens ? Il a l'air si convenable, ce monsieur.

Le maître d'hôtel s'avance.

LE MAÎTRE D'HÔTEL : M. Meyer vient ici depuis vingt ans. Je ne peux pas le mettre à la porte quand même.

LE MILICIEN : Toi, ferme-la, le loufiat. Je pourrais vous faire révoquer votre licence.

94

FRANÇOIS *(à mi-voix)* : Collabos !

L'autre milicien s'avance vers lui. Il est gros et vieux, avec une moustache.

LE MILICIEN : C'est toi qui as dit ça ?

MME QUENTIN : Tais-toi, François !
(Au milicien :) C'est un enfant. Il ne sait pas ce qu'il dit.

LE MILICIEN : Nous sommes au service de la France, madame. Ce garçon nous a injuriés.

Il y a des remous dans la salle, comme si l'assistance prenait courage.

UNE FEMME : Laissez ce vieillard tranquille. C'est ignoble ce que vous faites.

D'autres voix s'élèvent : « Allez-vous-en... Vous n'avez pas le droit... »

UNE VOIX *(stridente)* : Ils ont raison. Les juifs à Moscou !

Une voix allemande couvre le brouhaha : « Foutez le camp ! »

95

Silence. Derrière les Quentin, un officier s'est levé. Il a un bras en écharpe, porte monocle et beaucoup de décorations. Il est ivre, il a du mal à se tenir debout. Il s'approche du vieux milicien et le toise. Il a une tête de plus que lui.

> L'OFFICIER : Vous m'avez compris ? Foutez le camp.

Le milicien le regarde, hésite. Finalement, il salue l'Allemand et se retire, entraînant son jeune collègue.

> LE JEUNE MILICIEN *(à Meyer)* : On se retrouvera !

L'Allemand s'écroule dans sa chaise. Les conversations reprennent.

> MME QUENTIN : On peut dire ce qu'on veut. Il y en a qui sont bien.

> FRANÇOIS : Il a fait ça pour vous épater.

Bonnet regarde Meyer remettre son portefeuille dans son veston.

> JULIEN *(brusquement)* : On n'est pas juifs, nous ?

MME QUENTIN : Il ne manquerait plus que ça !

JULIEN : Et la tante Reinach ? C'est pas un nom juif ?

MME QUENTIN : Les Reinach sont alsaciens.

FRANÇOIS : Ils peuvent être alsaciens *et* juifs.

MME QUENTIN : Fichez-moi la paix. Les Reinach sont *très* catholiques. S'ils vous entendaient !

Remarquez, je n'ai rien contre les juifs, au contraire. A part Léon Blum, bien entendu. Celui-là, ils peuvent le pendre.

Julien, tiens-toi droit.

37.

Atmosphère de dimanche dans les rues de la petite ville. On entend un limonaire.

Mme Quentin et Julien marchent côte à côte. Elle a le bras autour de son épaule.

MME QUENTIN : Il est gentil, ton ami, mais il ne parle pas beaucoup.

JULIEN *(sentencieux)* : Il a ses raisons.

MME QUENTIN : Ce n'est pas un crétin, alors ?

JULIEN : Pas du tout.

Mme Quentin rit, et se retourne.

MME QUENTIN : Où est passé François ?

Un peu en arrière, François donne des renseignements à un groupe de soldats allemands.

FRANÇOIS : Vous passez derrière l'église, et vous continuez tout droit, toujours tout droit, jusqu'au pont...

Les Allemands le remercient chaleureusement.

JULIEN : Il les envoie de l'autre côté. Il fait toujours ça avec la verdure.

MME QUENTIN · C'est malin.

François les rejoint. Il est éméché.

FRANÇOIS : Qu'est-ce que vous diriez si je partais au maquis ?

MME QUENTIN : Ne dis pas de bêtises. Tu dois passer ton bachot.

FRANÇOIS : Le bachot, le bachot. Il y a des choses plus importantes...
Julien vous a dit qu'il voulait être babasse ?

JULIEN : Je ne veux pas être babasse. Je veux être missionnaire au Congo.

MME QUENTIN : Je vous défends d'employer ce mot stupide de babasse. C'est dégoûtant. Vous devriez être pleins de reconnaissance pour ces malheureux moines qui se crèvent la santé à essayer de vous donner une éducation.

François et Julien terminent la phrase à l'unisson avec leur mère.

MME QUENTIN *(riant)* : Parfaitement !

François pousse Julien du coude : Joseph, endimanché, débouche d'une ruelle, tenant par le bras une fille très maquillée.

LA FILLE : Tu m'énerves ! C'est fou ce que tu m'énerves ! Fiche-moi la paix.

Elle lui lâche le bras et fait demi-tour. Joseph lui court après.

99

JOSEPH : Fernande, Fernande !

FRANÇOIS ET JULIEN : Fernande ! Fernande !

MME QUENTIN : Vous la connaissez ?

Les deux frères rigolent.

MME QUENTIN : Mon petit Julien, tu es bien sûr que tu veux être prêtre ?

JULIEN : C'est contre vos idées ?

MME QUENTIN : Absolument pas. Ton père et moi serions très fiers. Mais je voudrais tellement que tu fasses polytechnique comme ton grand-père.

FRANÇOIS : Ne vous inquiétez pas. Il tombera amoureux et il défroquera. C'est un grand sentimental, comme Joseph.

Julien lui envoie un coup de poing. Les deux frères se battent.

Ils croisent une famille du collège : le fils, les parents, et la sœur, une jolie jeune fille de dix-sept ans. Le regard de la jeune fille croise celui de François. Celui-ci chuchote à son frère :

FRANÇOIS : Dis donc, elle est bandante, la sœur de Laviron. Je vais lui faire un frais.

Il fait demi-tour et rejoint les Laviron.
Mme Quentin regarde sa montre. Elle rejoint Julien et le serre contre elle.
Julien se dégage.

MME QUENTIN : Alors, c'est fini les câlins... Mais dis donc, tu as un peu de moustache.

JULIEN : Si je rentrais avec vous à Paris ? Papa ne le saurait pas.

Elle le regarde, déconcertée. Elle le serre dans ses bras.

38.

Bonnet et quelques élèves descendent l'escalier du collège, croisant Julien, trois pots de confiture dans les bras, l'air sinistre.
Bonnet fait demi-tour et le rejoint.

BONNET : Elle est gentille, ta mère. Qu'est-ce qu'elle parle vite !

JULIEN : Elle est folle.

BONNET : Tu vas la revoir bientôt.
Vous allez sortir pour le Mardi-Gras.

39.

Fin du dîner. Les élèves et les professeurs poussent
les tables du réfectoire, installent un écran pour la
séance hebdomadaire de cinéma. Le Père Michel
charge le projecteur, sous l'œil critique de Moreau.

MOREAU : Si vous faites ça, nous
allons casser comme l'autre fois.

LE PÈRE MICHEL : Je connais très bien
cette machine !

Encore attablés, Bonnet et Julien se partagent un pot
de confiture qu'ils étalent sur des biscottes.

BONNET : Qu'est-ce qu'elle est bonne,
ta confiture !

JULIEN . C'est Adrienne qui la fait.

BONNET : C'est ta sœur, Adrienne ?

JULIEN : Non. C'est la cuisinière... Pourquoi tu ris ? Vous n'avez pas de cuisinière ?

BONNET : Non.

JULIEN : Vous mangez au restaurant ?

BONNET *(riant)* : Mais non ! Ma mère fait très bien la cuisine.

Deux grands viennent prendre le banc où ils sont assis.

UN GRAND : Poussez-vous, les mômes.

JOSEPH : Dites donc, c'est mes confitures que vous bouffez.

JULIEN : Oh, ça va.

M. Florent accorde son violon. Il va accompagner les images muettes de Charlie Chaplin avec l'aide de Mlle Davenne au piano.

Bonnet et Julien sont assis côte à côte. La lumière s'éteint, le projecteur se met à cliqueter et le titre du film, *Charlot émigrant,* apparaît sur l'écran.

M. Florent et Mlle Davenne attaquent le *Rondo Capriccioso* de Saint-Saëns. Le pathos de la musique s'accorde avec le comique langoureux de Chaplin.

Les enfants regardent fascinés, moment tendre, moment d'oubli. François, debout à côté de Mlle Davenne, tourne les pages de la partition.

103

Quand vient une scène de poursuite, M. Florent enchaîne sur un mouvement rapide. La salle rit beaucoup. Ils connaissent le film par cœur et annoncent les gags à l'avance.

Ceux qui rient le plus sont Joseph et le Père Jean, côte à côte. C'est une surprise de voir ce prêtre austère plié en deux, riant aux éclats, se tapant sur les cuisses aux virevoltes du petit clown.

La musique se calme, Chaplin redevient sentimental. Il fait sa cour à la belle Edna Purviance. Enfants et professeurs ont l'œil rêveur.

Un petit cri aigu, une bousculade dans la pénombre. François tente d'embrasser Mlle Davenne, qui ne se laisse pas faire.

Le bateau des émigrants entre dans le port de New York. Négus, Bonnet et Julien regardent la statue de la Liberté apparaître sur l'écran.

40.

Le jour commence à peine à se lever à travers les fenêtres du dortoir. Les enfants sont écrasés dans leur lit. Personne ne bouge. On entend un « Merde » étouffé.

Julien se dresse sur son lit, glisse la main sous les draps.

JULIEN : Et merde...

Il rabat les couvertures et, avec sa serviette de toilette, éponge la tache humide. Cette fois, derrière son dos, Sagard l'observe.

Moreau rentre et allume.

MOREAU : Debout, c'est l'heure.

Julien, vite, recouvre le drap et fait mine de s'habiller. Mais Sagard attrape la serviette par le bout des doigts et la brandit

SAGARD : Quentin pisse au lit. Quentin pisse au lit.

Julien se rue sur lui et, méchamment, le jette à terre. Il récupère sa serviette.

Mais d'autres élèves reprennent, en faisant cercle autour de Julien :

LES ÉLÈVES : Quentin pisse au lit. Quentin pisse au lit.

Julien, humilié, fou de rage, les repousse. Bonnet est à ses côtés, deux contre tous les autres.

41.

Aux lavabos, Julien se confie à Bonnet, tout en se lavant les dents.

> JULIEN : A chaque fois, c'est le même coup. Je suis au milieu d'un rêve formidable, j'ai envie de pisser, j'ouvre ma braguette, tout va bien. Et puis je me réveille en sentant la pisse chaude couler sur mon ventre. C'est pas marrant, mon vieux.

42.

La neige tombe sur la cour de récréation.

Julien apprend à Bonnet à se tenir sur une paire d'échasses. Bonnet titube et tombe.

> JULIEN : Allez, remonte. N'aie pas peur.

> SAGARD *(en passant)* : Pisse-au-lit.

Julien lui court après.

> JULIEN : Toi, le gros Sagard, tu vas
> prendre une bonne raclée.

On entend des hurlements. La volumineuse Mme Perrin surgit de la cuisine, poursuivant Joseph qu'elle frappe avec un torchon.

> MME PERRIN : Salopard, espèce de
> salopard ! Tu vas voir...

On dirait le film de la veille et les élèves rient, mais la cuisinière est vraiment furieuse. Elle a un verre dans le nez, elle titube et manque de tomber.

Elle aperçoit le Père Michel parmi les joueurs d'échasses.

> MME PERRIN : Père Michel, Père
> Michel ! Je l'ai attrapé en train de voler
> du saindoux. Il le mettait dans son sac
> pour aller le vendre.
> Je vous l'avais bien dit qu'il volait...
> Voleur, voleur, saloperie !

Tout en parlant, elle continue à taper sur Joseph, acculé contre un mur. Il lève les bras pour se protéger et semble terrifié.

JOSEPH : C'est pas vrai, elle ment ! C'est elle qui vole !

Les jeux se sont arrêtés, tout le monde regarde. Le Père Michel prend Joseph par le bras et l'entraîne vers la cuisine.

LE PÈRE MICHEL : Pas devant les enfants, madame Perrin. Rentrez dans votre cuisine et calmez-vous.

FRANÇOIS *(à Julien)* : Je lui avais dit à ce crétin qu'il allait se faire piquer.

Ils lèvent la tête et aperçoivent le Père Jean, qui observe la scène de la fenêtre de son bureau.

43.

Sept élèves de différentes classes sont alignés dans le bureau du Père Jean. Parmi eux, François et Julien.

LE PÈRE JEAN : Joseph volait les provisions du collège et les revendait au marché noir. Mme Perrin aurait dû nous prévenir plus tôt et je ne crois pas qu'elle soit innocente.
Mais il y a plus.

108

Il montre sur sa table des boîtes de pâté, des bonbons, des pots de confiture.

LE PÈRE JEAN : Voilà ce qu'on a trouvé dans son placard. Ce sont des provisions personnelles. Il vous a nommés tous les sept.

Il prend une boîte de pâté.

LE PÈRE JEAN : Auquel d'entre vous appartient ce pâté ?

UN ÉLÈVE : A moi.

LE PÈRE JEAN : Et ces confitures ?

JULIEN : A moi.

LE PÈRE JEAN : Vous savez ce que vous êtes ? Un voleur, tout autant que Joseph.

JULIEN : C'est pas du vol. Elles m'appartiennent, ces confitures.

LE PÈRE JEAN : Vous en privez vos camarades.
(A tous :) Pour moi, l'éducation, la vraie, consiste à vous apprendre à faire bon usage de votre liberté. Et voilà le résultat ! Vous me dégoûtez. Il n'y a rien

que je trouve plus ignoble que le marché noir. L'argent, toujours l'argent.

FRANÇOIS : On ne faisait pas d'argent. On échangeait, c'est tout.

Le Père Jean s'avance vers lui, le visage dur.

LE PÈRE JEAN : Contre quoi ?

FRANÇOIS *(après une hésitation)* : Des cigarettes.

LE PÈRE JEAN : Quentin, si je ne savais pas tous les problèmes que cela poserait à vos parents, je vous mettrais à la porte tout de suite, vous et votre frère.
Je suis obligé de renvoyer Joseph, mais je commets une injustice. Vous êtes tous privés de sortie jusqu'à Pâques. Vous pouvez retourner à l'étude.

Les élèves sortent François chuchote à Julien.

FRANÇOIS : On s'en tire bien.

Dans le couloir, ils se trouvent en face de Joseph qui attend avec le Père Michel, le dos au mur. Il pleurniche comme un gosse.

JOSEPH : Et où je vais aller, moi ? J'ai même pas où coucher.

Les élèves sont très gênés. Julien lui met une main sur l'épaule.

LE PÈRE MICHEL : Allez en classe.

Ils s'éloignent. A l'extrémité du couloir, Julien se retourne et voit le Père Jean qui apparaît à la porte de son bureau.

LE PÈRE JEAN *(à Joseph)* : Allez voir l'économe. Il vous paiera votre mois.

JOSEPH : Y a que moi qui trinque. C'est pas juste.

LE PÈRE MICHEL : Allez, viens, Joseph.

Il l'entraîne, sous le regard du Père Jean, qui semble regretter la décision qu'il a prise

44.

Bonnet ouvre la porte de la chapelle, qui est déserte. Il fait quelques pas, s'arrête, enfonce son béret sur sa tête. Défi, prière, on ne sait.

Julien et les autres quatrièmes entrent les uns après les autres en chahutant. Le Père Michel surgit derrière eux, les bras chargés de fleurs.

> LE PÈRE MICHEL : Qu'est-ce que vous faites là ?

> BOULANGER : On a chorale avec Mlle Davenne.

> LE PÈRE MICHEL : Ça tombe bien. Vous et Babinot, vous allez m'aider à arranger les fleurs pour dimanche.

Julien est le seul à remarquer Bonnet qui recule derrière un pilier, son béret sur la tête. Leurs regards se croisent.
Mlle Davenne entre en courant. Elle s'installe à l'harmonium.

> MLLE DAVENNE : Bon ! Nous allons reprendre le *Je crois en toi, mon Dieu.*

Elle regarde autour d'elle.

> MLLE DAVENNE : Bonnet n'est pas là ?

Julien se retourne vivement.

> JULIEN : Non, mademoiselle. Il est à l'infirmerie.

MLLE DAVENNE : Ah bon.

Ils commencent à chanter : *Je crois en toi, mon Dieu, je crois en toi...*

45.

Bonnet joue un boogie-woogie sur le piano de la salle de musique.

Il s'arrête et montre à Julien comment faire la pompe sur les notes graves.

> BONNET : Tu vois, c'est facile. Avec la main gauche, tu fais ça.

Julien essaie. Il est interrompu par le bruit assourdissant des sirènes d'alerte.

> BONNET : Faut qu'on aille à l'abri.

On entend des coups de sifflets, des appels, un bruit de course qui se rapproche.

Julien entraîne Bonnet derrière le piano.

Moreau entre une seconde, croit que la pièce est vide et repart.

JULIEN : Ils sauront pas qu'on est manquants. Ils comptent jamais.

Plus tard.
Debout devant le piano, ils jouent un boogie à quatre mains. Julien fait la basse, Bonnet improvise sur le haut du clavier. Ils rient aux éclats.

46.

Le collège semble abandonné. Seules, deux silhouettes d'enfants au milieu de la cour enneigée.
Julien et Bonnet écoutent les bruits lourds des bombardiers et les rafales sèches de la D.C.A. allemande.

BONNET : J'espère qu'ils vont se décider à débarquer, les Américains.

JULIEN :Tu vas rester au collège quand la guerre sera finie ?

BONNET : Je ne sais pas... Je ne crois pas.

Il a comme un tremblement de tout le corps.

JULIEN : Tu as peur ?

BONNET : Tout le temps.

47.

Dans la cuisine, Bonnet et Julien profitent de l'alerte pour se faire rôtir des châtaignes. Ils se brûlent les mains en les dépiautant.

> JULIEN : Y a combien de temps que tu l'as pas vu ?

> BONNET : Mon père ? Ça fait presque deux ans.

> JULIEN : Moi, mon père non plus, je ne le vois jamais.

Il prend brusquement le bras de Bonnet et tous deux s'accroupissent sous la grande table.
Joseph entre dans la cuisine. Il va ouvrir un tiroir et fouille, leur tournant le dos.
Julien se relève.

> JULIEN : Qu'est-ce que tu fais là, Joseph ?

Joseph sursaute.

JOSEPH : J'ai oublié des affaires. Et toi, qu'est-ce que tu fais là ?

Il s'éloigne en claudiquant. Les deux amis échangent un sourire.

48.

Les élèves sont tous endormis. Au fond du dortoir, une lampe de poche troue la pénombre.

Bonnet est allongé et écoute Julien, assis au pied du lit, qui lui lit un passage des *Mille et Une Nuits*.

JULIEN : « Et d'un mouvement rapide, elle rejeta ses voiles et se dévêtit tout entière pour apparaître dans sa native nudité. Béni soit le ventre qui l'a portée !

« La princesse était d'une beauté douce et blanche comme un tissu de lin, elle répandait de toutes parts la suave odeur de l'ambre, telle la rose qui sécrète elle-même son parfum originel. Nour la pressa dans ses bras et trouva en elle, l'ayant explorée dans sa profondeur intime, une perle encore intacte. Et il se mit à promener sa main sur ses membres

116

charmants et son cou délicat, à l'égarer parmi les flots de sa chevelure.

« Et elle, de son côté, ne manqua pas de faire voir les dons qu'elle possédait. Car elle unissait les mouvements lascifs des filles arabes à la chaleur des Éthiopiennes, la candeur effarouchée des Franques à la science consommée des Indiennes, la coquetterie des femmes du Yamân à la violence musculaire des femmes de la Haute-Égypte, l'exiguïté des organes des Chinoises à l'ardeur des filles du Hedjza.

« Aussi les enlacements ne cessèrent de succéder aux embrassements, les baisers aux caresses et les copulations aux foutreries, jusqu'à ce que, fatigués de leurs transports et de leurs multiples ébats, ils se fussent endormis enfin dans les bras l'un de l'autre, ivres de jouissance. Ainsi finit... »

Julien lève la tête. Bonnet s'est endormi.

49.

Dans la salle de classe, M. Guibourg donne des nouvelles de la guerre, une règle pointée vers la carte d'Europe, sur laquelle des petits drapeaux marquent les positions respectives des armées.

> M. GUIBOURG : Les Russes ont lancé une grande offensive en Ukraine. D'après la radio de Londres, l'Armée rouge a crevé le front allemand sur 100 kilomètres à l'ouest de Kiev. D'après Radio-Paris, cette offensive a été repoussée avec de lourdes pertes. La vérité est probablement entre les deux.

Bonnet lève la tête. Par la fenêtre, il voit Moreau courir et rentrer dans le bâtiment d'en face.

> JULIEN et BOULANGER *(à mi-voix.*
> Radio-Paris ment,
> Radio-Paris ment,
> Radio-Paris est allemand

> M. GUIBOURG : En Italie, par contre, les Américains et les Anglais continuent de ne pas avancer d'un pouce devant le Mont Cassin.

Prenez vos cahiers. Nous allons faire un exercice d'algèbre.

Il écrit une formule au tableau noir.
Un élève pète. Rires. M. Guibourg ne se retourne pas.

SAGARD : Je peux sortir, m'sieur ? C'est la soupe du collège.

M. GUIBOURG : Il faut toujours que ce soit vous, Sagard. Allez.

Sagard sort. On entend une voix allemande : « Halt ! »
Sagard rentre dans la classe à reculons, poussé par un grand Feldgendarme casqué. Il porte un imperméable vert olive, une plaque de métal lui barre la poitrine, et il a une mitraillette en bandoulière. Il renvoie Sagard à sa place.
Julien et tous les autres ont les yeux fixés sur le soldat. Celui-ci s'efface pour laisser entrer un homme petit, vêtu d'un manteau marron.
L'homme remonte les pupitres, s'arrête devant le professeur, qu'il salue sèchement.

L'HOMME : Doktor Muller, Gestapo de Melun.

Il se tourne vers les élèves.

119

MULLER : Lequel d'entre vous s'appelle Jean Kippelstein ?

Il parle bien français, avec un fort accent.
Les élèves se regardent entre eux. Julien baisse les yeux, figé.

MULLER : Répondez !

M. GUIBOURG : Il n'y a personne de ce nom dans la classe.

Muller se met à marcher le long des pupitres, scrutant les visages des enfants.
Il se retourne, aperçoit la carte d'Europe avec ses petits drapeaux. Il va arracher les drapeaux russes et américains. Il tourne le dos à Julien, qui ne peut s'empêcher de regarder vers Bonnet, une fraction de seconde. Muller se retourne, intercepte le regard. Il traverse la classe, lentement, et vient se planter devant Bonnet.
Celui-ci le regarde, un long moment. Puis il se lève, sans un mot. Il est blanc, mais très calme.
Il range ses livres et ses cahiers en une pile bien nette sur son pupitre, va prendre son manteau et son béret accrochés au mur. Il serre la main des élèves près de lui, toujours sans un mot.
Muller crie un ordre en allemand. Le Feldgendarme vient tirer Bonnet par le bras, l'empêchant de serrer la

main de Julien, et le pousse brutalement devant lui. Ils quittent la pièce.

Le silence est rompu après quelques secondes par Muller.

> MULLER : Ce garçon n'est pas un Français. Ce garçon est un juif. En le cachant parmi vous, vos maîtres ont commis une faute très grave vis-à-vis des autorités d'occupation.
> Le collège est fermé. Vous avez deux heures pour faire vos bagages et vous mettre en rang dans la cour.

Il s'en va rapidement. La classe reste figée un moment.

Le Père Michel entre, parle à voix basse à M. Guibourg. Les questions fusent. Tout le monde se lève, sauf Julien qui reste à sa place, le regard droit devant lui.

> LES ÉLÈVES · Qu'est-ce qu'il se passe ? Où est-ce qu'ils emmènent Bonnet ?

> LE PÈRE MICHEL : Calmez-vous. Écoutez-moi. Ils ont arrêté le Père Jean Il semble que nous ayons été dénoncés

121

Un grand murmure des enfants répond à cette nouvelle.

JULIEN : Et Bonnet ?

LE PÈRE MICHEL : Bonnet, Dupré et Lafarge sont israélites. Le Père Jean les avait recueillis au collège parce que leur vie était en danger. Vous allez monter au dortoir et faire vos valises, rapidement et dans le calme. Je compte sur vous. Auparavant nous allons dire une prière pour le Père Jean et vos camarades.

Il leur fait réciter le Notre Père.

50.

Les élèves font leurs bagages, très vite et sans un mot. Julien finit de remplir son sac et s'assied sur son lit.
Quelqu'un rentre et chuchote quelque chose.
La rumeur se répand à voix basse jusqu'à Julien.

BABINOT : Négus s'est barré.

François pénètre dans le dortoir, son sac à la main, cherchant Julien.

JULIEN : Ils ont pas eu Négus.

FRANÇOIS : Je sais. Ils le cherchent, lui et Moreau. Ils ont trouvé des tracts de la Résistance dans le bureau du Père Jean.

Le Père Hippolyte frappe dans ses mains.

LE PÈRE HIPPOLYTE : Ceux qui sont prêts, prenez vos affaires et allez au réfectoire. Quentin, faites le sac de Laviron et portez-le-lui à l'infirmerie. Faites vite.

FRANÇOIS : Tu veux que je t'aide ?

Julien fait non de la tête et va vider le casier de Laviron. Les autres s'en vont.
Julien est seul dans le dortoir quand Bonnet rentre avec un Feldgendarme.

L'ALLEMAND : Schnell !

Bonnet va à son casier et rassemble ses vêtements, évitant le regard de Julien qui s'est rapproché de lui. L'Allemand allume une cigarette, leur tournant le dos un instant.

BONNET : T'en fais pas. Ils m'auraient eu de toute façon.

JULIEN : Ils ont pas eu Négus.

123

BONNET : Je sais.

Il lui tend une pile de livres.

BONNET : Prends-les. Je les ai tous lus

Julien sort un livre de sous son matelas.

JULIEN : Tu veux les *Mille et Une Nuits* ?

Bonnet prend le livre et le fourre dans sa valise. L'Allemand se retourne.

L'ALLEMAND : Schnell, Jude !

Bonnet ferme sa valise et se hâte de le rejoindre.

51.

Julien rentre dans l'infirmerie, portant le sac à dos de Laviron La sœur infirmière est très agitée.

L'INFIRMIÈRE : Qu'est-ce que tu viens faire ici ? File !

JULIEN : Je lui porte son sac.

Il pose le sac à côté de Laviron. Les autres lits sont vides.

JULIEN : Tu vas te lever ?

Au lieu de répondre, Laviron se dresse et, de la tête, lui indique une petite porte. L'infirmerie est sous les combles et elle donne sur le grenier.
Derrière la porte apparaît la tête de Moreau. Il fait signe à l'infirmière, qui a un geste d'agacement.

L'INFIRMIÈRE : Qu'est-ce que vous voulez encore ?

MOREAU : On ne peut pas rester là. Ils fouillent le grenier.

Il court vers la porte d'entrée, l'ouvre. On entend des voix allemandes venant de l'escalier.
Il revient vers le grenier, ramène Négus et le fait se glisser tout habillé dans un des lits vides.

MOREAU : Ma sœur, donnez-lui une compresse, vite !

L'INFIRMIÈRE : Fichez-moi la paix. Vous allez tous nous faire arrêter.

Moreau a juste le temps de se cacher dans un placard.
La porte s'ouvre, un Feldgendarme entre, avance dans la pièce.

Négus remonte la couverture jusqu'à son nez.

L'infirmière laisse tomber la compresse qu'elle tenait à la main. Elle tremble, littéralement, et s'assied sur une chaise.

L'Allemand la regarde, ramasse la compresse et la lui rend. Un autre soldat surgit, venant du grenier. Ils discutent en regardant autour d'eux.

> LE PREMIER ALLEMAND *(il renifle)* : Il y a un juif ici, je sais.

Julien fait un pas en avant.

> JULIEN : On n'a vu personne.

Les Allemands se tournent vers lui. Il n'en mène pas large.

> LE DEUXIÈME ALLEMAND : Viens ici, toi. Baisse ta culotte.

Julien défait sa ceinture.

Il voit l'autre Allemand, penché vers l'infirmière, se redresser, aller vers Négus et, d'un geste brusque, tirer la couverture, découvrant le garçon tout habillé.

L'Allemand éclate de rire, prend Négus par l'oreille et le sort du lit, rejoint par son collègue qui tient un pistolet dans la main.

Ils sortent, Négus toujours tiré par l'oreille.

Moreau sort du placard.

MOREAU : Qu'est-ce qui s'est passé ?

JULIEN : C'est elle.

L'INFIRMIÈRE *(presque hystérique)* : Foutez le camp !

MOREAU : Je vais passer sur le toit. Je sauterai dans le jardin du· couvent. Adieu, Julien.

Il l'embrasse, file dans le grenier, soulève un vasistas, et se glisse sur le toit.

52.

Julien dévale un escalier quatre à quatre, ouvre une porte et s'arrête au milieu d'une courette, regardant en l'air.

Il voit la silhouette de Moreau passer de l'autre côté du toit et disparaître.

Julien sourit. Il se retourne brusquement, entendant une voix.

Deux hommes se tiennent cachés dans un angle de la courette. L'un d'eux avance vers Julien et l'interpelle en allemand. L'autre reste caché. On voit à peine son visage.

JULIEN : Joseph !

Joseph se détache du mur et s'approche de Julien.

JOSEPH *(à l'Allemand)* : C'est un ami.

L'ALLEMAND : Zwei minuten.

JULIEN : Qu'est-ce que tu fais avec eux ?

JOSEPH : T'es content ? Tu vas avoir des vacances.

Joseph tend sa cigarette à Julien qui hésite, puis la prend. Il s'en allume une autre.
Julien le regarde intensément, comme s'il refusait d'admettre l'évidence.

JOSEPH : T'en fais pas. C'est que des juifs...

Julien tient la cigarette dans ses doigts, sans fumer.

JOSEPH : Bonnet, tu l'aimais bien ?

Julien recule. en fixant Joseph. Celui-ci brusquement le rattrape et le retient par l'épaule.

128

JOSEPH : Fais pas le curé. Tout ça c'est de votre faute. Si j'avais pas fait d'affaires avec vous, il m'aurait jamais foutu à la porte. La Perrin, elle volait plus que moi.

Julien se dégage et court vers la porte.

JOSEPH *(de loin)* : Fais pas le curé, j' te dis. C'est la guerre, mon vieux.

Julien se retourne un instant, et s'enfuit.

53.

Muller et quelques Feldgendarmes sortent du bâtiment et avancent rapidement dans la cour, où tous les élèves du collège sont en train de se mettre en rangs. Il fait un froid glacial, les garçons sautent sur place pour se réchauffer.

MULLER : Est-ce qu'il y a d'autres juifs parmi vous ?

Un grand silence lui répond.
Muller passe lentement devant les élèves alignés, les dévisageant.

Il s'arrête devant un jeune garçon qui a des cheveux noirs bouclés et une grosse bouche.

> MULLER : Toi, tu serais pas juif ? Ton nom ?
>
> LE GARÇON : Pierre de la Rozière
>
> MULLER : Va te mettre contre le mur.

Le garçon, tremblant, s'éxécute.
Muller donne un ordre en allemand. Un Feldgendarme s'avance, tenant une pile de cartes d'alimentation dans les mains Il met ses lunettes et commence à lire les noms sur les cartes. Chaque élève appelé va s'aligner contre le mur.

> LE FELDGENDARME : Abadie, Jean-Michel... D'Aiguillon, Emmanuel... Amigues, Dominique... Anglade, Bernard...

Boulanger, blanc, se penche vers Julien.

> BOULANGER : Tu crois qu'ils vont nous emmener ? On n'a rien fait, nous.

Des cris, des pleurs interrompent l'appel: Un Allemand entre dans la cour, poussant devant lui trois petites filles. Muller se dirige vers le soldat, lui parle un instant.

UNE PETITE FILLE *(en larmes)* : On était venues se confesser.

Muller sourit, les laisse partir et revient vers les élèves.

MULLER : Ce soldat a fait son devoir. Il avait l'ordre de ne laisser sortir personne. La discipline est la force du soldat allemand. Ce qui vous manque, à vous Français, c'est la discipline.

Muller s'adresse maintenant aux professeurs alignés devant la cuisine.

MULLER : Nous ne sommes pas vos ennemis. Vous devez nous aider à débarrasser la France des étrangers, des juifs.

L'appel reprend.

LE FELDGENDARME : Babinot, Jean-François... Bernay-Lambert, Alain... De Bigorre, Geoffroy...

A ce moment, le Père Jean apparaît dans la cour, une cape sur sa bure, tête nue, portant une légère valise. Il est suivi de soldats qui encadrent Bonnet, Négus et Dupré, eux aussi avec leurs sacs.

Quand le groupe atteint la porte de la rue, le Père Jean se retourne.

> LE PÈRE JEAN *(très fort, très clair)* : Au revoir, les enfants ! A bientôt.

Il leur envoie un baiser avec la main.
Un instant de silence.
Un élève crie.

> L'ÉLÈVE : Au revoir, mon Père.

Tous les élèves reprennent.

> TOUS : Au revoir, mon Père.

Un soldat pousse brutalement le Père Jean dans la rue. Bonnet, bousculé, se retourne un instant dans l'encadrure de la porte. Son regard cherche Julien, qui fait un pas en avant et lui fait un petit signe de la main. Bonnet disparaît.

On reste sur Julien un peu en avant des autres. Il regarde fixement la porte vide. Sur ce visage d'enfant, on entend une voix adulte.

> LA VOIX : Bonnet, Négus et Dupré sont morts à Auschwitz, le Père Jean au camp de Mauthausen. Le collège a rouvert ses

portes en octobre 1944. Plus de quarante ans ont passé, mais jusqu'à ma
mort je me rappellerai chaque seconde
de ce matin de janvier.

FIN

Composition Bussière
et impression S.E.P.C.
à Saint-Amand (Cher), le 17 août 1993.
Dépôt légal : août 1993.
1er dépôt légal : septembre 1987.
Numéro d'imprimeur : 2004.
ISBN 2-07-071187-0./Imprimé en France.

66487